Lotus
78 and 79
The Ground Effect Cars

Lotus 78 and 79
The Ground Effect Cars

John Tipler

The Crowood Press

First published in 2003 by
The Crowood Press Ltd
Ramsbury, Marlborough
Wiltshire SN8 2HR

www.crowood.com

Paperback edition 2009

This impression 2012

© John Tipler 2003

All rights reserved. No part of this publication may be reproduced or transmitted in any form or by any means, electronic or mechanical, including photocopy, recording, or any information storage and retrieval system, without permission in writing from the publishers.

British Library Cataloguing-in-Publication Data
A catalogue record for this book is available from the British Library.

ISBN 978 1 84797 143 2

Acknowledgements

Thanks to all who have given their time and assistance during the research for this book. I'm especially grateful to Peter Wright for an extensive interview on aerodynamics and the 'discovery' and evolution of ground-effect, and permission to quote from his piece on the twin-chassis Type 88 in Race Car Engineering. Tony Rudd also talked through his involvement with the Type 78 and the research into ground-effect. I spoke at length to Type 78 and 79 designers Martin Ogilvie and Geoff Aldridge, and Peter Riches who was racing manager at the time of the Type 80. Former Team Lotus chief mechanic Eddie Dennis described the build process of the cars at Ketteringham Hall. Mario Andretti gave great insight into what they were like to drive, applying his own particular techniques for set-up, and his former mechanic Glenn Waters vividly set the scene on the race circuits. Rex Hart also commented on aspects of life at Team Lotus. I particularly want to thank Bob Dance, who was Team Lotus chief mechanic at the time, for checking the text, providing background anecdotes and assisting with captioning photographs. Thanks to Noel Stanbury and Martin Treadway for advice on JPS graphics. Picture sources, for which I'm eternally grateful, were Ian Catt, Clive Chapman (Classic Team Lotus), the Ford Motor Company (with special thanks to Fran Chamberlain), LAT, Peter Riches, Glenn Waters and Tony Matthews, and I'm especially pleased to be able to feature Tony's fabulous cutaway illustrations of the Types 78 and 79.

Designed and typeset by
Focus Publishing
11a St Botolph's Road
Sevenoaks, Kent TN13 1AP

Printed and bound in India by Replika Press

Contents

	Introduction	7
1	Aerodynamic Developments	12
2	Coming Together at Lotus	23
3	Skirts	29
4	The Design Process and Build Programme	40
5	Specifications and Construction of the Type 78	60
6	Specifications and Construction of the Types 79 and 80	73
7	Ground-Effect in Action – The 1977 Season	93
8	The World Championship Year – The 1978 Season	115
9	Soldiering On – The 1979 Season	160
10	Epilogue: The Final Years of Ground-Effect, 1980–81	182
	Appendix I: Chronology of Team Lotus F1 Cars	195
	Appendix II: Race Record of Lotus Types 78 and 79	199
	Appendix III: Cast of Characters	203
	Appendix IV: Where Are They Now?	204
	Further Reading	204
	Index	205

Andretti's car at Monaco in 1978. Launched in 1977, the Type 78 introduced the concept of ground-effect aerodynamics to Formula 1. It was raced for a season and a half by Team Lotus. (Ford Photographic Archive)

The Lotus Type 79 took the concept of ground-effect a stage further, enabling Mario Andretti to clinch the 1978 world championship at Monza. (Ford Photographic Archive)

Introduction

The Lotus 78 and 79 were not only two of the most important Formula 1 cars built and raced by Team Lotus, but also hugely significant in the history of motor racing. Starting with the introduction of the Type 78 in 1977, they brought about a revolution in single-seater racing car design. For the first time, designers had to consider the behaviour of the air stream passing underneath the car and not just the effects of aerofoil-generated downforce.

Within two seasons, the epoch of 'ground-effect' racing cars was in full swing. It was relatively short-lived in Formula 1 – it was banned from 1983 – but its legacy was to prove all-pervasive, with CART and IRL single-seaters in the USA still using controlled ground-effect into the twenty-first century. Open-wheel single-seater racing cars were not the only vehicles to be affected by ground-effect aerodynamics; the phenomenon was applied to closed-bodied sports-racing cars as well.

The Types 78 and 79 were among Lotus's most successful F1 cars. Between 1977 and 1978 they won 13 races, bringing Mario Andretti the 1978 World Championship and Team Lotus the constructors' title. But the cars were also linked with tragedy, with the loss of Type 78 driver Gunnar Nilsson to cancer and the death of his fellow Swede Ronnie Peterson in the aftermath of a multiple crash at Monza in 1978.

Type Numbers and Years

One of the most perplexing things about Lotus 'Type' numbers in the 1970s and early 80s is the maddening way in which they coincide with – and then fail to coincide with – the year in which the cars were running. The company's Type numbering of its models was logical, pretty much in chronological order, with the racing cars being interspersed with the road cars. It was only in 1970 that the Type numbers caught up with the year in which the car was built. Thus, the Lotus Type 70 Formula 5000 car came out in 1970. That was also the year of the introduction of the Type 72 F1 car (which was used by Jochen Rindt in his title-winning season and brought Emerson Fittipaldi and Team Lotus the world drivers' and constructors' titles in 1972). This numbering created a precedent for the confusion into which the Types 78 and 79 found themselves locked.

The Type 78 was begun in 1975, launched in 1977, and was still running well into the 1978 season, when its successor, the Type 79, was launched. The Type 79 was still on the strength in 1979, but so was the ambitious but unsuccessful Type 80. In this book, the abbreviations T78 and T79 have been used as much as possible to differentiate the cars from the actual year. However, this should not be confused with the turbocharged F1 Lotuses, which used a 'T' suffix from 1983 to 1988 (for example, Type 93T).

The key years in the story of the Lotus T78 and T79 are 1976 to 1978, and this is the period with which this book is primarily concerned. By 1979, the Type 79 had been overhauled by the opposition and was barely a front-runner any more. Its intended replacement, the Type 80, proved unsatisfactory, and

Introduction

even two of the world's best F1 drivers, Mario Andretti and Carlos Reutemann, struggled to win many points using both the Type 79 and Type 80.

Turning Defeat into Victory

The inexorable rise and ultimate triumph of the Lotus ground-effect cars and Mario Andretti's 1978 World Championship title is one of the great stories of Formula 1. It was a time when seeds planted at BRM back in 1969 began to germinate; when previously unresolved technical solutions (such as side-pod venturii and sliding skirts) fell into place; and when attention to detail in the art of aerodynamics bore fruit, fostered by the far-sighted genius of Lotus boss Colin Chapman. In a serendipitous moment, the personalities and skills required to bring the concept to fruition were present at, or found their way, to Team Lotus; by 1975, the stage was set. The cast brought together old hands such as Chapman, Tony Rudd, Ralph Bellamy and Eddie Dennis, and up-and-coming design talent in the shape of Peter Wright, Martin Ogilvie and Geoff Aldridge. A year later, after long hours in the wind tunnel and on the race track, the Type 78 was a reality. The race team was in the safe hands of Andrew Ferguson and Bob Dance, while the driving talents of Mario Andretti and Ronnie Peterson were unsurpassed.

Although the T78 was not an instant success, it marked the beginning of a major renaissance at Team Lotus, which had been in the doldrums for three seasons. The World Championship victory of 1978, gained with both Types 78 and 79, is a milestone in the history of Team Lotus. It also represents the pinnacle of the team's achievements, since it never again

Andretti and Peterson on their way to a one–two victory at Zandvoort in the T79s. With two top-line drivers, Team Lotus completely dominated the 1978 F1 season with the Types 78 and 79. (Ford Photographic Archive)

The revolution in F1 aerodynamics that ground-effect caused was masterminded by Team Lotus boss Colin Chapman, a brilliant engineer, innovator and motivator. (Peter Riches)

enjoyed anything like the success of the first years of the ground-effect era.

The expansive T78 and sleeker T79 raced in the black-and-gold JPS colours during 1977 and 1978, the T79 and T80 running in the dark green Martini livery during 1979. The Type 79 remains the only Formula 1 Lotus to run in the livery of three different major sponsors during its racing career (mid-way through 1979 it wore the logos of Essex petroleum as well as those of Martini).

The Story Unfolds

This book begins with an appraisal of racing-car aerodynamics up to the point at which Team Lotus designers were given free reign in the wind tunnel to come up with the most

Introduction

The inverted wing configuration beneath the Type 79's side pods helped generate considerable downforce. Ronnie Peterson demonstrates at Anderstorp in 1978.
(Ford Photographic Archive)

radical new F1 car. It then traces the development of the crucial skirts that were the key to ground-effect, going on to examine the working practices at Team Lotus and the creation and specification of the Types 78, 79, and, because it sprang from the T79, the Type 80. The performances of these cars during the 1977, 78 and 79 F1 seasons are chronicled in three chapters, with a conclusion showing how the ground-effect era came to a close. This epilogue highlights one of Chapman's most innovative and radical aerodynamic creations: the twin-chassis Type 88, black-flagged every time they tried to race it.

The appendices include a chronology of Formula 1 cars built and raced by Team Lotus, which helps place the Types 78 and 79 in an historical context. There's a list of the key personalities involved, as well as an appraisal of the (by then) ubiquitous Ford-Cosworth DFV engine that powered the cars.

During the research for this book, Mario Andretti, his mechanic Glenn Waters and chief mechanic Bob Dance provided many fascinating observations into the way in which the cars were prepared and set up. Aerodynamicist Peter Wright and designers Martin Ogilvie and Geoff Aldridge gave an insight into the life and times of team Lotus in the mid- to late 1970s, while Eddie Dennis and Peter Riches described the construction process. They all describe fascinating times, far removed from the present day, yet still with us on the historic circuit and, conceptually at least, on the Indycar scene.

Introduction

Andretti at Buenos Aires at the beginning of the 1979 season. Team Lotus's major sponsor was the Martini & Rossi drinks firm, but the Type 79's side pods would later carry the logo of the Essex petroleum company. (Ford Photographic Archive)

Introduced in 1979, the Type 80 'wing car' had a complex system of sliding skirts and was originally designed to run without aerofoils. Development problems proved impossible to sort and Team Lotus reverted to the Type 79. Carlos Reutemann (right) rejected the car after testing at Silverstone. (Peter Riches)

1 Aerodynamic Developments

Pioneers in F1

Team Lotus was the first F1 team to build cars that harnessed the aerodynamic phenomenon that came to be known as ground-effect, redefining attitudes to racing-car aerodynamics that still hold good into the twenty-first century.

Ground-effect refers to the way in which the earth's surface – land or water – affects the aerodynamic characteristics of an object moving through the air. Racing cars use ground-effect in the opposite way to aircraft by inverting the wing-generated lift principle. As a convex-curve approaches the ground, the air flow between that surface and the ground speeds up. This reduces the air pressure and creates downforce, a phenomenon that was recognized in the 1930s and expressed theoretically in 1949, but not put into practice until the 1970s.

The man who brought ground-effect into widespread use in Formula 1 was Colin Chapman, while the person who applied the theories of ground-effect to the design of the cars that deployed it to such good effect was Peter Wright. According to Chapman, 'Ground-effect was something for nothing.' However, putting it into practice eventually meant that Lotus had to set up a separate team of fabricators.

Black Arts

In the 1960s and 70s, racing-car aerodynamics was a black art, a matter of trial and error as designers sought to create the downforce that increased the load on the tyres without increasing the mass of the car. In the 1960s, Colin Chapman and his designers Len Terry and Maurice Phillippe led the way in single-seater race-car design, with the streamlined cigar-tube monocoques that came in with the Type 25, and progressed into wedge-shaped cars such as the 56 Indy car. Lotus was at the forefront of the winged era that lasted from 1967 to 1969, out-doing all competitors for size and breadth of wing. While other teams were slow to copy Chapman's bathtub monocoque, pioneered on the Lotus 25, it took less than a year for wings to expand from the tentative devices fitted low down over the engine, to colossal full-width aerofoils, strut-mounted on the springs and flying high above both ends of the car. Driver-operated feathering mechanisms were the extra sophistication. However, while it was clear that these wings provided dramatic downforce, nobody understood the aerodynamic forces to which they were subjected, and Lotus suffered more than most from collapses and dreadful accidents.

Mario Andretti experienced the Lotus 49's lofty strut-mounted wings in his debut foray into Formula 1. This was Andretti's first direct contact with Chapman's fertile imagination at work, remembered as follows:

> They were certainly very effective. The most effective way to apply aerodynamics to the car is when you go straight to the uprights, right to the unsprung hub carriers. Then you could still run the car soft. You could have a car very pliable through the hairpins and slow corners, but you

The Lotus 49's lofty rear wing, used by Jackie Oliver at the 1969 British Grand Prix at Brands Hatch, was as high and as large as they came. (Ian Catt)

had the downforce for the high speed and everywhere else where you needed it. It was almost too efficient.

The wing on the Lotus was taller and wider than anyone else's. As Andretti said,

> Well, that's Colin, you know! If there was no limit, obviously the higher the better, the cleaner the air. He always understood all that, he was always a step ahead of everyone. But one of the drawbacks was that the aerodynamic oval tubing that he was using for the uprights was never as strong laterally, and we saw a couple of them collapse, with dramatic results. One time I got away with it was at the end of the straight in Kyalami, just under braking. We used to have a fourth pedal on the left of the clutch pedal where you could feather the wing. Down the straight you could just use your left foot to press on that pedal, and that would trim the wing out. It was almost like having an overdrive gear. But when you got down to the braking point, all of a sudden when the wing would take the maximum pitch it would be such a jolt that it could collapse the wing support tubes. And that could have been a total disaster for me, because there wasn't much of a run-off at the end of the straight. I got away with it and didn't crash, but that's more or less what happened at Barcelona in '69. It was probably much more downforce than Chapman ever calculated, and the wing just didn't have strong enough struts to support it.

The FIA soon banned the fitting of aerodynamic devices to the unsprung masses, outlawed movable aerodynamic devices, and restricted the height and width of bodywork and wings. The two latter regulations have survived since 1968, although they have been put to the test on occasion.

Aerodynamic Developments

So Long, Suckers

Some of the major breakthroughs in racing-car aerodynamics emerged from the world of sports-car racing. Chapman's equivalent in that world was Texan Jim Hall who, along with Hap Sharp, created the Chaparral series of alloy-block Chevrolet V8-powered Group 6 and 7 cars. In 1962, Hall was experiencing front-wheel lift at high speed in his Chaparral-Chevrolet; Chevrolet's R&D department duly investigated the problem. General Motors' chief stylist, the legendary Bill Mitchell, proposed the introduction of an inverted airfoil shape to create downforce instead of uplift. There was no radical solution, but the fitment of a bib spoiler negated the front-wheel lift.

The breakthrough for Jim Hall came in 1966 when the Chaparral CanAm cars were equipped with strut-mounted movable wings, hydraulically operated by a foot pedal into a virtually flat plane for minimum drag along the straights; when pressure was released, the wing moved into maximum downforce position. The following year, the Chaparral 2F prototype demonstrated just how effective a strut-mounted movable wing could be. Mike Spence and Phil Hill won the BOAC 500 at Brands Hatch, alerting everyone in Europe to the enormous increases in cornering, traction and braking grip that downforce provided.

Not only did Chaparral use (problematic) automatic transmissions and GRP chassis, it went on to develop the 7.0-litre Chevrolet-powered Chaparral 2J CanAm car of 1970. This car achieved ground-effect some eight years ahead of the Lotus 78, even though the means used were much more artificial. The 2J debuted at the Watkins Glen CanAm race in 1970, with Jackie Stewart at the wheel. With an angular midriff and unprepossessing rectangular back end, it was no beauty, especially compared with Jim Hall's earlier CanAm and Le Mans cars. In the rear panel

The lofty strut-mounted rear wing on the Chaparral 2F provided a great deal of downforce in corners, and could be feathered on the straight, enabling Mike Spence and Phil Hill to win the 1967 BOAC 500 at Brands Hatch. (Ian Catt)

were mounted two 17-in diameter fans, driven by a 45bhp JLO-Rockwell snowmobile engine. Their purpose was to suck the air from under the car and expel it from the rear.

Bob Dance was at Watkins Glen with Andretti when the Chaparral 2J was first run. 'The Snowmobile engine was the first thing to start up,' he said. 'That ran at a constant speed. The car was parked in the paddock, which was pretty dirty, so it sucked up all the muck off the ground and shot it out the back. It was known as the vacuum cleaner.'

From the front wheels back, the lower periphery of the 2J's bodywork was fitted with a skirt made of a new plastic called Lexan. The skirts ran off the wheels, so they could set the clearance and, as the suspension compressed, it would lift the skirt. The grip produced by the twin fans was prodigious and a blatant threat to the status quo, so the authorities allowed it to race for one season and then banned it. Jim Hall hired Vic Elford to drive the 2J in the 1970 CanAm series, and at the Road Atlanta race he was some 2.5 seconds a lap quicker than Denny Hulme's McLaren M8D-Chevrolet in practice. Elford repeated the exercise at Riverside, passing Hulme on the outside of notorious Turn 9, a 180-degree right-hander before the pits. The 2J's Achilles heel was its semi-automatic transmission, which meant it was slow off the line, but, once up and running, Elford was able to use ground-effect to drive around the opposition. The Chaparral 2J's trump card was the fact that the fans ran constantly, sucking the car down even at low speeds, so aerodynamics in the accepted sense were not that important. After the Chaparral 2J was banned, at the end of 1970, the team withdrew from racing completely.

Jackie Stewart in 1970 driving the 7.0-litre Chaparral 2J, the first racing car to exploit ground-effect. It used side skirts and a Snowmobile engine to power a pair of fans that sucked it down on to the track surface. (LAT)

The Search for Aerodynamic Efficiency

Over the years, numerous theories had been tried in the search for aerodynamic efficiency. Streamlining enabled smooth air penetration, and Auto Union's land-speed record attempts in the 1930s featured closed-bodied streamliners, while a version designed by Professor Ferdinand Porsche had proto wings that resembled flippers. F1 regulations in the 1950s allowed all-enveloping bodywork, and Mercedes-Benz (W196), Connaught (B-type) and Vanwall all took advantage of this. In sports-car racing, Porsche's engineer Michael May had erected a big, adjustable strut-mounted wing amidships on a 550 Spyder in 1956, but that was swiftly banned.

Further work on aerodynamic factors looked at the tendency of certain sports-racing cars with fully enveloping bodywork to flip over backwards. The aerodynamic Ford P68 F3L prototype of Chris Irwin became airborne at the Nürburgring's Flugplatz during the 1968 1,000-km; Irwin was lucky to recover from serious head injuries. The previous year, Donald Campbell had been killed during his attempt on the world speed record on Lake Coniston, when the streamlined *Bluebird* took off at 328mph (525km/h) and went into a back flip.

John Stollery had been involved with the *Bluebird* project, and he led an investigation into the effect that the ground had on vehicles travelling over it. He used the Imperial College wind tunnel, which had a conveyor belt serving as a moving ground plane, to test a quarter-scale streamlined model car known as the Whale. It had a cut-off Kamm-tail that was typical of something like the Ford GT40. A variety of nose shapes were tried, in order to assess such phenomena as lift, drag and pitch characteristics, and it was observed that, as the streamlined car body approached the ground, it generated negative lift, or ground-

Fan Club

The concept of fan-generated ground-effect was revived by Brabham with the BT46B Formula 1 car in 1978. Because their flat-12 Alfa Romeo engine obstructed the venturii, designer Gordon Murray installed a fan to draw air through the radiators. This had the incidental effect of creating a pressure difference under the car, sucking it on to the track, and led to victory in Sweden. It was swiftly banned, although the win was allowed to stand.

As a precaution, Lotus immediately designed a new version of the T79 – basically the T79 with a pair of fans in the venturii at the back of the side pods. The backs of the venturiis were blended into a pair of fan ducts, with a drive-train from the gearbox to power them. The concept was that, at low speed, the fans would draw the air underneath the car and suck it down on to the ground; at high speed, the velocity of the car would take over. The Brabham version worked only at low speeds; at high speeds it did not have any further benefit. The idea of the T79 fan car was that it had both. As Peter Wright recalls, 'Martin Ogilvie had it all drawn within a week, and we were going to race it just four weeks later. Then Chapman took some Polaroid photographs of the model with its twin fans, and probably showed them to Bernie Ecclestone who owned Brabham, and fan cars were banned soon afterwards. Our version never turned a wheel.'

The flat-12 Alfa Romeo engine powering the Brabham BT46B obstructed the venturii, so designer Gordon Murray installed a fan that created a pressure difference under the car and sucked it down on to the track. Seen in Donington pits before a demonstration run during the Gunnar Nilsson memorial day, the Brabham fan car was banned shortly after its victory in the 1978 Swedish GP. (Ian Catt)

Aerodynamic Developments

Land-speed record cars of the 1930s generally concentrated on streamlined bodies, but this closed-bodied Porsche Type 80 from 1937 featured inverted wing-profile fins on either side. This six-wheeler was powered by a supercharged V12 33.9-litre, 2,300bhp Daimler-Benz DB601 aero-engine (as used on the Messerschmitt Bf 109 fighter). (Porsche Photo Archive)

effect. Stollery defined the concept in a key paper, *Forces on Bodies in the Presence of the Ground* (J.L. Stollery and W.K. Burns, 1969).

Around the same time, similar work was going on in the wind tunnel at Kingston Polytechnic, on the 1969 Piper GTR Le Mans car. This resulted in a spoiler being fitted on the tail section so that the cooling air flow exiting under the car was not disturbed by the air also passing over it. At the Laboratoire Eiffel in Paris, research was being undertaken on the CD Le Mans car, while at MIRA a Rover-BRM Le Mans car was used for analysis. Designer Robin Herd explained that the McLaren M6 CanAm car was also achieving ground-effect at the front. They fitted an anemometer underneath the car and recorded negative pressure. 'I was in the passenger seat going round Goodwood and Bruce got very excited,' said Herd. 'I'd have been a lot happier if he'd concentrated on driving the car.'

The Wright Stuff

Peter Wright was the godfather of ground-effect. Though he had no background in Grand Prix racing, as a child he had been drawn to the sport and decided to follow the fortunes of Stirling Moss. As Wright recalls, 'Moss promptly went and had his accident on Easter Monday at Goodwood in 1962, so I thought, OK, it's either going to be Clark or Hill, and I chose Hill at BRM, and that was why I ended up at BRM in 1967.'

Back then, Peter Wright believed that he was going to make a major contribution to grand-prix engine design:

Aerodynamic Developments

That's probably the real reason why I chose BRM. But when I got there I realized engine design was all about thermodynamics and clearances, and manufacturing tolerances. It was very nice to work in a company that was making F1 engines, and I spent some time up at the test house at Folkingham. But then I started making comments about the aerodynamics, having done aerodynamics and thermodynamics at Cambridge.

It was Tony Rudd who advised Wright that aerodynamics was an up-and-coming subject, and encouraged him to concentrate on that area.

Forays into the world of ground-effect were at first vague and unfocused. As Wright remembers,

The whole ground-effect thing was rooted in the sixties. There were a lot of people dabbling in what turned out to be ground-effect, without necessarily realizing it. Funnily enough, Chapman had funded a guy in the States called Buckley, who had a Citroën DS with venturii underneath and suction fans leading on to the boundary layer, but he didn't have skirts. Chapman came to the conclusion that it was 'rubbish'. To a certain extent it was. I got into investigating ground-effect when I was at Specialised Mouldings at Huntingdon, looking at the under-trays of sports cars, seeing how you could affect the compression distribution. I was also doing research on lifting ground-effect boats in the wind tunnel, so the whole time I was thinking about surfaces in relation to the ground.

In his book *Formula 1 Technology* (SAE International, 2002), Wright describes the way heavy birds like swans employ positive ground-effect aerodynamics as they fly close to the surface of the water,

gaining speed before climbing into the sky. Ground-effect is how the characteristics of the wing vary as they come close to the ground. Whether the wing is creating downforce or lift doesn't really matter, ground-effect comes into everything.

Looking to Stollery's work at Imperial College for inspiration, Wright said, 'All we did at Lotus was stumble across how important the skirts were. That was the key.'

The BRM Connection

One of the threads that came together to create the Lotus Type 78 began at Bourne, Lincolnshire, in the BRM headquarters. After the debacle of the H-16 engine, there was a slight recovery of BRM fortunes with the P133 in 1968 in the hands of Pedro Rodriguez. John Surtees then came on board, with great expectations, but the uncomplicated organization that he sought proved an illusion, while the 48-valve V12 engine grew steadily worse.

Racing manager and chief engineer Tony Rudd left under a cloud:

Peter Wright began researching the aerodynamic effects of cars passing over the ground in the late 1960s, and joined Lotus in 1974. A year later he had embarked on the wind-tunnel tests for what would become the Type 78. (Peter Wright)

There were too many chiefs at BRM. Peter Wright, my design assistant, was working on a revolutionary new car shaped like an inverted wing that used the airflow underneath the chassis to generate downforce. We moved him and about ten fabricators in great secrecy into the chapel at the other end of Bourne. The plan was that we would race it at Monza in 1970. Then Surtees got wind of it and found out that I'd got this pirate operation under way, that none of the management knew about. I had told Sir Alfred about it, since it was his money, but I hadn't told anyone else. As far as Surtees was concerned, this ground-effect project was a secondary issue and the main aim should be to concentrate on the P139. There was a row at Zandvoort. Jackie Oliver wouldn't drive the new car and Surtees went to the Stanleys and told them the new car didn't work, and all the key personnel including me seemed to be involved with some experiment. They instructed me to stop what I was doing at once. That was the final straw and I resigned there and then. I went to Chapman and said, 'That job you offered me a year ago, is it still going?' And he said, 'Yes it is.' And I left and the whole BRM ground-effect project was abandoned.

At BRM, Tony Rudd had been dismayed by the rapid growth of wings in Formula 1 and the cataclysmic effect when they failed, as the works Lotus 49s of Hill and Rindt did at Barcelona in 1969. He hurried Wright into investigating the generation of downforce without using strut-mounted wings, testing potential in the Imperial College wind tunnel.

Wright worked with chassis designer Alec Osborne on an inverted aerofoil-shaped body that consisted of a slender central fuselage to accommodate the driver and engine. The internal radiators were fed by NACA surface intakes, while nose wings and a spoiler at the trailing edge allowed the distribution of the overall downforce to be adjusted. In the wind tunnel they established that the overall downforce would be similar to that produced by a winged car and that lift versus drag would be significantly improved. In the secret workshop they adapted one P126 V12 chassis by bolting aerofoil-section side panniers on to the sides of the monocoque in order to assess how the new car would perform. They ran it at Snetterton, but, due to a lack of measuring equipment, there was no way of evaluating it. Then before any further work could be carried out, Tony Rudd and BRM parted company.

Opposite: *Designed by Robin Herd, Bruce McLaren's McLaren M7C of 1969 not only featured front and rear strut-mounted aerofoils but also pannier side tanks, which could have produced superior ground-effect characteristics. (John Tipler)*

Aerofoil Side Tanks

Peter Wright left BRM shortly after Tony Rudd, joining Huntingdon-based Specialised Mouldings, pioneers of composite structures in motor racing. One of his first assignments was to work with Robin Herd, chief designer of March racing cars, on the design of the bodywork for its Formula 1, 2, and 3 cars. The results were trend-setting cars like the 732, which won the European F2 championship in the hands of Jean-Pierre Jarier.

The March F1 car of 1970, the 701, needed greater fuel capacity for certain races. Harking back to his recent experiment at BRM, Wright proposed using inverted aerofoil-shaped side tanks that occupied the space between the front and rear wheels. The 701s appeared in this format in several races although Wright doubts that they generated much downforce. In reality, the benefit was that they housed the fuel with no additional drag. 'They were a solution to the fuel problem,' he said, 'but I never heard a driver say, "Yes, I can feel the lift." Any underside aerodynamic effect was lost because the air could simply spill out sideways as there were no side plates or skirts. The only advantage it had in that respect was the wind pressure on the top surface.'

Aerodynamic Developments

Mario Andretti drove the March 701, and he believed there had been something in it:

I was doing a test in South Africa, and you are running at altitude there, so in a normally aspirated engine you are down on power. That car had wing-shaped pods on both sides of the cockpit. We were talking away at Granatelli's [the STP Corporation team owner], and I thought the pods may be producing more drag than we need here, so I said, 'Why don't we take those off and see what reaction we get out of the car?' In those days, when cars were designed, they were not studied very much in the wind tunnel; in fact they didn't even have a moving-road wind tunnel yet, so whatever information they had from a wind tunnel was erroneous anyway. So we did that, and my straight-line speed did not change at all. However, I noticed that I lost some front-end downforce. So even though the pods were between the wheelbase, and you would think that we should have got just overall downforce, the pods actually moved the centre of pressure forward and affected the front end more than the back.

There is another example of side-pod-generated downforce from the same era. In 1969, Colin Crabbe Racing ran Porsche race and rally expert Vic Elford in the Antique Automobiles' ex-works McLaren M7C in most of the European rounds of the World Championship, until it was written off at the Nürburgring. Designed by Robin Herd, this car had pannier side tanks blended into the monocoque, and was sold off because Hulme did not get on with it. However, at one point in practice at the Nürburgring, Elford in the side-tank car proved quicker than Hulme in the regular cigar-tube chassis of the works M7A, suggesting that the broader chassis might have had superior ground-effect characteristics.

During his four years at Specialised Mouldings, Peter Wright designed and ran a one-quarter-scale wind tunnel. Most of the work was conducted on sports-racing cars for Lola, March and GRD, which advanced the thinking on sports-car aerodynamics. Wright also carried out tests on OMC (manufacturers of Johnson-Evinrude outboard motors) Formula 1 catamaran racing boats and some water-speed record boats powered by outboard engines. All were ground-effect craft with the potential to lift and flip over backwards when travelling at more than 100mph (160km/h).

Wind-Tunnel Tests for Lotus

In 1974, Peter Wright rejoined Tony Rudd at Lotus to run the Lotus Group's composite R&D facility Technocraft. This was a period when Team Lotus was starting to flounder, and was introducing the Type 76 in a bid to replace the phenomenally successful Type 72. The latter had become obsolete largely due to the understeer caused by Goodyear's new generation of tyres, which suited McLaren, Tyrrell and Ferrari better. Towards the end of 1974, Colin Chapman asked Tony Rudd to put a team in place, to run independently of the racing team, to look at the whole Formula 1 car concept from first principles. Wright's task was to devise and conduct a wind-tunnel programme in support of this, working closely with chief designer Ralph Bellamy.

Wright was somewhat taken aback when Rudd first approached him:

> When the T78 project got started, I was working at Technocraft doing composite research on the Moonraker boats. Tony said, 'Oh, you've not got much to do' (I was working about a 16-hour day), 'in your spare time you can do the wind-tunnel programme for the Type 78.' So he put Ralph and myself together, and I worked very well with Ralph – we just got on, and understood what we were trying to do. We set it out as a research programme, and the key decision that I made was that we would do it in a wind tunnel with rotating wheels and a moving road. That was crucial because it was the only way to simulate the ground accurately. If you're going to investigate the airflow characteristics in relationship to the ground, you'd better simulate the ground properly.

Lotus did not have a wind tunnel of its own. According to Wright, this was simply because 'people didn't build wind tunnels in those days'. The first motor-racing wind tunnel built was at Specialised Mouldings, where Peter Jackson had had the foresight to take on an aerodynamicist. Initially, a Volkswagen engine was used to drive the fan and then, when Imperial College uprated the electrical power system on their wind tunnel, their old

The Lotus 78 had a slim nose that housed the oil radiator and fire extinguisher; a pedal can be seen through the hole between the suspension assemblies. Water radiators were housed in the leading edges of the side pods. (Tony Matthews)

one was acquired and installed. Later, Williams bought the tunnel from Specialised Mouldings, and put a rolling road in it. Then Team Lotus bought it from Williams, and it has now been installed at Hethel since the 1990s.

Without a Lotus wind tunnel at his disposal, Tony Rudd did a deal with Imperial College in London to use theirs in the evenings, outside college time. This cut costs and prevented outsiders from knowing about the secret programme. The team started with a model of the Type 72. As Rudd says, 'This was long before the days of CAD, of course, and the models were modified as we went along, with cardboard, modelling clay and sticky tape.'

Peter Wright describes the methodology:

> Charlie Prior was the fabricator who made the scale models for the wind-tunnel tests. He was one of Chapman's right-hand men. Frank Irving was an aerodynamics consultant, Ralph dealt with how the tunnel was set up, and I ran the wind-tunnel programme. They were long shifts, way beyond when everyone had gone home at Imperial College. We had the tunnel all day, and worked on into the evening, basically until we were too tired to go on. There comes a point when you're doing that sort of testing when you have to go away and think. You can't just keep testing. It's not like nowadays, when the programmes are all thought through and planned and schedules are shifted. It was a totally different thing: we were just going step by step and you had to think about the result before deciding on the next one, where-

as now they test all these things before looking at the results.

First, the team wanted to find out whether a chisel nose with two aerofoils worked better than the inverted-shovel nose (as used by Tyrrell, March and Chevron) that was the full width of the car. Alternatively, should they favour the narrowest nose with the biggest aerofoils? They ended up with something in between. Quite early on they noticed that, when the model was closer to the 'road', the down-thrust suddenly increased. That was ground-effect. Rudd recalls those days of testing:

> We saw that the rubber-band [the 'road'] had lifted up under it, so the forces were obviously quite considerable. We agreed that we would have to modify the tunnel to keep the 'road' down, but we didn't know how we could tell Imperial College that we wanted to modify their tunnel without telling them why. We used air pressure to suck the 'road' down. We didn't tell Colin about it until we were pretty sure of what we'd found, because once he'd got the idea into his head, he would move the whole caboodle full speed in that direction. We used to have a big session at Imperial College on Friday night, and then be back at Ketteringham Hall [Team Lotus HQ] on Saturday morning to compare notes. At about 10.30am Colin used to come in…and we'd tell him what we'd found and what we thought we needed. He'd contain himself for a bit and then, one time, he said, 'Well what we want is a car shaped like a wing.' We agreed that that was a possibility, but not at that stage. The ideal arrangement was the fuel tank at the back of the driver, between the driver and the engine, on the centre of gravity of the car, so that as the fuel was used up, the balance wouldn't change. That was a key feature of the Type 79.

The tank behind the driver was also the safest place to put the fuel.

The most significant aspect of the Type 78's aerodynamic make-up was its side pods. As Rudd says,

> We got the idea of using the radiators for downthrust because I knew that the radiators gave you thrust, and Peter was prepared to believe me. He spent the day at the Science Museum, looking at the aeroplanes to see how the radiators worked. He came up with a quarter-scale model of the radiator, which discharged heat. That was the next stage, assembling and incorporating the oil and water radiators and the ducts, and the vents at the back of the radiators and the flat panels at the side.

It was a long process but, by late summer 1975, the overall configuration of the Type 78 was more defined. The slim nose with oil cooler and front wings were in place, along with aerofoil side pods to clad the fuel tanks, and the water radiators accommodated in their leading edge, similar in concept to the De Havilland Mosquito aircraft of the Second World War. Although the side pods appeared to generate only a little downforce, they had the advantage of accommodating the fuel and radiators with no drag penalty. At the rear of the car was a large, conventional rear wing. By Christmas 1975, project was well on the way.

2 Coming Together at Lotus

Think Tank

By the middle of 1975, the situation at Lotus was looking decidedly insecure, compared with the glory days of 1972 and 73, and Chapman urgently needed to find a solution. According to designer Martin Ogilvie, the light at the end of the tunnel was considered to be ground-effect:

It was seen as something that could radically change the whole picture. We were definitely lost at the time, at the end of the Type 72 and the 76, just flailing around. We didn't know what to do. One week it was falling rates of suspension, then it was 2mm of movement, the next minute it was 3in of movement. At that point Chapman gathered Rudd and Wright together and said, 'We need to do something, we've lost drivers, and we've lost

Lost souls. Team Lotus race crew fettle the unsuccessful Type 76, intended as a replacement for the Type 72. Looking for answers are Peter Warr (rear), Dougie Garner, Glenn Waters, Stevie May (behind car), Keith Leighton, and Ralph Bellamy (right). (Ian Catt)

Coming Together at Lotus

As powertrain manager and a director of Team Lotus in 1975, Tony Rudd was given a twenty-eight-page list of Colin Chapman's requirements for the new Formula 1 car. (Tony Rudd)

director of Team Lotus in 1975. He describes his role in the genesis of the Type 78 project:

> When I got back from holiday [late in 1974], Chunky [Chapman] handed me this 28-page document, all in his own handwriting. It was a list of everything he could think of, all the unknowns that needed to be considered for building a new F1 car. He told me to read it and draw up a programme and recruit a team that would answer all the questions. I realized that the key man I needed was an aerodynamicist, and I had just the right one. I said to Colin, 'I must have Peter Wright.' There was a hell of a row about that because he was involved with the boats at the time. Colin interviewed him and they took to each other instantly. He told me that we could have the orangery to work in and suggested Ralph Bellamy as a designer. Ralph worked hard and was clever and I liked him, so I said I'd have him. Colin asked me, 'What else?' and I said, 'Well, I need Charlie Prior, the pattern maker.' Charlie could work in wood to the sort of tolerances I worked in steel. He was a fabulous man. He made the moulds for the Esprit on the VARI system in 1974.

Ketteringham Hall is a Victorian Gothic mansion set in acres of parkland. Most Lotus people referred to it as 'Kett Hall', or, back in the 1970s, 'Fawlty Towers'. Initially, Rudd and his team worked at the Hall in an office built on to the end of the orangery, but, because of the confidentiality of their material, Chapman soon moved them to a palatial office overlooking the rear garden, with an enormous antique desk and a gun cabinet in corner. As Rudd remembers, 'Colin used to put his head round my office door as the light was fading, and ask, "What about the ducks then?" He liked to shoot duck.'

Saturday-morning meetings with Chapman only lasted half an hour, and Chapman would have separate talks with Rudd to see if he was satisfied with the team. He often urged Rudd to keep the pressure on Bellamy, which Rudd

direction.' They then came with a dossier, and set out to find out the things we didn't know about, like suspension geometry. The graphics boys worked out that they'd found this aerodynamic downforce, and Chapman saw that as a way of gaining an unfair advantage. He was paranoid about secrecy and if something got out he would come storming in, saying, 'I told you it was a secret! If someone's been blabbing down the pub I'll dock people's pay!' But it always ended up being him because he was always blabbing to his mates, because he had a massive ego.

A Serendipitous Moment

Tony Rudd joined Lotus Cars on 3 September 1969 as Powertrain manager, becoming a

Coming Together at Lotus

Ralph Bellamy, Team Lotus's chief designer from 1973 to 1977, with Colin Chapman, in the Monaco pits. Bellamy was closely involved with the conception and wind-tunnel testing of the Type 78. (Ian Catt)

felt was unfair: 'Ralph did his share of the stress calculations, and it was a job keeping the peace.'

Andretti Comes on Board

Tony Rudd and Colin Chapman knew that Mario Andretti's commitment was crucial to keeping the sponsors happy and the project running forward. It was Rudd's job to sell the project to the driver:

> Andretti came to meet me in the office, surrounded by the models, and asked me a lot of questions – I'd known him from my BRM days. I said, 'It's so good that a baboon could win races with it.' He was a bit put out by that but we got him on board, and from then on, it went at full speed.

Andretti played a crucial part in the genesis of ground-effect and the Type 78. He recalls the meeting at Ketteringham Hall at which the way ahead was discussed:

> Obviously there was going to be a clean sheet of paper for next year's car because the Lotus 77 was obsolete and we had tremendous drag with it. We

Coming Together at Lotus

Colin Chapman and Mario Andretti confer over the set-up of the Type 77. The American's commitment was crucial to the development of the Types 78 and 79. As the 1976 season progressed, the T77 incorporated flexible side skirts and, here, a twin aperture type of air-box. (Ford Photographic Archive)

managed to win in Japan with it before the season went out, so we were competitive towards the end, but the objective was to try to do something quite different. When it came round to me and Colin said, 'Mario, what would you like to see?', I said, 'Well, as a driver I would love to have downforce without drag penalty.' I started explaining to them about the March 701 that I had driven in 1970. I said, 'You know, there is something to those wings; we were getting downforce without drag penalty.' There were no fences [skirts] – the side pods were just a clean shape. Can you imagine if maybe we put fences on there – we would control the flow better, there would be no spillage. This is how the Lotus 78 was born, with that idea in mind. The ground-effect situation came later when we had discovered that, by lowering the fences more and more, we were creating this vacuum underneath by speeding up the air.

Money Matters

The project was taking on a life of its own and finance became a priority. As Tony Rudd recalls,

Colin had a meeting with Geoffrey Kent of Players and said it would cost about £345,000 to build the new car. He didn't quite fall out of his chair! But I was given a bollocking on the way back for not trying to sell the project. I just said what we wanted the money for. So we fixed another appointment with Geoffrey Kent and I gave him the performance predictions as to how much faster it would be than the existing cars. I didn't see Colin for a couple of days,

Boarding School

Martin Ogilvie describes what it was like working at Team Lotus:

> It's difficult to imagine the environment of Lotus. It was very much like a boarding school, with pranks and bullying, and all sorts of things going on. Everyone had a nickname, sarcasm was rife, and you learned to give as good as you got. A lot of that was pretty unpleasant, I have to say. It used to be quite brutal.

F1 teams continue to be split between the going-away team and the home-based team, with very different rules in place. At Team Lotus, this led to much aggravation, because the employment terms were very different between mechanics and fabricators. The mechanics put the car together and went racing while the build team made the parts for the car. But the home-based build team worked more regular hours, five days a week, and could take three-week holidays. The mechanics on the race team went away on the Thursday, came back on the Monday and perhaps went into work again on the Thursday after a few days off. And at the end of the season they might stay three or four weeks in Australia. When they were away, however, they would work weekends, often all through the night. 'They were very different types of people,' said Ogilvie, 'and they all thought the grass was greener on the other side. It wasn't always the most amicable working environment.'

Team Lotus in those days comprised about 60 people, running a raft of cars including Cortinas, Type 30s, 47s and Indy cars, as well as F1 and F2. An F1 team today would probably comprise a workforce of about 200.

Designer Martin Ogilvie and Team Lotus's former F2 chief mechanic Ian Campbell work on the rear wing and side-plates of the Type 79 prototype in December 1977. (Tony Matthews)

but then he said, 'We've got a bit of a problem. We've got some of the money, but the question is whether we spend it all in one go and move the project on, or whether we just use it to build the prototype.' I said, 'The snag is, until we build the car and run it, we won't have any numbers to convince anybody.'

Martin Ogilvie thought Lotus never invested in its own wind tunnel simply because they were always short of money. According to Ogilvie, the company employed a common trick:

> Team Lotus's financial year used to be about six months different from Lotus Engineers and Lotus Cars and they just used to swap the money around. Fred Bushel got the money in and looked after it, and Chapman used to spend it. He would say, 'Fred, your job is just to get the money so I can spend it.' But the money was never there, so they had to do a sponsorship deal as early as possible. Sponsorship got more and more difficult to come by, as it was realized by sponsors like Camel that their money was paying off the previous year's debts. So there was little capital outlay.

There never was much in the way of equipment, and the value of Team Lotus must have been practically zero, because there was no machinery. In Ogilvie's opinion, things would have been substantially better in the end if Team Lotus had been self-sufficient in machine tools and a wind tunnel, because they would not have had to rely on outside suppliers.

Harbour Lights

Tony Rudd was less directly involved in the detail work on the Type 78. Lotus was building luxury cabin cruisers, and Rudd's expertise was in demand there too:

> Colin Chapman had got me working on my next projects by then, and I was spending nearly half the day down at Brundall [at Chapman's JCL Marine], sorting out hydraulic drives and all manner of troubles with the Marauder and Moonraker boats.

Rudd used to spend part of the day in the workshop watching the car being built, and part of the day in the office with Peter Wright and Ralph Bellamy, who were developing the detail. He recalls some of the progress made:

> People were starting to use the gearbox bellhousing to put the oil in, because there's a space there with nothing in it. Ralph and I were trying to evolve an oil gallery, and the snag was to go through the oil tank to get at the clutch, so we tried to evolve a different form of clutch mechanism, a hydraulic one. All we had to do was to put in oil down the middle, down the housing of the gearbox. I was working with Keith Duckworth as to how much oil we'd got to carry, and Duckworth was darkly suspicious of Chapman because he never put enough oil in, or so he reckoned. Weight distribution was another factor. We had the idea of moving the driver further forward, because there was no weight on the front wheels, and I had this theory that the driver's ears sensed the balance of the car. It was where his ears were that counted, so we should move his head. But it was a very big problem moving the oil cooler about. It did finish up in the nose, but it was quite a problem as to how to run the oil pipes.

3 Skirts

Dream to Reality

The Type 78 project evolved in the wind tunnel. Preliminary tests revealed that the model had sagging side pods, which indicated that they had started to generate downforce. This must have had something to do with the gap between their edges and the ground. Peter Wright explains it as follows:

> When you run a wind tunnel non-stop, it gets very warm, and the clay and sticky tape perform worse and worse as it gets hotter and hotter. It wasn't a refrigerated wind tunnel like they have now, with temperature control, so we started getting very inconsistent results.

The research team inserted thin wire supports to restore the side pods to their correct position and to stop them from sagging. Cardboard skirts were taped along the bottom to seal the gap between the edge of the side pods and the ground, leaving a gap of approximately 1mm (0.04in). Astonishingly, the total downforce on the car doubled for only a small increase in drag. According to Peter Wright,

> Ralph [Bellamy] looked quite startled, and I don't think either of us could believe the results. The tests were repeated, with and without the skirts, and, sure enough, ground effect was happening, provided the outer edges of the side pods were sealed to the ground.

Skirting the Issue

Tony Rudd remembers how Peter Wright was 'beginning to feel his way towards skirts; they'd done quite a bit of work as to how the side panels would look, how close to the road they'd got to be, and, because they really needed to rub on the road, how they'd got to have a special tip.'

Peter Wright describes the moment when the key was discovered:

> One day we were watching the model, trying to see what was happening to it, and we noticed that this gap was closing up between the bottom of the model and the road surface. What was happening was that the gap under the side pod was getting smaller. We decided to try fixing the side pods on and sealing the gap, designing the gap to become fixed, in fact. We taped some card along the bottom of the side pods, and there it was – double the downforce. So we took it off, and put it on again, and found out that it was a real effect.

First tests indicated that skirts were worth about 2 seconds per lap at Snetterton. Rudd recalls Andretti taking him round to the back of the pits, and asking him to explain how the car worked. Andretti knew it was different, and had spotted a lot of the characteristics of it, but the car had a lot more drag than it was supposed to have. As Rudd says,

> At that stage we didn't really understand how much downforce we'd got from the underpan.

Skirts

There were a lot of things we didn't understand very well, but it had got a lot more drag, even if you took the wings off, by virtue of its shape. It wasn't as fast in a straight line as it should have been.

Later on, Colin Chapman sent for Tony Rudd and held a formal meeting with him in the office at Ketteringham Hall:

> I got the hard chairman treatment. Chapman said, 'This is going to be very disagreeable. I've been talking to Mario and we've been looking at the time it'll take us to build an improved car, because we're not sure if the first one is good enough to race as it stands. We've decided that we won't race it this season.' He waited for me to explode, because of all the effort that had gone into it, getting it ready for the [1976] American Grand Prix. I told him, 'Well, the first time everybody sees it going back up the ramps into the truck, and sees the underside of it, they'll see what we've done and suss out how it works, and they'll copy it.' So it was best not run until the start of the new season.

Although there were flashes of inspiration during the gestation period, the realization that they had something of real potential only dawned on the team by degrees. According to Peter Wright,

> Mario was into it eventually. When the car came out, it went off testing and the brushes [see below] didn't really work. Then it got to South Africa and Chapman insisted on trying to get the skirts to work. Bob Dance bolted on some aluminium skirts with steel springs acting as hinges to stiffen the whole thing up and keep the skirts pointing downwards, and Mario said he could actually feel it working. We had pressure tappings, and as the

After mid-season tests in 1976 revealed that trapping the air under the car produced a modicum of downforce, the Type 77s were equipped with brush skirts. Gunnar Nilsson drives the T77 in its later format with air-box and brush skirts around the radiator side pods. (Ford Photographic Archive)

car went through a dip, you could see all the pressure going whoosh because the skirts sealed off the underneath. Chapman was pretty excited about it. So that summer [1976] I just really worked on skirts.

Mario Andretti talks about the time when he discovered the effectiveness of the addition of skirts:

> We were testing the 77 at Hockenheim, and we were running the car fairly soft in those days. I noticed that, through the Bosch curves, when we were getting roll in the car, all of a sudden I was experiencing a heaviness in the steering. The car was sticking more on the left side because we were closing the gap to the ground. I came in and told Colin about it, and immediately he sent out for some strips of plastic, which we fitted to close the gap on both sides. I went out there and, immediately, on the first lap, set a new lap record. Of course, the more I kept running, the slower I was going, because we were wearing the plastic away and then it was becoming less and less effective. But it told us what we needed to know – that we had to close that gap.

The next step was to maintain consistency between skirt and track and Colin Chapman came up with the idea of using brushes. Andretti explains the process:

> The brush didn't wear out as much as the plastic strips, but it wasn't as effective, because air would still slip through the bristles. We raced the 77 with brushes a couple of times. Colin hired David Phipps to photograph the car everywhere on the circuit to see what the brushes were doing. We saw that, at speed, the forward part of the brushes were sucking in and, just in front of the rear wheels, they were blowing out. So we realised how effective this venturi was, but also how important it was to control that flow. Whatever was blowing out ahead of the rear wheels was loss of velocity, downforce, because we were wasting all that energy. Colin and the group designed sliding skirts – solid skirts that would go up and down. Once we did that and started reshaping the diffusers, it all came together. It was a series of fascinating trial-and-error sequences before we truly had a ground-effect car.

The Evolutionary Key

The development of the skirts was the key thing throughout the evolution of the Type 78. The shape of the car was not changed at all, according to Peter Wright; the skirts were simply put on:

> We started altering the venturii under the side pods in the T79 because Chapman told us to compromise the rest of the car for the aerodynamics. The layout of the 79 chassis was different: the engine was all tucked in, the exhaust tucked in, the suspension designed for the aerodynamics, so we had a lot more freedom. The side pod was something you could just fit, whereas on the T78 it was part of the chassis structure so it wasn't easy to change.

The nature and configuration of the skirts evolved through four distinct phases: from brushes via hinged polythene 'suck-up' and aluminium 'suck-down', to the fully sprung 'board-in-a-box' sliding skirts on the Type 79. The T78 never had sliding skirts, because, to begin with, the team was very unsure about the rules. As Peter Wright recalls,

> We decided that everything had to flex, because people had already run flexing skirts – Brabham had done it transversely across the front of the car towards the end of 1974. That idea was to stop the air going underneath the car, and then you get a low-pressure area behind the skirt. All our skirt work related to the way we could make something that sucked the car down. The big problem with the later 'board-in-a-box' sliding skirts was that rubber off the tyres got in the cavity and jammed them. The brushes were installed to keep that out.

Skirts

Above: *With air trapped under the car, low pressure built up behind the skirt, causing the vacuum that glued the car to the ground. At Jarama in 1977 Andretti was uncatchable, his Type 78 running with 'suck-up' skirts. (Ford Photographic Archive)*

Andretti's Type 79 shows the 'suck-down' ceramic-tipped skirt bearing on the kerbs at Jarama in 1978. (Ford Photographic Archive)

While the nylon brushes swept the track, they proved to be incapable of sealing the gap between car and track. Winter tests at Kyalami in 1976 using polypropylene skirts demonstrated that these sucked inwards and distorted. There had to be measures in place to prevent excessive wear, and one way was to suck the skirts up using the low pressure beneath the car. They were loaded down by steel shim springs and, inevitably, there was a compromise between their performance when they were new and when they were so worn as to be ineffective.

Peter Wright was instructed to devote all his time to the development of rubbing strips:

> Whereas before we'd been using plastics and PTFE rubbing strips, if we were really going to suck it down hard, we had to have something that wouldn't wear. So I talked to my brother-in-law, who was a potter, and he suggested ceramic. Through Imperial College we got to the School of Mining, and were told about a company that made moulded ceramics.

Using ceramic tips on the skirts transformed the wear rate and allowed the skirts to be spring-loaded harder on to the road, via Peter Wright's new skirt design, which was sucked down instead of being sucked up. It was similar in design to a twin, unequal link suspension, which took up little width and had a small area for the suction beneath the car to act on, to minimize the wearing load.

Eddie Dennis (second from right) fits the bodywork on the Type 79 prototype in December 1977. It never raced with this configuration of curved side pod. (Tony Matthews)

Skirts

Evolution of Lotus ground-effect skirts

(drawn by John Tipler, with reference to Tony Matthews' illustrations in Peter Wright's Formula 1 Technology*)*

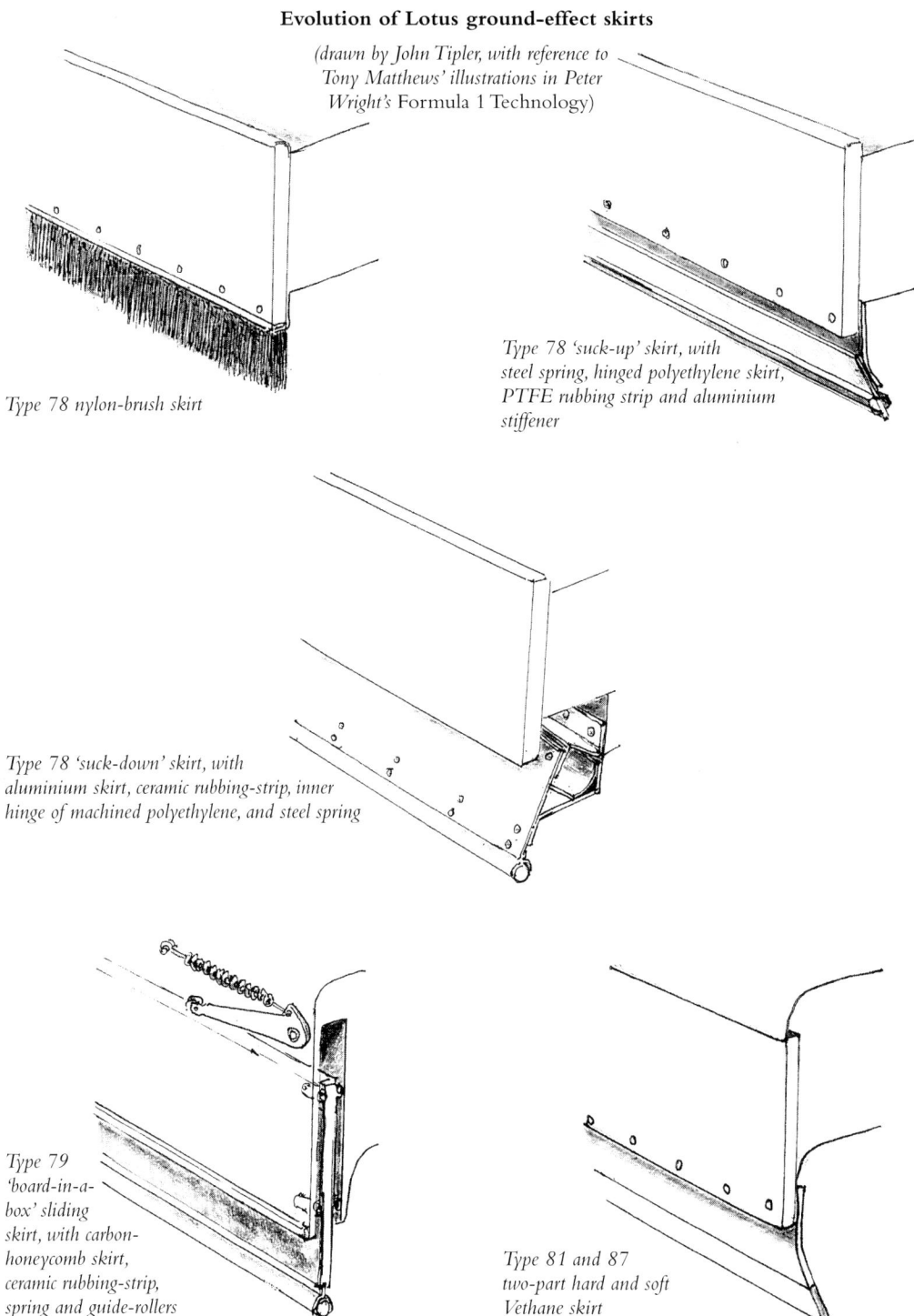

Type 78 nylon-brush skirt

Type 78 'suck-up' skirt, with steel spring, hinged polyethylene skirt, PTFE rubbing strip and aluminium stiffener

Type 78 'suck-down' skirt, with aluminium skirt, ceramic rubbing-strip, inner hinge of machined polyethylene, and steel spring

Type 79 'board-in-a-box' sliding skirt, with carbon-honeycomb skirt, ceramic rubbing-strip, spring and guide-rollers

Type 81 and 87 two-part hard and soft Vethane skirt

The Type 79's Skirts

The T79 prototype had cut-outs in the bottom of the monocoque with 'sword blades' on which the skirts were mounted. 'The skirts would articulate on these projecting blades,' recalled Glenn Waters (Andretti's race mechanic). 'If the car came off on the grass, you'd have a pretty effective grass cutter!' The blades were made of sprung steel and they would articulate up and down with the skirt on the end.

The construction of the Type 79's skirt box consisted of two outer panels and one inner panel – literally a 'board-in-a-box'. The inner

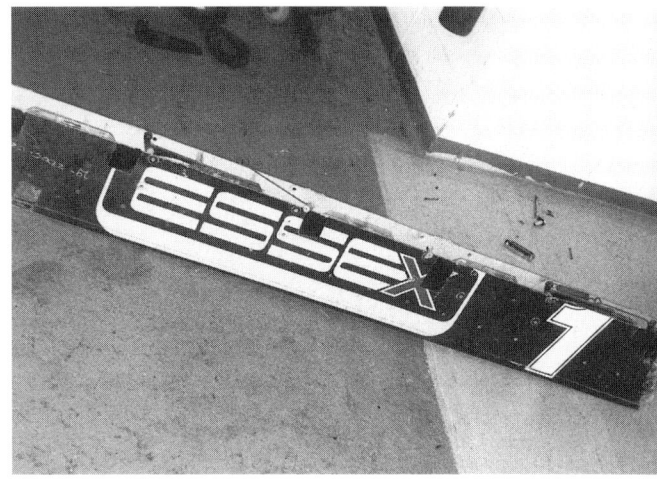

The 'board-in-a-box' side skirts rode up and down within these frames, which fitted on the bottom of side pods. (Tony Matthews)

The skirts were forced down by strong springs, and pegged up when the car was off the circuit. (Tony Matthews)

Skirts

Above: Andretti at speed in Type 79/4, its sliding skirts sweeping the Interlagos track surface during the 1979 Brazilian Grand Prix. The fixings on the side pods indicate the extent of the skirt boxes. (Ford Photographic Library)

The Type 80's ceramic-tipped side skirts ran right to the back of the car, curving round inside the wheels and sliding up and down within the boxes on the bottom of the tail plates and side-pods. The springs that pressured them down were so strong that the car could sit on the skirts with no jacks. (Peter Riches)

The Type 80 wing car of 1979 was designed with a pair of skirts running underneath the nose in triangular boxes, as indicated by chief mechanic Bob Dance. The air passing under the front of the car was channelled between the skirts and exited via an opening in the upper surface of the tub just ahead of the cockpit. The intention was to create a low-pressure area under the front of the car and exert downforce on the front wheels. (Peter Riches)

Originally conceived as a pure wing car, the Type 80 took the ground-effect aerodynamics a stage further than the Type 79, with side skirts that ran the length of the car and twin plates at the tail. The nose skirts are absent here at Zolder in 1979. (Peter Riches)

> **More Rear Wing**
>
> The problem with the Type 78 aerodynamics was that the downforce generated by the side pods occurred too far forward relative to the central point of balance. For this reason there was a need to run with a lot of rear wing to stabilize the car, and this had an adverse effect on the top speed along the straights. Clearly, modifications on the Type 79 would seek to redress the balance. The centre of pressure underneath the car was shifted backwards, increasing the car's pitch sensitivity. The throats of the venturii were extended as far back in the side pods as possible and, following Chaparral's wind-tunnel tests, the T79's suspension and engine ancillaries were tidied up for better airflow.
>
> Meanwhile, the sliding skirt proved to be the optimum version. Peter Wright points out the following:
>
>> At a fast circuit like Kyalami, in 1977, it wasn't really in the picture. But by the following year, when we were still using the T78 at Kyalami, Mario was on the front row and Ronnie won, because by then we'd realized that we had so much downforce that we could just take the wing off altogether. We'd learned how to balance the car a bit and it was very good.
>
> When the Type 78 started to realize its true potential, Bob Dance created a diversion by running the cars without a differential, making rivals think that this was where the advantage lay. It seemed that only Postlethwaite had twigged what they were on to – Ferrari were reputed to have tested a ground-effect car in the Pininfarina wind tunnel in 1976. However, the tunnel did not have a moving road, and no positive effect was evident.
>
> There was more to come, as Wright recalls:
>
>> At the end of 1977 or early 78, we did a long winter test down at Ricard with the Type 78, and we had our very first instrumentation in the car, so we could measure downforce, suspension deflection, pressures, speeds, and so on. Mario, Ronnie and Jackie Stewart drove the car (he was doing a series of magazine articles about the current Grand Prix cars). That was one of the most interesting things that we did because we could gauge what was actually going on.

panel articulated up and down between the two outer panels. It was suspended on a piece of mylar film, which was attached like an S-bend to the top of the outer box. The film ran down and around quarter-inch diameter aluminium tubes, which acted as roller bearings. Any thrust on the skirt would allow the rod to roll up and down. The idea behind this was twofold. First, the film would not allow any air leakage up and inside and, second, the negative pressure vacuum caused by the ground-effect would pull on the film and pull the skirt down on to the surface of the road.

The aluminium honeycomb skirts were 7ft (210cm) long, with a channel section at the bottom, and ceramic rods inserted as rubbing strips. A complicated spring-and-arm, fastened at one end to the inside top of the side pod and to the top of the sliding board at the other, ensured that downward pressure was maintained. The ends of the 'box' were capped, and the skirts were pegged up within the box when the cars were off the circuit.

The T79 first raced at Zolder in 1978 with the 'board-in-a-box' skirts, and ran them for the rest of the year and, indeed, for 1979 as well, alongside the fully-skirted Type 80. The T78 made do with the 'suck-down' skirt with the ceramic rubbing strips.

Eddie Dennis was in charge of the build shop. He describes how the rubbing strips fitted into the T79's board-in-a-box sliding skirts:

> An aluminium extrusion was set in the bottom of the board with a slot in it, a bit like a guide channel for a sail in a mast. We inserted a series of half-inch round ceramic rods, each about 7in [17.5cm] long, and they were glued into the extrusion and bolted into the rubbing strip for the skirt. These ceramic tips would last about the length of practice and do one race if we were lucky.

The ceramic rods could disappear, they could shatter, the extrusion could wear away and they would drop out, or the heat of the friction could cause the glue to soften, with the same result. According to Glenn Waters, 'After the third iteration, the skirts actually worked quite well. They were a pain to assemble. We had this sub-assembly shop which used to make the bits that would wear out, like the skirts.'

Predictably, there were many complaints that the skirts marked the track, although Peter Wright claims that the load was not that significant. All that was needed was something that rested on the ground, so that it actually sealed the gap. Wright goes on to say, 'It needed three people to arrange the skirt, and servicing the channel above the skirt was a complete nightmare from an access point of view.'

To ensure that no air escaped from under the car, except in the required direction, the gap between the front of the engine and the rear of the monocoque was stuffed with sponge rubber. A sausage-like air bag was also tried, but that proved to be too vulnerable to being punctured on sharp edges when it was being installed.

The sliding skirt is clearly visible on Mario Andretti's Type 79 at Zandvoort, 1979. (Peter Riches)

4 The Design Process and Build Programme

Drawing Office

Four people worked in the Team Lotus drawing office at Ketteringham Hall: Martin Ogilvie, Geoff Aldridge, Keith Lane and Mike Cook. Subsequently appointed chief designer, Martin Ogilvie joined Team Lotus in 1973 and went right through to the Type 100 of 1988:

The design team joined Lotus in the heyday of the Type 72, here in the hands of Ronnie Peterson in 1973, with the rear wing set back at its fullest extent. (Ford Photographic Archive)

Inevitably I saw some amazing changes in that period. In the days of the Types 77, 78 and 79, I worked alongside Geoff Aldridge and Mike Cook, with Tony Rudd, Peter Wright and Colin Chapman, who were a sort of think tank. It was people like Ralph Bellamy and myself and Geoff Aldridge who did the actual bits and pieces, so it's difficult to actually identify who did what. There was quite a divide as to what came out of the think tank and came to us, which we had to draw.

When I joined, in 1973, Ralph had just started, having been at McLaren and after a short stint at Brabham. He did the Type 76 Lotus, which wasn't

The Design Process and Build Programme

The Type 78 was a wide car, with double air-scoop engine cover and broad side pods containing water radiators. The oil radiator was in the nose, and the nosecone merged with the upper rockers of the front suspension. (Ford Photographic Archive)

a huge success – Chapman said it was a Type 72 with a hundred more mistakes. Ralph was a super guy but very conservative. He wasn't dynamic enough for Chapman's liking, and they didn't get on at all well, so it wasn't long after the Type 76 came out that Chapman felt he couldn't really work with him any longer and found an alternative role for him. That's when it all started to happen with the Type 77. Geoff Aldridge and I worked together on that.

Geoff Aldridge joined Team Lotus as a junior draughtsman in 1972 after Maurice Phillippe left and Martin Wade was acting as chief designer in a caretaker role. He had a degree in mechanical engineering:

Although I'd never really been a motor-racing enthusiast, it was just such a good opportunity. There were only 23 people working on the team then, and we ran two Grand Prix cars and two Formula 3 cars. I was working on the Type 72, and the Type 73, which was the Formula 3 car. Maurice [Phillippe] had designed them both. The Type 73 was in many respects a miniature 72. It was very complicated for a Formula 3 car, and there was a lot of work in the double curvature chassis. The 72 and 73 tubs were made by Frank Cubitt, who was brilliant at rolling aluminium panels. He'd been in the aircraft industry, which is where all this stuff came from.

Geoff Aldridge drew the chassis for the Types 77 and 78, working for Ralph Bellamy; as he remembers, the inspiration came from Bellamy. Ogilvie did the suspension drawings,

41

The Design Process and Build Programme

The Type 79 had a cleaner shape than its predecessor; Ronnie Peterson gave a ground-hugging demonstration at Hockenheim in 1978. (Ford Photographic Archive)

Billed as the wing car, the Type 80 should have been the sleekest of the ground-effect designs, but it did not work without wings. On Andretti's car at Jarama in 1979, the horizontal lines on the sliding skirts show where they marry up with the fixings within the side pods. (Ford Photographic Archive)

The Design Process and Build Programme

and Aldridge did all the chassis and some of the body design. 'And the other two did other stuff.'

There's an aesthetic aspect to this, too. Compared with the elegant Type 72, the T76 and T77 were the ugly ducklings of Lotus's F1 cars of the 1970s. The Type 78 had a much cleaner shape, surmounted by the twin air-scooped engine cover. Sleekest of all was the T79. Its successor the T80 should have had that accolade, by virtue of its wing configuration in its purest form, but it was compromised by the addition of fins and the over-complication of its skirts.

Rip it Up

Ralph Bellamy supplied the draughtsmen with sketches and measurements for the Type 78. According to Geoff Aldridge,

> They were very accurate, very neat, and very pedantic for the 78. But he [Bellamy] wasn't involved on the 79. He'd fallen out of favour then, so he was tucked away in a little room at Ketteringham Hall and Chapman had given him the gearbox to design, or something. That was the Lotus way. There was something in Chapman's philosophy that said when things aren't working you either start again, or you change the personnel, or you do both. I think that's why Lotus ceased to be successful in the later years, because there was more to motor racing than just tearing it all up and starting all over again. There was an evolutionary thing which Lotus never managed to grasp.

The drawing office was just outside Colin Chapman's office in Ketteringham Hall, separated by a pane of silvered glass. He could see what Ogilvie was doing, but Ogilvie could not even see whether Chapman was in or not. As Ogilvie recalls,

> Ketteringham Hall was a quiet environment, and that was where they did prototypes of some of the road cars as well. The drawing office was in the old orangery. You could walk out of the door and stroll down to the lake, which was a fantastic environment for being creative. Ketteringham Hall also encompassed boat-design people, so it was really quite fun up there. It was all youngsters, fighting for position in the company, supercharged people, with Colin Chapman driving us on like mad, churning out boats and racing cars. He certainly was an amazing bloke to work with and he treated me exceptionally well, almost like a father.

The designers rarely went to the Grand Prix races. Chapman preferred them to stay at their drawing boards thinking pure thoughts, unsullied by the goings-on at the circuits. Martin Ogilvie went to a few races but saw himself very much as 'a backroom boy. I didn't seek publicity at all, and it suited Team Lotus very well to have one man in the public eye all the time, and that was obviously Colin Chapman. He didn't like other people to be a deflection really, he liked to take the credit for everything.'

Ogilvie's colleague Geoff Aldridge felt much the same:

> I went with Martin and Brian Spooner [gearbox specialist] to the first test of the Type 79 at Paul Ricard. We realized that we were either going to stand around getting bored, or we were going to get stuck in, so we worked on the car all week. And thoroughly enjoyed ourselves. But generally I don't feel comfortable going racing because there's nothing for me to do. My job is the designer. You can offer advice and go round looking at people's cars, but it's a rather tedious time, and if you don't go on a regular basis you don't actually know what's happening.

View from the Front Line

At the sharp end of racing-car construction are the mechanics. Glenn Waters' opinion of the cars in his charge was not always positive:

The Design Process and Build Programme

Drawn by Martin Ogilvie and pictured with Gunnar Nilsson at the wheel at Monaco in 1976, the Type 77's suspension consisted of fabricated double wishbones, coil springs and dampers with outboard brakes, and parallel links, twin radius rods and outboard springs and dampers at the back. (Ford Photographic Archive)

My definition of Lotus racing cars would be their structural inadequacy. We were always chasing inadequate structures, while most of the other teams would build robust cars. I always felt that it was a negative thing at Lotus that the designers never got to go to the races, because they'd never see other the teams' solutions to the same problems.

Martin Ogilvie described some of the idiosyncrasies of the braking systems that he drew:

The suspension that Colin Chapman got me to do for the outboard brake system of the Type 77 basically consisted of fabricated double wishbones and outboard coil springs and dampers up front, and parallel links and twin radius rods and outboard springs and dampers at the back. The back suspension of the Type 77 went on the 78 and the same principle was used on the 79. We did all this brake work, which had repercussions on the rear of the Types 78 and 79. The Types 72 and 76 suffered from their inboard brakes, the 76 particularly as they were quite small bits. In fact, the rear brakes of the 79 were always running hot and it wasn't until the end of the 1978 season that the problem was traced to the brake fluid. They had magnesium gearbox side cases, and when it got hot the brake fluid attacked the magnesium, creating air bubbles or gas bubbles.

The Design Process and Build Programme

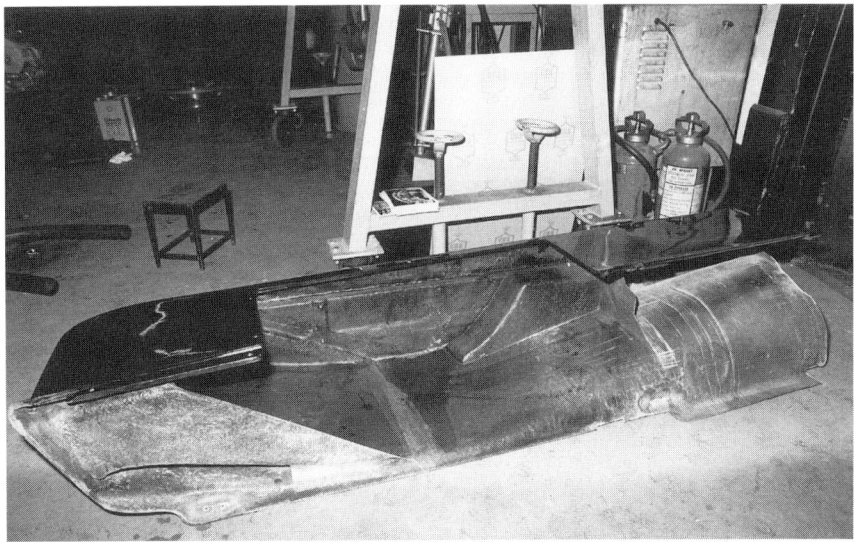

The side pods of the Type 79 were quite different from each other on the inside, because the oil and water radiators were of a different shape. The right-hand one (shown here) would accommodate the water radiator. The venturi is the up-swept area running underneath it from left to right. (Tony Matthews)

Under-Body Shapes

The wind tunnels were quite small in those days, using quarter-size scale models. According to Martin Ogilvie, 'We developed a way of doing the under-body shape, evolving from a straightforward curve like the 78's into a more complex shape with the Type 79.' The other aspect they concentrated on was tripping the flow at a consistent point, because with a generally curved shape, the centre pressure moves backwards and forwards as the car pitches in acceleration and under braking.

Geoff Aldridge believes that at some point between the Lotus 78 and the Lotus 79 they stopped thinking about wings on the side of

The left-hand side pod for the Type 79 reveals the air scoop for the oil radiator and the curvature of the venturi beneath it from which the ground-effect was derived. (Tony Matthews)

The Design Process and Build Programme

cars, and started thinking about ducts underneath cars. 'Suddenly the side of the car was now a duct,' he recalls. 'It wasn't a wing at all.'

Martin Ogilvie agrees:

> The 79 side pod was a completely different structure to the 78. In some ways, it was a bit of a retrograde step because, for the 79, Chapman wanted the air to be made to flow right out through the back, whereas with the 78 there was a fuel tank present. So we ended up with these two C-shaped fibreglass mouldings, which were not very stiff and, structurally as a whole, the 79 was a bit of a disaster.

When Williams introduced its FW07, in 1979, its designers had come up with a much more rigid chassis, which proved superior to that on the Lotus 79. As Ogilvie affirms,

> It was a stiff, tautly sound bed to hang all its loads on, while the 79 was a very floppy car. In those days you used to get some quite good slow-motion shots at Monaco on the television. The 79 came down the hill from the casino and through the hairpin in slow motion, and you could see the whole car was alive and twitching. That was the first time I'd seen it in slow motion and really understood what it was all about. It was not good! In fact when they were built they were originally about 3,000 per degree, which is not high, but by the end of the season it was down to 1,500 per degree, which is about the same as a Caterham Seven without the side panels on. These fibreglass side panels could be deflected all over the place, but Colin Chapman wouldn't allow us to put anything else in. The actual fibreglass had to be structural, and those were the days before proper carbon fibre. We bonded in some aluminium hoops, which didn't really make an awful lot of difference.

Chapman Breezes In

Geoff Aldridge describes the division of responsibilities within the design office:

A Type 79 in build in April 1978, with fibreglass side pod attached, demonstrating the slant of the water radiator installation. Fixing holes and slots for the side skirts are also visible. Whereas the T78's side pods incorporated part of the car's chassis, the T79's were essentially bolt-on items. (Tony Matthews)

Andretti rounds Rascasse in 1978. When Martin Ogilvie saw the Type 79 on TV during the Monaco Grand Prix, he was surprised how much the chassis flexed. (Ford Photographic Archive)

The Design Process and Build Programme

Designer Martin Ogilvie examining the front suspension of the Type 79 prototype on 10 December 1977. Ogilvie had a hands-on role during the car's construction, and instigated crash tests on the rocker arms prior to fitment, the first time this had been done. (Tony Matthews)

Ralph used to spend hours a day with Chapman, but he fell out of favour because of the Type 76. Martin [Ogilvie] and myself and Mike Cook then did the 77. And Chapman of course. Then we heard that Ralph was working on another car, which was the Lotus 78. So we all went to work for him down at Ketteringham Hall. And then it swung back the other way again with the 79, because Ralph wasn't involved with that at all. [By 1980, Bellamy was working for Mo Nunn, and designed the Ensign N180-B F1 car.]

The 79 was me, Martin, Peter Wright, Chapman and Brian Spooner, who did the transmission. It was a super time. The inspiration came from Chapman, as I suspect it always did.

Martin Ogilvie talks about about the reality of the design work within Team Lotus – how the instructions came through from Colin Chapman and how they were interpreted:

He was very good at leaving you to find your own way around the problem. He would never allow for compromise, and would always find the 'unfair advantage'. Whether it was downforce, sticky Goodyear tyres, or Nicholson engines, that had to take precedence over everything else. So he would actually present you with a problem, saying, 'I want this feature. Design me a car that incorporates it.' He wasn't one to have design meetings. He would breeze into the drawing office and go around the drawing boards having a look, offering a bit of advice here and there, and then back out again. It was immensely frustrating, because you could be beavering away for hours or days, and he would come in and within ten seconds spot the obvious mistake. He loved to do that, to come in and show that he was right on top of it, which he was in those days. But what it did mean was that he would make us work ridiculous hours. For three to four months a year I would be doing 100 hours a week, from September through to Christmas, twelve to fourteen hours a day, seven days a week.

The Design Process and Build Programme

It was all pencil drawing in those days and it was slow work, not like CAD [computer-aided design], which is so quick. It's a very lengthy process to draw by hand. You scheme it out, then you draw it again about four or five times, full size on squared paper, then write down all the co-ordinates from that, and then draw it again full size using the co-ordinates. And then you had a first machine drawing and a second, and these used to take about four days to accomplish.

If Chapman was happy with the design, he would go away and do something else and then come back a month later. It was down to Ogilvie, as chief designer, to report to Chapman how much the chassis weighed. They would usually have a sweepstake on it; this still goes on in motor racing, with bets being made on the weight of a new chassis, and the winner taking all. As Ogilvie testifies, 'It would have to be about 30 to 40lb. We still worked in pounds, although we went metric on the T78 almost ahead of the industry.'

Colin Chapman would come and have a look at the car, and always took great delight in coming up with a 100-item job list just by looking at it. Martin Ogilvie, in particular, was proud of the fact that, by the time he had done his last car with Chapman, he was no longer able to produce a list with 100 items on it.

Life in the drawing office was not without its humorous side, as Ogilvie explains:

Front view of the Type 79 chassis showing how slim it was. The prototype is being assembled by former Team Lotus chief mechanic Eddie Dennis (left), who was in charge of the fabrication and assembly shops at Ketteringham Hall between 1976 and 1979. Also at work are Reg Underhill and signwriter Paul Crowland, right. At the rear are Roy Franks and, facing camera, designer Geoff Aldridge. Although Team Lotus used Valvoline engine oil, there were problems with crownwheels and pinions at the time, and Texaco's gear oil was thought to be the best lubricant to use. (Tony Matthews)

The Design Process and Build Programme

On the Type 77's job list we would often come across the letters 'MCTR' at the end of an item; none of us knew what it meant and we didn't dare to ask him. We had this bloke called Mike Cook who was more of a development engineer – he did the test work and fibreglass information – so I came up with the idea that MCTR stood for 'Mike Cook To Rectify', and he got given all the difficult jobs to sort out. In fact it was 'More Careful Thought Required'. It meant that Colin Chapman didn't know the answer himself; he was just saying, 'It's not right, so go and have another go.' It was ages after that we found out what it really meant; Chapman thought it was quite funny.

This process was fairly typical of the way Chapman worked. Some vital procedures were overlooked – for example, the Type 74 Texaco Star F2 car was never weighed. 'It caught fire and was destroyed first time out. Colin Chapman went absolutely berserk,' says Ogilvie. 'It meant we had to make another complete car before we knew whether the weight of it was right or not. That car and the Type 76 had a lot in common in terms of construction.'

Chapman's Influence

Once the concept and figures were fed into the drawing office, work could begin on designing the car. Geoff Aldridge describes the way the drawings were produced:

> You got the basic scheme, then you drew it up. Typically, a chassis drawing in those days would be on an A0 sheet because you'd draw it full scale. Drawn in quarter scale, various parts, the assembly and so on, would be detailed on a second sheet. It would be in plan, side elevation, front elevation, whatever it took to get the information down.

The designers produced GA (general arrangement) drawings on big-scale A0-sized sheets. This is the Ralph Bellamy/Martin Ogilvie rendering for the Type 78. (Classic Team Lotus)

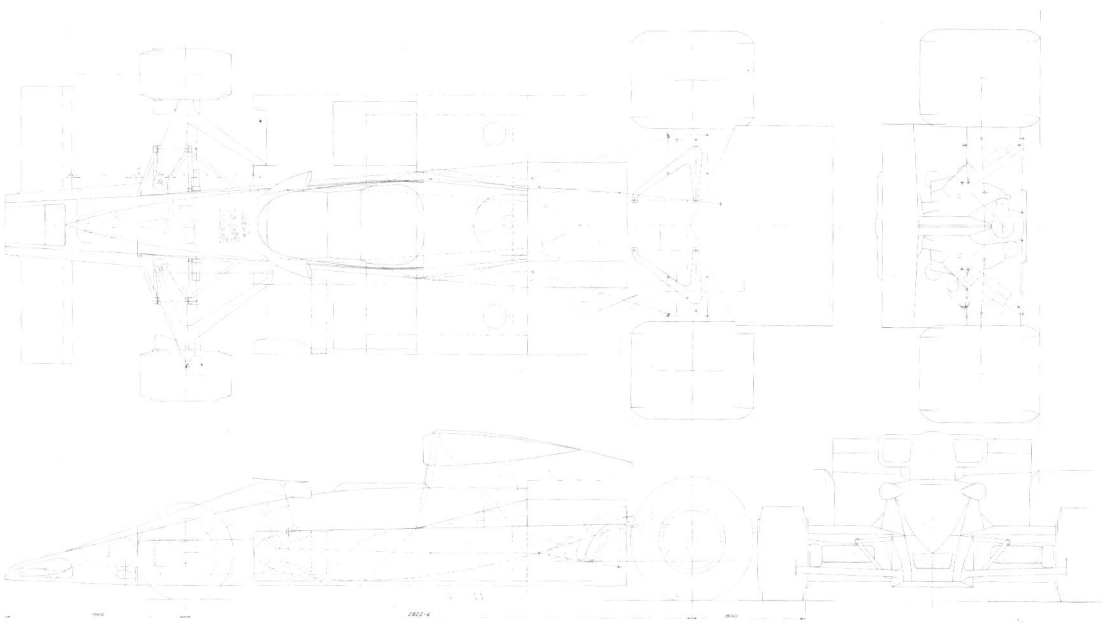

Not isometric. Then you spent a fair bit of time playing around, ultimately trying to get at what Chapman wanted. He'd have ideas in his head. All the time I worked at Lotus I never saw him do a proper drawing at a drawing board. I know he was well capable of it because I've seen his stuff. But we'd get sketches on cigarette packets, or whatever, and then lay it out as best we could. And then of course he'd come in and have a look and say, 'No, that wasn't quite what I wanted.' And it was a sort of to and fro situation . . . until we ended up with something that he was happy with. We might be given a sketch by Chapman or Peter Wright with the brief that the chassis ought to be a particular shape. You'd try and draw it that shape and realize that maybe the steering column went though the middle of it, or whatever, so you'd have to thrash it out between you. But, in terms of chassis design, we were aware at the time that we were breaking new ground.

Colin Chapman's expectations of his staff were high, but he was not unreasonable in his demands of them. He wanted the people who worked for him and were being paid by him to do what he asked them to do. As Aldridge remembers,

With bodywork fitted, the Type 79 takes on a wider stance. At the rear, model maker Charlie Prior (smoking) and designer Martin Ogilvie reflect, while graphic artist Paul Crowland works on the car's JPS livery. Even while the car was in build, the signwriters made use of every opportunity to complete the colour scheme and logos. (Tony Matthews)

Rolling chassis of the Type 79 chassis with left-hand side pod attached. The corners of the single-skin tub were prone to crack due to flexing. The front 'canard' fins provided downforce on the front tyres, affecting handling and steering. End-plates stopped the air from spilling off the upper surface of the wing. (Tony Matthews)

If you couldn't do what he wanted for very good reasons, that was fine, but if you couldn't do what it because you couldn't be bothered, or it was too difficult, he got quite angry. I never saw a bad side to him, but I know lots of people did. There were stories of him tearing drawings up. It never happened to me. I always found him very approachable; he would sit down and explain things to you if you said you didn't understand. Chapman was first and foremost a very good engineer, far-thinking, innovative, and he was a very shrewd businessman. Thirdly, and more important than both those things, he could motivate people, and he could charm the birds off the trees. He'd come in, put his arm round you, and you'd work all night. And with those three things going for him, he couldn't fail.

Mario Andretti recalls the motivation within the team that paved the way towards the world title:

Everybody was highly motivated to create something different and pursue whatever we needed, including a lot of testing and good preparation. This was one of the periods when Colin Chapman and the troops [Martin Ogilvie and Peter Wright] were keeping their senses as stimulated as possible. Colin really wanted to make the difference, and as a driver, to have Colin himself so motivated was a good chance for me to go for the championship. Every time Colin was on that particular path he produced a world champion. His career was one of peaks and valleys – you had to ride the peaks with him. I was riding that crest with him as a driver, and that was awesome, tremendously motivating for all of us. That's how we were making these strides, because we were constantly searching for that elusive unfair advantage.

Martin Ogilvie is convinced of Chapman's influence over his designers:

It's interesting looking at various cars and the people who designed them, like Maurice Phillippe and Martin Wade, but when they left Lotus they never seemed to progress. They did advance well at Lotus under Colin Chapman but after they left they always turned out the same thing. He never gave any words of praise. I threatened to leave Lotus at one stage and join McLaren and John Barnard, Colin Chapman got to hear about it and he said, "You can't leave, you're the only designer I've had whose cars didn't fall to pieces.' That was the only compliment I'd had in 15 years. So they gave me a company car and I decided to stay.

Slim Chance

The Type 79 might have looked like a wide car, but its chassis was actually very slim. Geoff Aldridge explains why:

Chapman wanted the smallest possible chassis so that he could have maximum ground-effect down the sides. To give more room for the aerodynamics down the sides it had to have a slim chassis, and we knew it needed to be as stiff as possible. And there was a contradiction here, because you can't necessarily have small things very stiff. While the 78 chassis had two skins, the 79 was in fact single-skinned, with just one skin down the side. The tub of the earlier 77 was a single skin from the front bulkhead back to the dashboard. From the dash bulkhead rearwards it had side tanks so it was double-skinned at the back.

The 79's chassis was not without its flaws, according to Martin Ogilvie:

Another problem we used to get was in the corners of the chassis, and they always used to crack there due to flexing. There were beaded edges, which were difficult for the poor fabricators to make. And because of its relatively unsophisticated construction, the old DFVs used to rattle the chassis to pieces like nobody's business. The engine mountings used to destroy themselves in no time; they cracked and fell apart inside the car and we were for ever taking the fuel tank out and

The Design Process and Build Programme

inspecting the engine mountings. The other thing on the T79 was that our roll-over hoops were always illegal. Andretti really didn't worry about roll hoops and seat belts, because of having done Midget racing and that sort of thing. Chapman was actually quite blatant about it at one time. And no one ever protested. Nobody even thought about it. You still get the same thing today – if you can provide documentation on tests that your roll hoop survives at 7.5G then you can get away with it. But, contrary to a lot of people's protestations, we never cheated. People would say, 'Oh, Chapman always cheats,' but that really wasn't the case. We did not cheat.

The Type 79 was the first car to put all the fuel behind the driver, and that was another factor in determining how slender its chassis was. It had just one tank whereas the T78 had three, and it had a very complex fuel-collection system. Geoff Aldridge explains as follows:

> In F1 these days they just put a couple of submersible electric pumps in, get the fuel up and blow it into a collector. We had to use gravity or induced gravity feed. No one thought of the pumps, or maybe they just weren't available.

The rectangular fuel tank had a central collector with four tubes running from bell-cup reservoirs in the corners of the tank uphill into the collector. The bell-cups picked the fuel up and, as the car braked and dipped forward, the fuel ran up the four tubes and into the aluminium collector pot towards the back of the tank. Aldridge drew the tubes again and again to get the system right. He describes the set-up:

> They used electric pumps to pressurize the fuel-injection system. But it was just a can with four tubes running to the top of it. They were all spring-loaded and the filter was in the middle, and that was also spring-loaded. The fuel system for the T80 was similar.

Conflict of Interests

The chassis for the Type 80 was Geoff Aldridge's last piece of work for Team Lotus before he went freelance. The 80 had skirts on the front and skirts on the rear. As Aldridge explains,

> It's very difficult to get a curved skirt to move freely up and down. Some cars just go well and some don't, and this was not a nice car. It was very complex and, because of the constraints of ground-effect, fitting everything else in became very difficult. Lotus had lost it again at this point, and I think they should have developed the 79. It's easy with hindsight to say that. But Chapman saw it as the next step. Even now I'd have to say that, aerodynamically, it was ahead of its time. Nowadays, Formula 1 teams have an aerodynamic programme running alongside their race programme, and therefore they've become very good at it. But in those days it was Peter Wright's view against Chapman's view against mine and Martin's. It was all about making up your theories to fit the facts.

According to Geoff, there was always a divide between the staff in the drawing office and Peter Wright: 'He [Wright] was a great theorist, but not always the most practical of people. And whilst we always got on well together there was this gap between the drawing office and the boffins. There was no stifling of ideas though. If you had an idea, you said so.'

Despite all the hard work of the team, Geoff Aldridge still regrets the lack of development on the Type 79:

> We did the 79 and it was so successful, then Williams copied it [with the FW07 in 1979], and there were things on the car which they'd copied that there was no logical reason for copying. They obviously didn't understand exactly what it was

The Design Process and Build Programme

The left-hand side of the rose-jointed front suspension of the Type 78, which consisted of upper rocking arms, lower wishbones, coil springs and dampers, with outboard disc brake, air scoop and steering arm prominent. (Tony Matthews)

fabricators stayed behind at Potash Lane to do the maintenance, and there were six of us at Kett Hall: Roy Franks, Eric Gray, Billy Monaghan, Nick Paravani, Jim Bamber, and me. Eric Gray could do beaded and wired edges in L72 aluminium, which is pretty much a lost art nowadays. We had most of the tooling there, like the guillotine, although there wasn't a great deal of machinery. The limited number of tools provided says a lot for the skills of the fabricators.

There was sometimes friction between the designers and the fabricators, with the fabricators accusing the designers of not considering exactly how something was going to be put together. Eddie Dennis recalls, 'There'd be a confrontation while we sorted out what they wanted and how we'd make it.'

Another first was the test rigs that were assembled at Ketteringham Hall, ten years before five- and seven-post testing rigs became standard in F1. 'We built rigs for testing components like the top rocker arm, which had never been done before,' says Eddie. They also built a heavy-duty wooden table with a number of block-and-pulley devices to put loads in the car, described by Glenn Waters:

> The car sat on the table with its tyres on pads with small nails protruding through them to give it the type of grip level the tyre would see when it was warm and the downforce was on it. We would put sandbags on top of the wheels and apply various loads to try and pull it about and see what we could change in the suspension, whether it moved about in the monocoque or whatever.

The data was recorded by Mike Cook from the design office. Later, by the mid-1980s, they were using hydraulics rather than blocks and tackle.

At this point, Colin Chapman decided to embrace metric weights and measures. 'The Type 78 was the first Lotus to be built in metric,' says Eddie. 'No more feet and inches – although we were using imperial bolts for some time.'

Another novel feature of the ground-effect Lotuses was homogeneous body parts. 'The Types 78 and 79 were the first cars that had a

The Design Process and Build Programme

inspecting the engine mountings. The other thing on the T79 was that our roll-over hoops were always illegal. Andretti really didn't worry about roll hoops and seat belts, because of having done Midget racing and that sort of thing. Chapman was actually quite blatant about it at one time. And no one ever protested. Nobody even thought about it. You still get the same thing today – if you can provide documentation on tests that your roll hoop survives at 7.5G then you can get away with it. But, contrary to a lot of people's protestations, we never cheated. People would say, 'Oh, Chapman always cheats,' but that really wasn't the case. We did not cheat.

The Type 79 was the first car to put all the fuel behind the driver, and that was another factor in determining how slender its chassis was. It had just one tank whereas the T78 had three, and it had a very complex fuel-collection system. Geoff Aldridge explains as follows:

> In F1 these days they just put a couple of submersible electric pumps in, get the fuel up and blow it into a collector. We had to use gravity or induced gravity feed. No one thought of the pumps, or maybe they just weren't available.

The rectangular fuel tank had a central collector with four tubes running from bell-cup reservoirs in the corners of the tank uphill into the collector. The bell-cups picked the fuel up and, as the car braked and dipped forward, the fuel ran up the four tubes and into the aluminium collector pot towards the back of the tank. Aldridge drew the tubes again and again to get the system right. He describes the set-up:

> They used electric pumps to pressurize the fuel-injection system. But it was just a can with four tubes running to the top of it. They were all spring-loaded and the filter was in the middle, and that was also spring-loaded. The fuel system for the T80 was similar.

Conflict of Interests

The chassis for the Type 80 was Geoff Aldridge's last piece of work for Team Lotus before he went freelance. The 80 had skirts on the front and skirts on the rear. As Aldridge explains,

> It's very difficult to get a curved skirt to move freely up and down. Some cars just go well and some don't, and this was not a nice car. It was very complex and, because of the constraints of ground-effect, fitting everything else in became very difficult. Lotus had lost it again at this point, and I think they should have developed the 79. It's easy with hindsight to say that. But Chapman saw it as the next step. Even now I'd have to say that, aerodynamically, it was ahead of its time. Nowadays, Formula 1 teams have an aerodynamic programme running alongside their race programme, and therefore they've become very good at it. But in those days it was Peter Wright's view against Chapman's view against mine and Martin's. It was all about making up your theories to fit the facts.

According to Geoff, there was always a divide between the staff in the drawing office and Peter Wright: 'He [Wright] was a great theorist, but not always the most practical of people. And whilst we always got on well together there was this gap between the drawing office and the boffins. There was no stifling of ideas though. If you had an idea, you said so.'

Despite all the hard work of the team, Geoff Aldridge still regrets the lack of development on the Type 79:

> We did the 79 and it was so successful, then Williams copied it [with the FW07 in 1979], and there were things on the car which they'd copied that there was no logical reason for copying. They obviously didn't understand exactly what it was

The Design Process and Build Programme

Andretti at Monaco in 1979. The motion of the T80's suspension made the car pitch up and down, causing a phenomenon known as 'porpoising'. This was further aggravated by the inability of the skirts to follow suit, and was both uncomfortable and unsettling for the driver. (Peter Riches)

they were copying. For instance, Chapman wanted a curved panel over the driver's legs, which is difficult to do because of the double curvature. And he wanted wired edges to the apertures, also incredibly difficult. The Williams actually copied both those features, which were nothing but an aggravation. But after copying it they worked on it and made it better. If Lotus had done that, they'd probably still have had a winning car. But that wasn't Chapman's philosophy.

Build Programme

Up to 1976, Team Lotus racing cars were built by the mechanics, the people who raced them.

The Type 78 programme marked a major change in policy, with a dedicated team of designers and fabricators based at Ketteringham Hall. The racing team remained ensconced in the former wartime blockhouses a mile or so away along Potash Lane. Today, this austere complex is home to Clive Chapman's Classic Team Lotus operation, and is more or less opposite the Lotus car factory, which, with its test track, stands on the site of the demolished Hethel Hall.

Heading the construction team at Ketteringham Hall was Eddie Dennis, a veteran from the latter years at Cheshunt and Team Lotus chief mechanic from 1971 to 1974 and from 1975 to 1976. In the late 1960s, Dennis had worked on the Lotus 47 sports racers and the Winkelmann Type 48 F2 cars of Rindt and Hill, as well as servicing F1 gods such as Fittipaldi and Peterson in the early 1970s. As he recalls,

The Design Process and Build Programme

Above: *Fabricator Eric Gray, a veteran from the Team Lotus days at Hornsey and a virtuoso with aluminium. The Type 78 tub was constructed out of sheets of aluminium honeycomb, riveted together, with brackets and plated sections at the sides for the fuel tanks and brackets for mounting the water radiators and fuel tanks. (Tony Matthews)*

It was a major departure from what had gone before. The idea was to set up a research and development facility and a build shop. I was in charge of the machine shop, the fabrication shop and the build shop. There were ten or twelve people there. We'd build the cars and hand them over to the racing team. It was more of a half-past eight to half-past five regime. And it was pretty calm most of the time because we were working ahead. A couple of

Right: *Close-up of the Type 79's single-skin chassis, showing beaded edges to some of the apertures. The two brake and single clutch fluid reservoirs are prominent. (Tony Matthews)*

The Design Process and Build Programme

The left-hand side of the rose-jointed front suspension of the Type 78, which consisted of upper rocking arms, lower wishbones, coil springs and dampers, with outboard disc brake, air scoop and steering arm prominent. (Tony Matthews)

fabricators stayed behind at Potash Lane to do the maintenance, and there were six of us at Kett Hall: Roy Franks, Eric Gray, Billy Monaghan, Nick Paravani, Jim Bamber, and me. Eric Gray could do beaded and wired edges in L72 aluminium, which is pretty much a lost art nowadays. We had most of the tooling there, like the guillotine, although there wasn't a great deal of machinery. The limited number of tools provided says a lot for the skills of the fabricators.

There was sometimes friction between the designers and the fabricators, with the fabricators accusing the designers of not considering exactly how something was going to be put together. Eddie Dennis recalls, 'There'd be a confrontation while we sorted out what they wanted and how we'd make it.'

Another first was the test rigs that were assembled at Ketteringham Hall, ten years before five- and seven-post testing rigs became standard in F1. 'We built rigs for testing components like the top rocker arm, which had never been done before,' says Eddie. They also built a heavy-duty wooden table with a number of block-and-pulley devices to put loads in the car, described by Glenn Waters:

> The car sat on the table with its tyres on pads with small nails protruding through them to give it the type of grip level the tyre would see when it was warm and the downforce was on it. We would put sandbags on top of the wheels and apply various loads to try and pull it about and see what we could change in the suspension, whether it moved about in the monocoque or whatever.

The data was recorded by Mike Cook from the design office. Later, by the mid-1980s, they were using hydraulics rather than blocks and tackle.

At this point, Colin Chapman decided to embrace metric weights and measures. 'The Type 78 was the first Lotus to be built in metric,' says Eddie. 'No more feet and inches – although we were using imperial bolts for some time.'

Another novel feature of the ground-effect Lotuses was homogeneous body parts. 'The Types 78 and 79 were the first cars that had a fair chance of coming out with identical body parts,' says Dennis. 'Previously, the panels were fitted individually on cars like the 72 and, because there was so little time, different people fitted them in different ways. The Dzus fasteners on one car wouldn't line up with the holes on another car's bodywork. With the moulds for the 78 and 79 bodywork, all the holes for the fixings lined up.'

The new machine shop at Ketteringham Hall contained a jig on which the fabricators could manufacture skirts. Eddie Dennis explains how they were made:

> The Type 78 skirts were a 5mm-thick strip of polypropylene. We milled a groove about 2mm deep along the full length of the skirt, and that formed a hinge that allowed it to bend inwards and follow the contours of the road. We were experimenting on various types of skirt rubbing strips to see what would work. We had a chassis tub bolted on an angle-iron subframe fastened to the back of a Renault 4 van, and thrashed that round the lanes and the test track. Peter Wright was hanging out of the back watching how the skirts on the test rig behaved. Of the materials we tested, PTFE had very low friction and wear rate, but the ceramic-tipped one came out best in the end.

Glenn Waters reflects on the genesis of the Type 78:

> The 78 first ran after the August Bank Holiday in 1976. We took one of the 77s along to Silverstone with it to use as a benchmark. The only other team there was Tyrrell. Ken Tyrrell came up to look at the 78 and walked away quietly, talking about it. A lot of people were curious about it because, by contemporary standards, it was enormous. Everybody else was trying to make small cars, and suddenly Lotus brought this car out, which, superficially, looked like a tank.
>
> A big effort was made to take all the friction out of the suspension. If you look at the cars in detail, you'll notice that all the suspension joints – the rose joints, the bearings, or whatever – on the 78, appear to be massive. There was an attempt to have every joint as a rolling friction joint rather than a sliding friction joint.

When the car ran, the drivers remarked on its Rolls-Royce ride. Eddie Dennis was the first person to drive both the T78 and T79 prototypes on the Hethel test track, 'blatting up and down to sort out problems before the drivers tested them. The 77 was a darting sort of car – if you hit a bump on the straight it would dart 3 or 4ft to left or right. But the ride of the 78 was excellent.' At first it was the set-up of the suspension that was deemed to be the reason for this, as no one understood initially how ground-effect was working on the car. As Glenn Waters recalls,

> The second time we took the 78 to Silverstone it had a completely flat plywood floor. At that time the car had fixed brushes along the side of the skirts, like those little nylon brushes you'd find on a revolving door. They weren't that efficient then, but we put the plywood on the bottom and it didn't seem to make any great difference.

Tyre Factors

One of the most crucial factors in the fortunes of a race team is tyres, and it was this that had torpedoed the Type 72. The handling characteristics of a car originally designed to run on a Firestone specification no longer suited the new generation of Goodyears in 1974, despite the heroic efforts of Ronnie Peterson to demonstrate to the contrary. Predictably, the whole ground-effect phenomenon put much bigger loads into the tyres, which meant that they needed to be stiffer. Over the years, suspension systems came to be massively stiffened, which meant that tyres needed to be softer, in order to give the car a modicum of suspension. That produced conflicting

The Design Process and Build Programme

> **Working with Andretti**
>
> Mario Andretti's mechanic in 1977 and 1978 was Glenn Waters. He found Andretti a straightforward person, with the experience to know just what he wanted from a car:
>
> > He had some favourite tricks, especially to do with the tyres, which owed much to his career in oval racing. When it came to putting the qualifying tyres on, they would normally increase the camber of the wheels by about half a degree for him. Then they would give him about three more flats on a camber adjuster, because he was going to lean a little bit harder on the qualifying tyres. Andretti was more particular about those than other drivers of the era.
>
> As well as the stagger of the tyres, Andretti frequently asked Waters for another clip on the dampers. Indeed, he would often get out of the car, ask for the spanners and adjust it himself, which was completely untypical of a racing driver of the time. Again, that went back to the days when Andretti worked on his own racing cars. He would always take the time to be involved in the set-up of the car.
>
> The only time Andretti was less than amiable was when he had made a mistake. As Waters says,
>
> > If he'd made an error then he was wild with himself. When things went wrong, or we had let him down, he always took the view that there was another race next week and didn't let it get to him.
>
> Andretti and Colin Chapman never got angry with one another, although the American was unimpressed when the car ran out of fuel. According to Waters,
>
> > There would be a bit of ridicule, but never any screaming or shouting, and this attitude was common to other teams. They were different days. There was much more of a feeling that we were all in it together, since there were so few of us compared with today.

results – compounds also had to be harder because they had to do more work – but, in general, ground-effect pushed the loads up so that bigger, stiffer, higher-load capacity tyres were required.

Nobody exploited the omnipresent fluctuations in tyre quality as cleverly as Mario Andretti, who brought the practice of measuring tyres to Formula 1. In those days, F1 tyres were not radials but bias-ply, and they were not particularly accurately manufactured. Two seemingly identical tyres pumped up to the same pressure might have a discrepancy of circumferance of up to an inch. From his experience with oval racing, Andretti understood the sensitivities of adjusting the handling of the car by making a tyre on one side slightly bigger than its opposite number. The mechanics would frequently over-pressurize a tyre overnight to expand the carcass slightly, so it would be slightly different from the other.

When two tyres of slightly different sizes were fitted on the car, and the differentials were set up quite tight, this would have the effect of making the car want to go to one side all the time. Andretti would be able to ascertain this by the position of the steering-wheel arms. If the tyre was trying to drive the car to the left, and he was having to restrain it with a certain amount of right-hand down, he would know that his right-hand tyre was slightly large. He would come in and ask his mechanic Glenn Waters or tyre man Kenny Szymanski to 'check the stagger', which meant measuring the circumference; sometimes they would have to swap them from side to side. According to Waters, 'The Goodyear

Opposite: *Andretti's Type 80 has its Goodyear slicks checked by Team Lotus tyre man Clive Hicks (right). The American driver knew how to use the fluctuations in tyre manufacture to best advantage, insisting the diameters be measured, 'checking the stagger' for optimum set-up. In 1979 the Goodyear runners had their work cut out to match the Ferraris, which were running Michelin tyres. (Peter Riches)*

guys didn't like that, because the tyre has a splice on it, and running it against the splice you'd get a line of wear building up – you were sort of going against the grain, as far as they were concerned.'

They would run the front tyres contrary to the official direction of rotation, but the splice wasn't an issue there, although they took the biggest braking loads. The rear tyres would be run the right way round because the biggest load was obviously the driving force. Waters explains further:

> It became apparent that there was a line across the tyre, which was the splice, the place where the last bit of rubber went on during the manufacturing process as they wound it up. So if you run the tyre the correct way round, the rubber melts over the top and you never see the line. But if you go the other way with it, the rubber is abraded and the line appears.

As Peter Wright observes,

> It was a competitive era, and the tyre companies were into that. By the time ground-effect had finally arrived and been widely accepted, Lotus weren't the leaders any more. And since nobody really cottoned on until after 1978, ground-effect didn't really affect tyre design until after that.

5 Specifications and Construction of the Type 78

Meet the Ancestors

A number of cars make up the background to the Type 78. In Formula 1 in the early 1970s, the trend-setting wedge profile was the Type 72. Its top-line career lasted from 1970 to 1974 and it ended up with three constructors' titles to its credit. The failure of its successor, the Type 76, meant that it soldiered on into 1976. The relatively limited evolution in the Type 72's aerodynamic appendages over that period show how locked-down the thinking had become on the subject. Nevertheless, the basic wedge shape of the Type 72 endured up to the introduction of the torpedo-shaped cars of the early 1980s.

The Type 76 was unveiled at the New London Theatre, Drury Lane, in 1974, in one of the first presentations of its kind. It was all suits and laboured formality, with showbiz personality William Franklin acting as host. The Ralph Bellamy-designed T76 consisted of a delta-

Specifications and Construction of the Type 78

The dart-shaped Type 76, driven by Jacky Ickx at Kyalami in 1974, originally featured electronic clutch, four pedals and biplane rear wing. By the South African GP Ickx had reverted to the conventional three-pedal layout. (John Tipler)

shaped monocoque made of 16-gauge aluminium alloy sheet. It had T72-style torsion-bar suspension and fabricated double wishbones at the front, and twin parallel upper links, single lower links and twin radius rods at the rear, with inboard-mounted 10in disc brakes all round. The Cosworth engine, an integral part of the chassis, was mated to a Hewland FG400 five-speed transaxle, but here the formula parted company with accepted practice. The T76 was equipped with an electronic clutch, oper-

Opposite: *Ronnie Peterson flings the Type 72 around the Dijon-Prenois circuit on his way to winning the 1974 French Grand Prix. The 72's career lasted from 1972 to 1975, during which time it was pensioned off more than once, only to be reinstated as Team Lotus's front-line weapon. (John Tipler)*

ated by a button on the gear lever that activated the hydraulic system via a starter motor-driven pump. It also had four pedals: the one on the left worked the clutch to get the car away from a standstill; the right-hand pedal was the accelerator; and the two in the middle provided a facility for left- and right-foot braking. It was also fitted with a staggered biplane rear wing, the most notable attempt at advancing the rear-wing configuration.

The T76 (or 'JPS 1', as sponsor John Player insisted on referring to it) promised a great deal more than it ever delivered. At Kyalami 1974, Jacky Ickx reverted to the normal three-pedal layout while Ronnie Peterson had the left-foot brake pedal relocated to the extreme left (so it was outside the clutch pedal). With throttle jammed, he inadvertently took out both 76s at the first turn. Peterson also reverted to the conventional pedal layout and led the *Daily Express* race at Silverstone until his engine seized. Gradually, the gizmos fell by the

Specifications and Construction of the Type 78

wayside and, with regular clutch control, Peterson led in Spain until his engine failed again. When both 76s packed up in Belgium, the old faithful Type 72s were reinstated and the Type 76s were condemned to be, at best, back-up cars; mostly, they were cannibalized for spares.

Disgruntled Drivers

Colin Chapman was faced with two very disgruntled drivers in Peterson and Ickx. On the advice of his manager Staffan Svenby, Peterson had written to Chapman on 12 June, 1975, expressing grave concerns about repeated brake and driveshaft failures on the Types 72 and 76. As for Jacky Ickx, he simply walked away after the 1975 French GP. Chapman pushed through the Type 77 for the 1976 season, and it was launched in September 1975. The chief sponsor – by now wavering on whether to pull out or not – required that it be known as the 'John Player Special Mark II'.

The idea of the Type 77 was to produce an infinitely variable car with subframes that could be swapped as and when required so that the track and wheelbase matched the requirements of a particular circuit. Ronnie Peterson wanted to race it straight away, but Chapman insisted that it should be fully tested first. Team Lotus had experimented with the concept of variable chassis lengths and widths, using a variety of bolt-on subframes, to provide a multi-adjustable car. Tests at Paul Ricard in November 1975 showed that the T77 seemed to work best with a long chassis and wide track configuration. It was as they were returning from this particular session that Graham Hill's Embassy Hill team was wiped out in an air crash. But for a last-minute switch to Colin Chapman's plane, Peterson would also have been on Graham Hill's flight. The Swede may have been shaken by this but, in the event, it was the scary nature of the short-wheelbase T77's handling on its debut at Interlagos in 1976 that prompted him to leave immediately and rejoin his former employers at the March team.

The Cosworth DFV-powered Type 77's aluminium monocoque chassis, designed by Geoff Aldridge, had a central fuel cell and a pair of side tanks, a triangulated section over the driver's legs, and the now customary side radiators. The suspension, designed by Martin Ogilvie, consisted of fabricated double wish-

Andretti dives into the Karussell at the Nürburgring in 1976 with Scheckter's Tyrrell P34 in the background. The Type 77 was pushed through for the 1976 F1 season, and componentry such as the rear suspension and the air-box design were carried over to the Type 78. The JPS logos were absent at the Nürburgring because of German tobacco advertising rules. (Ford Photographic Archive)

Specifications and Construction of the Type 78

Type 77 (1976)	
Designers	Geoff Aldridge, Martin Ogilvie
Chassis tub	aluminium monocoque
Engine	Cosworth DFV
Gearbox	Hewland FG400
Front suspension	double wishbones, outboard coil spring/damper units, anti-roll bar
Rear suspension	single lower links, parallel upper links, twin radius rods, outboard coil spring/damper units, anti-roll bar
Wheelbase	9ft 2in (2795mm)
Front track	4ft 2in (127mm)
Rear track	5ft 1in (155mm)
Weight	11.60 cwt

Spooky Handling

Mario Andretti declared that the Type 77's handling was 'spooky', in that it was erratic. 'Spooky means exactly that,' he says. 'The 77 was a flexible flyer.' It was not unusual for F1 cars in the mid-1970s to flex to such an extent that their handling behaviour would be unpredictable. In the case of the Type 77 it was partly to do with the way the front bulkhead was fabricated. 'Under braking you never knew which way it was going to go,' says Andretti. Chapman was aware that he didn't have a very good car, but he and Andretti resolved to make it a winner before the end of the 1976 season. Indeed, the last race of the year at Fuji was won by Andretti and the Type 77. According to Mario, 'The car was coming around, but it was definitely at the end of its life, no question. Colin knew that he needed to do something really drastic.'

bones, outboard coil springs and damper units up front, with single lower links, parallel upper links, twin radius rods, outboard coil springs and damper units at the back. The inboard braking system was notable in that the calipers doubled as pick-ups for the suspension links and wishbones.

Initially, Peterson had been joined by Mario Andretti on a one-race deal, but after the Brazilian debacle, when both Lotuses collided, Gunnar Nilsson effectively traded places at March with Peterson, and was joined for a few races by F5000 stalwart Bob Evans. The Type 77s were dogged by rear-suspension maladies, and for the *Daily Express* International Trophy, Nilsson's solo entry had a redesigned front suspension and brake system, hurriedly provided by Team Lotus's former designer from the early 1960s, Len Terry. Brakes were now outboard, suspension uprights were Ralt F2 items, with new bottom wishbones and upper rocking arms. Such was the improvement that Nilsson achieved fourth-fastest practice time and finished sixth in the race.

After his brief sojourn with the Parnelli squad, Mario Andretti returned to Team Lotus full-time for the Spanish Grand Prix, for which the T77s had air-boxes mounted on either side of the engine cover. Nilsson came in third, with blistered hands from incessant gear changing, while Andretti was forced to retire. Evidently, Team Lotus was still some way from the podium. A string of retirements was relieved by Nilsson's third place at the Österreichring – crossing the line with a blown engine – and Andretti taking third at Zandvoort and Mosport. In Canada, the cars ran with a wheelbase that was 4mm shorter, and, significantly, were fitted with brush skirts. As the world championship reached a dramatic finale – with Hunt and Lauda vying for top spot – at a wet and misty Fuji, Andretti took pole and, by dint of conserving his tyres in the appalling conditions, scored the Type 77's single race victory.

Glenn Waters recalls that season:

> We worked through the year [1976] with the 77, and the car got incrementally better. The weight distribution of the car kept changing, with radiators in the front to keep the car down to the lightest weight. From the middle of the year onwards

Specifications and Construction of the Type 78

we copied McLaren and developed a compressed-air starter-motor system for it.

From the Dutch Grand Prix onwards, a real effort was made to exclude the air from underneath the car using nylon industrial brushes and, latterly, ethane mouldings with a 45-degree angle in them, which could be attached to the bottom outer edges of the side pods. These provided a wear strip that ran along the leading edge of the radiators and went down and prevented some of the air from going

Right-hand side pod of the Type 78, showing brush skirt, water radiator at the front, battery and fuel filler cap; riveted sections to cockpit and central fuel tank are also evident. (Tony Matthews)

The cockpit of the Type 78 was made as narrow as possible, with water radiators housed in the leading edges of the side pods and hot air expelled from vents behind them. Filler caps for the fuel tanks were in the top of the side pods. Rear-view mirror housings helped stiffen the bodywork and mirrored the air-box shape. (Classic Team Lotus)

under the car. By the last two or three races of the season, the Type 77 was a reasonably competitive car.

Sometimes, a season has to be sacrificed in the interests of developing a new racing car. This was pretty much the case in 1976.

The Type 78

In deference to sponsor John Player, the Lotus 78 was identified as 'JPS Mk III'. Whereas the Type 77s were slim cars with side radiators located at the rear end of the chassis, similar to the T72, the T78s were broad, full-width monocoques made of stiff L72 aluminium honeycomb sandwich, with radiators in the leading edges of the side pods, just behind the front wheels. Fuel tanks were housed in the sides of the monocoque behind the radiators. The hot air from the radiators exited on top of the side pods by the cockpit, while under the side pods towards the rear, the inverted aerofoil created downforce. The underneath of the pods sloped upwards to the rear and stopped level with the engine mounts, forming the inverted wing section, which generated an area of low pressure to suck the car down towards the track surface. The side structures were completed by Cellite closures at the rear, and at either side bristle skirts bridged the gap between car and track. The brushes actually swept the track surface to control the air flow.

'The Lotus 78 was not designed as a ground-effect car out of the box,' says Mario Andretti. 'The shape was there, and it had the wing-shaped pods on the side with fences, but initially the fence only went to a certain level, because obviously it was going to touch the ground. But that's how we discovered the importance of closing the sides.

The rest of the car's aerodynamics were trimmed with nose fins and a rear wing. The chassis also had a stressed section behind the upper cockpit area and a structural section around the front of the cockpit, while the front

Shown before being connected up, the Type 78's rear suspension consisted of parallel links, twin radius rods and outboard coil spring and dampers. Installation of the inboard brake discs and calipers was facilitated by the casing of the Lotus/Hewland gearbox that was designed to accommodate them. (Tony Matthews)

bulkhead and side skins were formed from aluminium honeycomb sandwich. As Tony Rudd explains, 'Ralph Bellamy sourced the aluminium honeycomb for the chassis, and he was the one that developed the techniques so we could use it.' Eddie Dennis adds, 'The fact that the monocoque was in honeycomb caused a few problems, mostly with glueing the sandwich together.'

65

The Type 78 was unveiled at the Royal Garden Hotel in London in December 1976, with 'draught-excluder' brush-type side skirts prominent under the side pods. (Ian Catt)

One of the main problems with the honeycomb chassis was that it was irreparable. According to Tony Rudd,

> If you stuffed it, it couldn't be hammered straight. I wanted to test the strength of it, because the forces were going to be about four times as great as anything we'd ever used before and we needed to understand it. It could well break something that had always worked OK. The aerodynamic loads we were going to put on it were going to be colossal, and I didn't believe some of the suspension systems were going to work in the same way. So, a test rig was in my scheme of things, and, although Ralph recognized the need for it, I'm not sure he was overly enthusiastic.

Although the body of the car was of the maximum permissible width, the cockpit itself was extremely narrow, tapering forwards almost to a point. The engine received its air supply through ducts that protruded like ears from each side of the cockpit roll-over hoop.

Front suspension was by upper rocking arms and lower fabricated wishbones, inboard coil springs and damper units, complemented by lower wishbones, parallel upper links, twin radius rods, outboard coil springs and dampers at the back, with a rear anti-roll bar that could be adjusted by the driver. The wheel bearings were a new and unique one-piece fitting with the constant velocity joint. The wheel bearing was machined into the outer rim of the constant velocity joint by RHP (Ransomes-Hoffman-Pollard).

Public Debut

The Type 78 was taken to the Paul Ricard circuit in the south of France for its public debut, by this time painted in JPS colours. According to Glenn Waters, 'It posted respectable times, but it wasn't doing more than the 77 which we had there at the same time. The 77 had a

Opposite: *Rear quarters of the Type 78, showing suspension linkages, inboard brakes, driveshafts, starter gas bottle, and brackets for mounting the aerofoil. The oil tank was located behind the engine in the bell-housing of the Hewland gearbox. (Tony Matthews)*

Specifications and Construction of the Type 78

Amid all the razzmatazz of the Type 78's launch, drivers Gunnar Nilsson and Mario Andretti are pensive about their prospects with the new car. (Ian Catt)

quick run to put in a base lap time as a target for the 78, and the rest of the effort was devoted to the 78.'

The Type 78 was officially launched at the Royal Garden Hotel in London in December 1976. Although both Andretti and Nilsson were cheerfully present, for Colin Chapman the occasion was marred by the loss of his father Stan in a road accident on the way to Norfolk. Chapman stayed away and relied on Tony Rudd to deputize for him. After the launch, two cars were shipped off to Argentina, with only 78/1 having actually run.

There were a number of issues that still had to be worked through. Glenn Waters recalls the process:

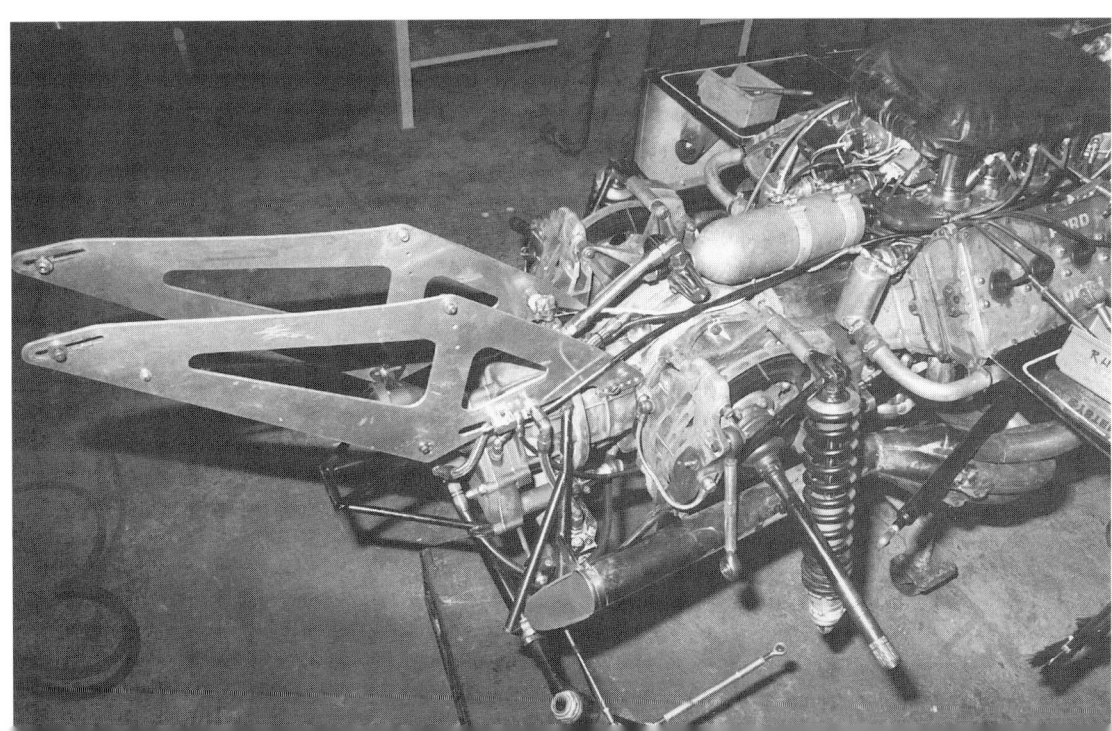

Specifications and Construction of the Type 78

Type 78 (1977–78)	
Designers	Ralph Bellamy, Martin Ogilvie
Chassis	aluminium monocoque, with Cellite sheets enclosing aluminium honeycomb incorporated in front bulkhead and side skins; three fuel cells
Engine	Cosworth DFV
Gearbox	Hewland FG400, Lotus-Getrag
Front suspension	upper rocking arms, lower wishbones, inboard coil spring/damper units, anti-roll bar
Rear suspension	lower wishbones, parallel upper links, twin radius rods, outboard coil spring/damper units, anti-roll bar
Wheelbase	8ft 11in (2728mm)
Front track	5ft 7in (1702mm)
Rear track	5ft 3in (1600mm)
Weight	11.70 cwt

We never ran the fully blocked up flat wooden floor again. It always ran with the tunnels. We changed the profile of the parts which ran alongside the engine to give the under-wing a bit more camber. Every time something was changed, the car did a few laps. It had the ground-effect side pods with the radiators inside the wings each side, and it had three fuel tanks which was in the regulations at that time. There was a driver-operated fuel switch, and the driver could select not to use the inside tank until a certain proportion of the fuel load had been used, thereby keeping the weight inside the car.

The Type 78 prototype (78/1) was about 4in (100mm) longer than subsequent chassis because initially it had an oil tank between the back of the fuel tank and the engine. In the interests of a long wheelbase layout, it also had a bell-housing oil tank, making it the first car to have the oil tank incorporated in the bell-housing with a coaxial clutch. There was a hole through the centre for the clutch shaft, the clutch being operated axially through this shaft. If the bell-housing oil tank had failed to work there was the possibility of reverting to the normal metal oil rig. Subsequent cars did not have the extra oil tank, so they were 4in shorter in the wheelbase.

The Type 78 was popular with the people who worked on it, including Glenn Waters:

> The 78 was one of the better cars I had to deal with at Lotus. It was the most structurally complete car. From a racing operator's point of view, we weren't continually having to rebuild the structure of the monocoque just to maintain the car. On the 77, and latterly the 79, we were for ever fiddling with the engine mountings because they were pulling out. Various parts of the structure were actually failing. The 78 was nicely done because it had a completely full double-skin monocoque. Those two little wings down the side of the driver in the sides of the cockpit were an attempt to circumvent the regulations. It was deemed that they defined the cockpit entry, not the smaller aperture that the driver actually got in. The advantage was that they made the cockpit surround torsionally better. There were some oddities structurally to it. For instance, they attached the fuel tank base and didn't run it all the way through to the back of the monocoque.

The Verdict

One of the few shortcomings of the Type 78 was the fuel system, which, under certain circumstances, failed to pick up all of the fuel. As Glenn Waters states,

> When we ran the car at Interlagos, which was a left-hand circuit, we knew the car couldn't run the race without being refuelled. In those days

Specifications and Construction of the Type 78

As well as the fuel tanks housed in both side pods, the Type 78 also carried a fuel cell behind the cockpit. One of the original flaws to this layout was that not all the fuel could be accessed, so eventually a fuel pick up tank was installed in the forward section of the cockpit floor. The T78 was equipped with the air start system and used a small, lightweight motorcycle battery. The battery's connection to the Zenar diode is also visible. (Tony Matthews)

the bend after the pits was a very long flat-out left-hander, not a chicane like it is now. We seemed to slosh all the fuel to the wrong side and then not pick it up. So the panel that went down behind the driver's calves was removed, and I'm sure that would have had some effect on the torsional rigidity. This little fuel tank was put down there beside the driver's left knee inside the car.

Waters is convinced that the location of the tank contributed to the severity of Ronnie Peterson's fatal accident at Monza in 1978, since it burst and caught fire.

The footwell area of the Type 78 reveals pedal and steering-column layout, demonstrating how the driver's feet had to tuck behind the steering arrangement, with heels resting on a ledge on the floor. (Tony Matthews)

Specifications and Construction of the Type 78

The Ford-Cosworth DFV Engine

The 3.0-litre Ford-Cosworth DFV (double-four-valve) V8 engine used in the Lotus T78 and T79 made its debut at the 1967 Dutch Grand Prix and powered Jim Clark's Lotus T49 to a maiden victory. Funded by the Ford Motor Company to the tune of £100,000, the Cosworth-built engine was available exclusively to Team Lotus for that season, and Clark won again with it at Silverstone, Watkins Glen and Mexico City. The following year, Matra and McLaren also had use of it, and by 1969, two-thirds of the cars on Grand Prix grids were powered by the same engine.

Although the Cosworth DFV power unit held sway throughout the 1970s, it gave best to Ferrari in the constructors' tables in 1975, 1976, 1977 and 1979. During the ground-effect era, the Cosworth V8 was used by all but Ferrari, Matra, Brabham (Alfa Romeo engines) and Renault. It was affordable, available and reliable, and was the natural choice for the vast majority of non-factory-backed constructors who could bolt on a competitive motor. However, after Nelson Piquet won the 1983 world title with a turbocharged Brabham BT52B-BMW, other teams took the forced-induction route, and by 1985 only Tyrrell and Minardi were running Cosworth DFVs.

The DFV was the most successful engine in the history of the World Championship, racking up 155 Grand Prix victories between 1967 and 1985. Its origins lay in a deal brokered by Colin Chapman in the summer of 1966 between Ford Motor Company UK, under Walter Hayes and Keith Duckworth, and Mike Costin of Cosworth Engineering. Designed by Duckworth, the Cosworth power unit was a doubling-up of the existing 1600 FVA unit that had been immensely successful in Formula 2. The DFV For-

mula 1 engine introduced the concept of systems integration to racing-car builders – the engine could be a stressed chassis member, in a configuration pioneered by Lotus with the Type 49.

Announced on 25 April 1967, the Cosworth DFV's principal characteristics were a 90-degree V-shaped layout, 2,995cc capacity, a single flat-plane crank, pent-roof combustion chamber with four valves per cylinder (hence DFV) with a valve-included angle of 32 degrees. Power output was 450bhp at 9,500rpm. Each bank of double overhead camshafts was driven by a series of spur gears from a half-speed compound gear in the centre of the engine's V, itself driven by a compound gear running off the crankshaft gear. Using belt-drive, its half-speed shaft drove ancillaries, including a pair of water pumps, fuel pump, oil pressure pump and two oil scavenge pumps, as well as driving another shaft for the distributor, alternator and fuel-injection-metering unit, located in the central V of the engine within the fuel-injection induction trumpets.

It was a compact, lightweight unit, wider than its length, although no broader than the shoulders of the average racing driver. With the fuel cell occupying a similar dimension between cockpit and powertrain, as in the case of the ground-effect Lotuses, the venturii tunnels on either side of the chassis were not obstructed by cylinder heads and induction systems, as they were with the rival flat 12 Ferrari and Alfa Romeo engines.

The Cosworth DFV engine proved a crucial factor in the success of the Types 78 and 79. As Mario Andretti points out,

> We came to realize how important it was to have as free an exit of air as possible from the venturii. Even changing the offset of the rear wheels would affect that. The Lotus 78 was very cluttered back there, but by the time we got to the 79, that area was all cleaned up.

Opposite: *The 3.0-litre Ford-Cosworth DFV V8 engine as fitted to the Type 79. Mountings were prone to crack and fall apart inside the car. Coolant pipes were routed to the radiator in the right-hand side pod. Typically, the Type 79's exhaust pipes were tuned lengths, designed to take advantage of pressure drop and pulsations, and provide better engine breathing and higher rpm. (Tony Matthews)*

By 1977, Cosworth was building 'development' F1 engines that produced more horsepower than its normal 'customer' DFVs. A handful of the leading teams, including Team Lotus, received these engines, but they proved to be fragile, and Mario Andretti preferred to rely on the standard unit:

> In 1977 with the Lotus 78, Cosworth were really on our side, and they wanted to do everything possible to help us win races. So they said, 'We'll give you development engines and make sure that you have the most horsepower.' Huge mistake for us, because all of that cost me the championship. The engine was our Achilles heel in 1977. For instance, in Sweden in mid-race, it went to full rich. I knew at that point that it might be a problem for me finishing the race because Colin always wanted to finish the race with maybe half a litre of fuel in the car. The Ligier was running second to me, and I let him creep closer and closer because I was trying to save fuel. We didn't have radios in those days, and I kept trying to motion to them to prepare for a splash-and-dash, and they had no idea what the hell I was trying to say. The engine sputtered, and I came in with two laps to go to get half a gallon of fuel, and by the time they'd realized what I needed and I went out again, I was down to sixth.
>
> We ran out of oil in the Canadian GP. They were running one-ring pistons for less friction. I had a one-lap advantage on Jody Scheckter, and my oil pressure started fluctuating with ten laps to go. I started slowing down and on the last lap, at the end of the straight, the engine scattered. The straightaway at Mosport is uphill, so I didn't get much of a run and I thought I could coast through the next couple of corners. I was 50 yards from the start-finish line when I stopped, and there again I was classified sixth and got one point. That should have been another easy win. In fact, when I count all of the debacles to do with the engine, I probably should have won the championship even easier than in 1978.

Apart from Cosworth, other specialist DFV engine builders used by Team Lotus during this period were Nicholson Racing Engines, Swindon Racing Engines and Euroracing Engines.

Specifications and Construction of the Type 78

Instrument panel of the Type 78 contains rev counter, fuel and oil-pressure gauge to the right and oil and water-temperature gauge to the left. The lens on the steering wheel holds an oil-pressure warning light. A second tachometer is set to the left of the steering column, and the adjuster for the rear anti-roll bar is visible to the left of the cockpit. The padding is support for the driver's thigh. (Tony Matthews)

The Type 78 changed little from the beginning of its race career to the time when it was superseded by the Type 79. Mario Andretti assesses it as follows:

> Inside the cockpit there was no question that the 78 and 79 felt very different. Overall, the 79 was the better car because, with everything inside, it was cleaner and quicker on the straightaway. The 78 was like a brick down the straight. The 79 had more downforce, and the quality of the 78, but tremendously polished up.

In spite of all the evidence, at the end of 1977, hardly anybody else decided to build a ground-effect car, probably because, when the car went to the really fast circuits such as Hockenheim, it did not have the edge. There was still some scepticism about whether the ground-effect car worked or not. As Glenn Waters explains,

> The Type 78 was a hedge-your-bets wing car. It had all of these other more conventional aerodynamic features, and the air flow over the car was not ideal. It had big inboard brakes at the rear, which were in the way of the tunnel. It just wasn't done as effectively as it was on the Lotus 79. On the 79, everything was sacrificed for ground-effect, so you had a quite superior wing car, which was structurally inadequate.

By the end of 1978, when the loads generated by the downforce were enormous, and heavier springs were fitted on the T79, the structure could no longer take the inputs. That was why the Ligier and subsequently the Williams FW07 were so much more effective; they were better structured cars, although neither had such an ideal aerodynamic shape.

6 Specifications and Construction of the Types 79 and 80

The Type 79

Skating Off

The Type 79 was built at Ketteringham Hall and tested at Hethel, Silverstone and Paul Ricard during the winter of 1977–78, although conceptual work started early on in 1977. The Type 79 prototype (79/1) was used only as a development car, and a second chassis, 79/2, was built up. This car made its debut at the *Daily Express* International Trophy race at Silverstone; in appalling weather conditions, Mario Andretti lasted only three laps before skating off, along with most other runners. The car was badly damaged when it struck Regazzoni's abandoned Shadow, and a major rebuild ensued.

With the T79, Colin Chapman fully embraced the ground-effect principles that

Reg Underhill works on the prototype in November 1977. The tub of the Type 79 was very slim and made of single-skin riveted aluminium panels. Underhill's main role was to put together component and suspension sub-assemblies ready for the racing team. (Tony Matthews)

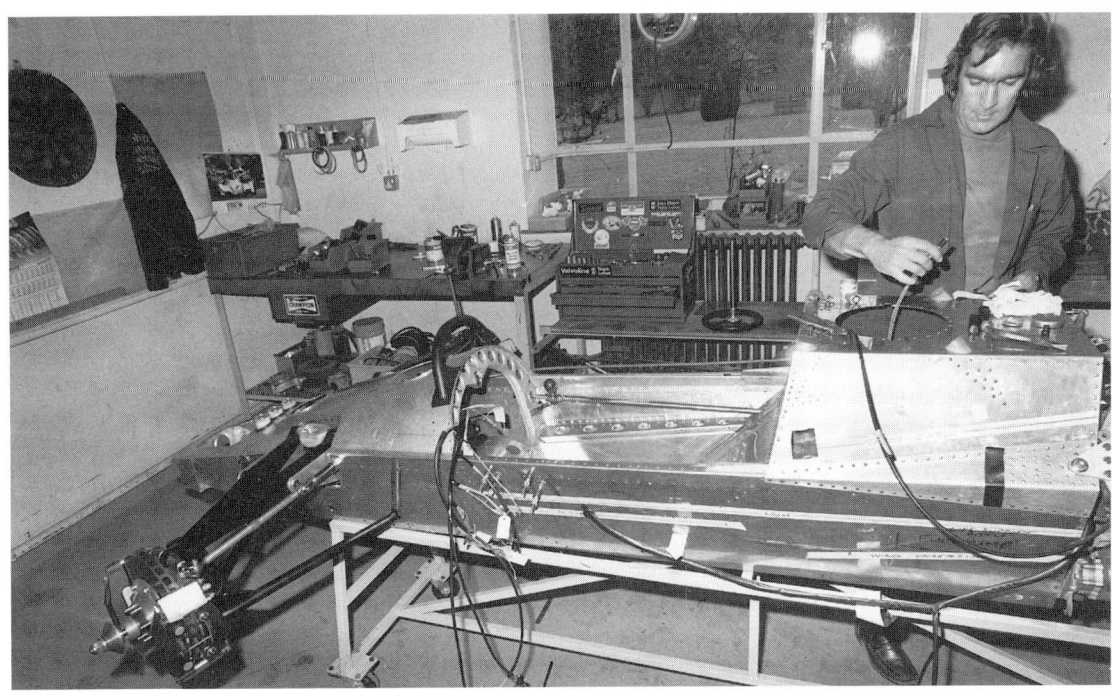

Andretti fires up the Type 79 prototype for the benefit of the press and hardy observers in the snow-lined Silverstone pits in April 1978. (Ian Catt)

were beginning to bear fruit with the T78, and was much involved with its detailing. The T79 was a whole-hearted attempt to make the underside of the car work towards increasing downforce. It was a major leap forward, with only Harvey Postlethwaite's Wolf WR5 operating on anything like the same lines; the rest of the grid was still trying to get on terms with the Type 78 in its 1977 configuration. At Chapman's behest, the T79 monocoque consisted of sheet aluminium rather than honeycomb, which was only used for the clean, smooth floor. It was a slimmer chassis than the T78, without the sideways

Specifications and Construction of the Types 79 and 80

Cockpit shot of the Type 79 prototype under construction. The Momo steering wheel and gear lever are in place, while the perforated front bulkhead that provided much of the rigidity in the scuttle area is also visible. 79/1 also had a separate front roll-over hoop. (Tony Matthews)

Dashboard of the Type 79, showing the raised front roll-hoop that superseded 79/1, ignition cut-off on the Momo wheel, central tachometer, with fuel and oil-pressure gauge to the right and oil and water-temperature gauge on the left. The fire extinguisher button and tail-light switch are to the right of the dash. (Tony Matthews)

Opposite: *The first person to drive both T78 and T79 prototypes was fabrication shop boss Eddie Dennis, seen here assembling the Type 79 prototype. Signwriter Paul Crowland (closest to camera) is at work inscribing the aluminium cover over the roll-hoop with the name of the driver. This section of bodywork was later extended to provide more surface for sponsor advertising. The oil radiator is mounted on the left-hand side of the tub. (Tony Matthews)*

extensions that housed the T78's fuel tanks. Apart from containing the oil and water radiators, the T79's side pods performed the fundamental aerodynamic function and were attached to the sides of the monocoque. Its cockpit was strengthened around the dash by a perforated bulkhead similar to the Type 77's

Specifications and Construction of the Types 79 and 80

Close-up of the Type 79's water radiator, inlet and outlet tubing and flimsy-looking bracing, showing also the angled top and bottom which maximized the usable area within the side-pod housing. (Tony Matthews)

and 78's, and by another panel enclosing the pedal area.

Instead of a water radiator on either side, the T79's water radiator was located in the right-hand side pod and the much smaller oil cooler in the left-hand one. While the oil cooler was upright, the water radiator was inclined at a steeply rearward-raked angle, with a flattened-off top and bottom (making a parallelogram when viewed in profile) for maximum use of the space. The car's single 34-gallon-and-1-pint capacity fuel cell was located behind the driver, rather than in the side pods, meaning that the driver had to sit further forward than in the T78 cockpit. The work's Renault 4 van was also used to test the Type 79's fuel tank as well as towing the sliding-skirt test rig. The full-size mock-up tank was made of perspex so they could see what was going on inside it, to make sure that the fuel was sluicing into four 'feet' at each corner of the tank under braking and cornering, and passing up the tubes that fed the catch tank. According to Eddie Dennis, 'It worked well even with just half a gallon in.'

Transmission Test

The T79's DFV engine was at first allied to a Lotus-Getrag gearbox and sequential shift. This unit proved to be insufficiently strong and, by the time of its reappearance at the 1978 Monaco Grand Prix, the in-house transmission had been replaced by the Hewland FG400 transmission. Meanwhile, further development work was carried out on the Lotus-Getrag transmission using the prototype 79/1 to test it in.

One of the main issues surrounding the Type 79 concerned the designated gearbox. Martin Ogilvie has a particular view on this:

The choice of gearbox stemmed from Colin Chapman's antipathy to Mike Hewland. Whether they crossed swords at an earlier time I don't know. At any rate, Chapman didn't have much regard for him, and he didn't like the weight of all the gears hanging on the back axle. He wanted the car to have a much more compact gearbox, and he came across this layout on something like a Goggomobile where all the gears were trussed together and selected from the inside. The gears were on a big hollow shaft and selected by going up the shaft; it

Specifications and Construction of the Types 79 and 80

The compact Lotus-Getrag gearbox was a prominent feature of the original Type 79, as was the oil tank between engine and gearbox – in this case, still in plywood mock-up. The gearbox castings incorporated housings for the inboard brake callipers. The Lotus-designed casings were made by GKN. (Tony Matthews)

picked up the gears through slots in the shaft and that saved an awful lot of room. The second Type 79 did have the Lotus gearbox back end and they did a lot of revisions at the same time. Whilst that was happening we modified the bodywork, and that was the car that was taken and practised at Monaco, and then went on to Zolder and won there first time out.

The old Lotus 'queerbox' that formed the basis for the transmission described by Ogilvie dated from the late 1950s, when it was used in the Lotus Mk 15 sports racer and Type 16 F1/F2 cars. The job of reviving it was given to Tony Rudd and Brian Spooner. On Colin Chapman's insistence, the sequential-shift box was designed around the ZF crownwheel-and-pinion and differential assembly from the Type 56 four-wheel-drive Indianapolis gas-turbine car. According to Rudd, his argument was that, since the Pratt and Whitney PT6 tur-

	Type 79 (1978–79)
Designer	Martin Ogilvie
Chassis	aluminium monocoque, honeycomb sandwich floor, perforated stressed bulkhead, single fuel cell; sliding skirts
Engine	Cosworth DFV
Gearbox	Hewland FG400, Lotus-Getrag
Front suspension	upper rocking arms, lower wishbones, inboard coil spring/damper units, anti-roll bar
Rear suspension	lower wishbones, upper rocking arms, inboard coil spring/damper units, anti-roll bar
Wheelbase	9ft 0in (2743mm)
Front track	5ft 8in (1727mm)
Rear track	5ft 4in (1625mm)
Weight	11.32 cwt

Specifications and Construction of the Types 79 and 80

Transmission of the prototype Type 79, showing how the rear brake assemblies were housed in the castings of the Lotus-Getrag gearbox. Also visible are inboard spring and dampers, adjustable anti-roll bar, oil tank, and the original parallel exhaust pipes that pre-dated the eventual twinned solution. (Tony Matthews)

The Type 79 mostly ran with the ubiquitous Hewland (six-speed) gearbox, as installed here. It was quite common to have different back ends on the later cars. The Lotus-designed inboard brake assembly, oil tank and twin upward-pointing exhausts are also prominent. (Tony Matthews)

Specifications and Construction of the Types 79 and 80

bine of the T56 had much more torque than a 3.0-litre Cosworth DFV engine, it would therefore have adequate strength. Rudd advised Chapman that turbine torque was different from piston engine torque because it was constant, whereas with a piston engine it would be the average of a fluctuating amount. The solution was to use balls in tangential holes to lock the desired gear in place, activated by pulling a cone through the driveshaft to select the gear needed.

With the aim of obtaining a prototype, they went in the first instance to see ZF, who were too busy to oblige. However, Getrag recognized the idea as being the transmission they had developed for the Messerschmitt bubble car in the late 1940s, and were able to produce exactly what Team Lotus had in mind. As it turned out, the cars ran mostly with Hewland transmissions, with the Lotus-Getrag gearbox ultimately being shelved.

The drivers had different gearbox preferences. Gunnar Nilsson used a six-speed Hewland gearbox a number of times, but Mario Andretti refused to have anything to do with it, claiming, 'I'd had this five-speed gearshift pattern imprinted on my hand for 20 years and wasn't about to change now.' Although the Lotus-Getrag gearbox was phased out, Andretti had no problem with it:

> The Lotus-Getrag gearbox was fine from a driver's point of view. The reason for using it was to clean up the back end, to benefit aerodynamically, and to bring the weight more inside between the wheelbase, with the minimum amount of weight hanging out behind the rear axle.

Right: *View of the Type 79's rear upright/hub carrier, upper linkages, lower wishbone and driveshaft. The Lotus-made CV joint was outboard with the wheel-bearing built on to it. Marked on the tyre are 'For racing purposes only. Not for highway use. Made in England' and the initials 'ACBC'. (Tony Matthews)*

Joint Issue

Another problem area on the Type 79 concerned the CV (constant velocity) joints, as Martin Ogilvie remembers:

> We did our own CV joints. These were the outboard CVs – what's called a third-generation wheel-bearing – where, on a conventional car, you get a CV joint and then it goes through some wheel-bearings in an upright and the wheel goes on the outside. This third-generation set-up had the wheel-bearing built on to the CV joint – you get these sort of applications nowadays, but that was the first time it had ever been done. We did that with RHP and Lobro. It was quite a saga, something like an eight-month process. The actual harness was not very satisfactory, and the CV joints and the wheel-bearings used to clap out. In the first two races the retirements were due to CV and wheel-bearing failure; they used to run hot and wear out. Poor old Mike Cook – one of his jobs was to keep refurbishing these things. They used to get their little drum sanders and sand out the area that had got destroyed and put in bigger balls, and we even ran one race with five balls in because we'd run out. It wasn't a very rigid set-up anyway because you couldn't put any pre-load on these to assemble them. All you could do was push the balls in and then push the cages in around the balls, but it enabled us to get very thin uprights. Hardy Spicer did the original CV joint, which was a parallel tract, and on the early ones you got quite a lot of angularity and they used to get very hot. We had a great deal of trouble getting the driveshafts absolutely dead straight so there was no plunge at all; Lobro joints aren't used very often now.

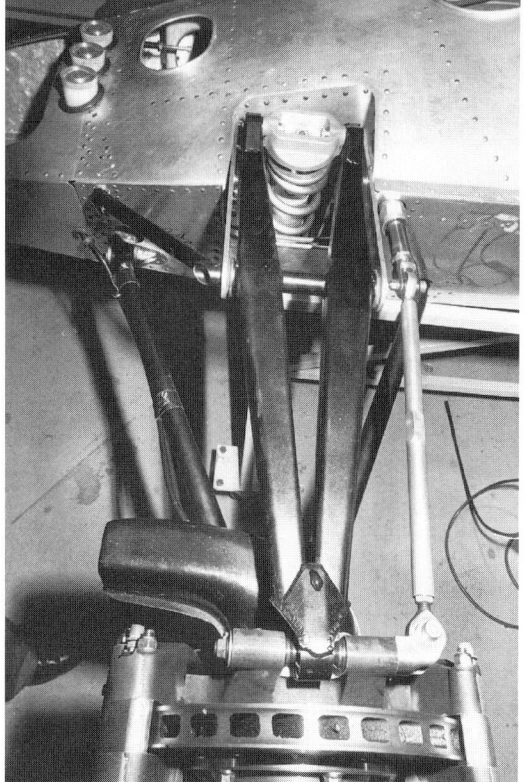

The Type 79 used narrow-angle fabricated upper wishbones and broader-based, tubular lower wishbones. Also visible here are the steering arm, ventilated brake disc and air scoop, while coil spring and damper units are inset in the chassis. (Tony Matthews)

Glenn Waters had a different opinion:

> I don't think it was really up to the job, particularly as F1 cars' rev levels were going up along with the ground-effect loads. At one point we tested with just a freewheel spread clutch so that the car would freewheel when you backed off the throttle.

Waters recalls the Lotus–Getrag gearbox failing in South Africa in 1977:

> The nut on the lay-shaft came loose and machined its way through the back of the gearbox, which then let all the oil out. Of course, the car ground to a halt on the circuit with the gearbox locked solid. About 30 people went out and literally picked it up and put it on the trailer. It just wouldn't move.

Tubular Wishbones

The rebuilt T79 now featured slim, tubular wishbones at the front, instead of its original box-section fabricated wishbones, to operate

The footwell of 79/1, showing the steering column and pedal assembly. The pedal space was more cramped than that of the Type 78 because of the insets that housed the coil spring and damper units. (Tony Matthews)

the springs. The braided brake pipes now ran inside the wishbones, emerging at the outer ends to activate the twin calipers without being in the air stream. The suspension units were actually located within the footwell and covered by aluminium plates with access holes. At this point the T79 also had wishbones at the rear to control the lower ends of the hub carriers, and the inner pivots of the wishbones were located virtually on the car's centre-line underneath the gearbox. This fairly major redesign of the back end was to facilitate the use of the Hewland gearbox.

The rear uprights operated box-section rocker arms, the inner ends of which operated on the inboard spring unit, while an adjustable strut at the rear of the upright or hub carrier provided the means of altering rear-wheel angles. By the time of the T79's launch, most other teams had incorporated Lotus's pioneering adjustable anti-roll bar mechanism. One arm of the roll bar took the form of a steel blade that could be rotated about is longitudinal axis by a small lever (like a gear knob) in the left-hand side of the cockpit, operating a Bowden cable and linkage. The required stiffness was achieved by altering the angle of the blade, with maximum stiffness at one extreme, passing through 90 degrees to obtain minimum stiffness.

The Lotus T79 had taken another leap forward by providing its driver with a very short adjustable front anti-roll bar, operated via a push-pull control to the left of the cockpit instrument panel. These were configured originally for Mario Andretti, and Ronnie Peterson did not use them very much because his taller build made fiddling with them awkward. So cramped was the cockpit that Peterson could only operate the one for the rear mechanism with his right hand; at Jarama he got his glove trapped in the linkage while preparing to alter the stiffness at the end of the main straight.

The T79's nosecone was very narrow compared with the T78, the oil radiator now being

The Lotus T79's front-brake assembly included a ventilated disc with twin Lockheed calipers fore and aft of it, and an air scoop supplied cooling draught. The whole assembly was busied within the wheel, which was attached by a small nut and conical spacer on a solid shaft, the wheel seating on the shaped bush and pins. (Tony Matthews)

housed in one of the side pods, and it featured wide canard fins. The rest of the bodywork extended back over the engine and gearbox and under the rear aerofoil, with the twin exhaust pipes emerging through a slot in the middle above the gearbox, instead of via the traditional DFV route alongside the bottom of the transmission. The side pods that housed the all-important venturii were bolt-on items. The venturi shape underneath extended rearwards from the radiators, and the whole aerodynamic effect took place further forward than on the T78 because there were no fuel tanks to accommodate.

Team Lotus knew that air passing through a venturi drops in pressure as it expands, exerting a negative force on the walls of the venturi. Since the ground cannot rise up to

Specifications and Construction of the Types 79 and 80

After 79/1, all subsequent Type 79s had a taller front scuttle area. The driver-operated knob that controlled the front anti-roll bar setting is to the left of the front bulkhead and the lever for the adjustable rear anti-roll bar is at the left of the cockpit. (Tony Matthews)

meet the car, the car is pulled down towards the ground, with consequent beneficial weighting up of the tyres. The air flow was optimized by making the passage through the venturii as clear as possible, by elevating the exhaust pipes and cleaning up the linkage, so the rear suspension was well inboard alongside the brake discs, for example. Twenty-five years on, some things have not changed much. As Mario Andretti points out, 'While current F1 cars must have flat bottoms, Champ cars still have those Lotus-type venturii tunnels in their side pods.'

The venturii also worked as cooling ducts, accelerating the air over their inverted wing profile and expelling it at the rear, and the low-pressure U-section air chamber was sealed with the track surface at the bottom by the complex system of sliding skirts. The board-in-a-box skirts rode up and down, remaining in contact with the ground as the chassis rose and fell on its suspension. There were limit stops that prevented them from coming out completely should the car become airborne.

Compared with the Type 78's succession of brush, 'suck-up' and 'suck-down' skirts, the T79's board-in-a-box skirts were very sophisticated. By the time T79/2 appeared at Zolder, the board-in-a-box skirts were fitted, and that was how subsequent cars ran.

Brake Problems

The Type 79s often had problems with their rear brakes. They were cast as the gearbox side-plate, all as one casting. Being magnesium, when they got hot, they would become porous and let off gas in the brake fluid. As a result, brake-pedal pressure would disappear. Glenn

Specifications and Construction of the Types 79 and 80

The Type 79's rear-suspension assembly, showing the relationship of the brake disc to caliper housings on the Lotus/Hewland gearbox casing. Also evident are the inboard spring and damper units, driveshaft, anti-roll bar and adjustable blade, top link, box-section rocker arm and lower wishbone. (Tony Matthews)

Waters drove Andretti's car from the finish line to the pits at the end of the 1978 Italian Grand Prix; his admiration for the drivers increased considerably:

> There weren't any fluid leaks, it was just the castings getting porous. You could pump the brakes up because there wasn't a leak. When the brakes have failed because the system's got a leak, the pedal goes straight to the floor. When they've got air in the system, you can actually pump the thing up, so they'd be going along maybe left-foot tapping it up. Whatever he was doing, he was doing a bloody good job because he had Gilles Villeneuve behind him and no doubt the Ferrari did have some brakes. There are three big chicanes at Monza, and you've got to slow down for those. It certainly impressed me no end.

Team Lotus tried to solve the problem by impregnating the magnesium with Loctite sealants in the casting. However, they eventually went back to outboard brakes with the Type 79, which were really what a wing car needed, with the brake buried in the wheel, making the tunnels even more efficient.

Unbeatable Combination

The Type 79 had superb turn-in, matching that of the T78, combined with a rear-end layout that kept the power down and an aerodynamic configuration that was way quicker in a straight line than its predecessor. It was an unbeatable combination during the 1978 season, and took the concept of a Formula 1 racing car on to an entirely new level.

Time has been kind to the Type 79 too. Twenty-two years on, Mario Andretti was

Specifications and Construction of the Types 79 and 80

doing a track test for *Road & Track* magazine in Duncan Dayton's restored Type 79. Dayton's Highcroft Racing team had acquired a dossier of photocopies of the original worksheets for every circuit on which the car had raced, making it possible to achieve an authentic set-up. The track test was written up by top motor-racing journalist Pete Lyons and, in the piece, Mario points to the old T79 and exclaims, 'Look at this car. I mean, this car to me looks contemporary right now.'

The Type 80

The Type 79's monocoque chassis structure was torsionally weak because it was too narrow, and its magnesium brake calipers could not do a whole race without experiencing some degree of deterioration. According to Eddie Dennis, 'In some respects the Type 78 was a stronger chassis than the 79, because of the open cockpit area of the 79. On the Williams FW07, which copied it, that area was all sheeted in.' The T79's exhaust system also suffered due to inadequate cooling inside the bodywork. These aspects could have been sorted out had the Type 79 been refined like the Type 72. Colin Chapman, however, chose to move on to the next thing, which he perceived to be a chassis offering still more downforce and more pitch sensitivity; this became the disastrous Type 80.

GA drawings of the Type 80 demonstrate the front- and side-skirts that were fundamental to the wing-car aerodynamics. (Classic Team Lotus)

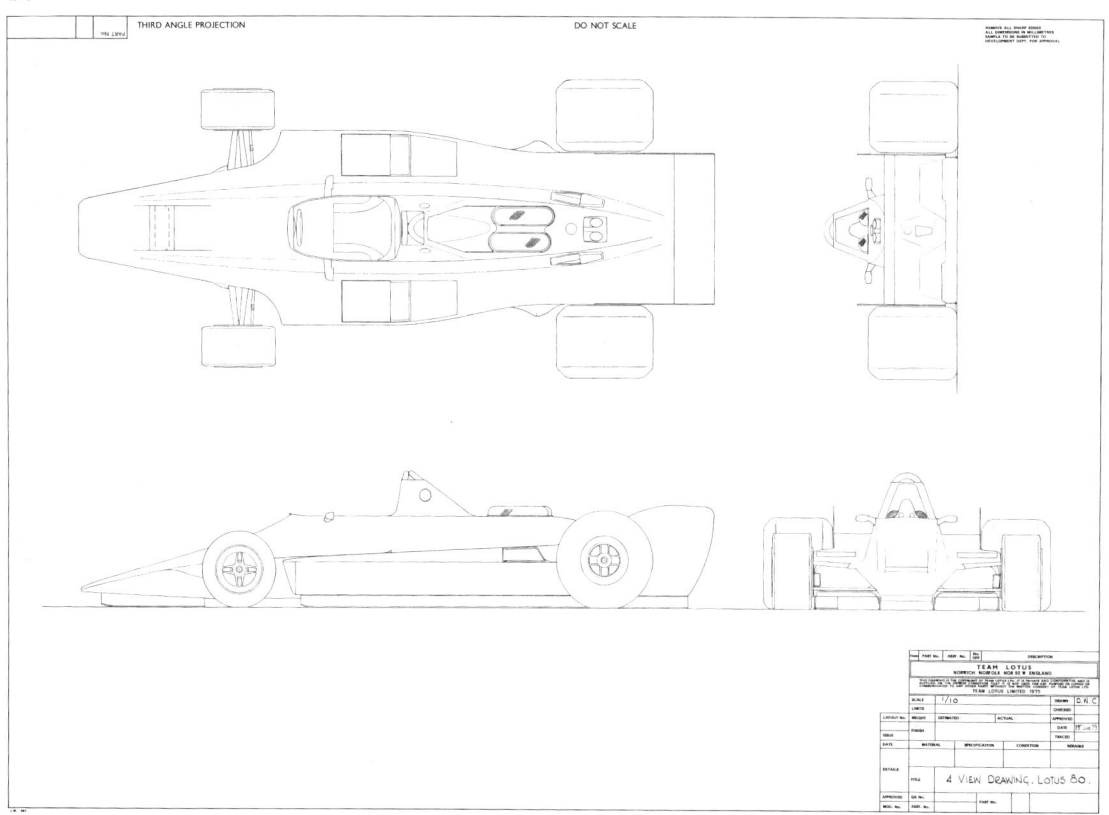

Specifications and Construction of the Types 79 and 80

Type 80 (1979)	
Designer	Martin Ogilvie
Chassis	aluminium monocoque, interior and exterior aluminium honeycomb panels, titanium reinforcement. Side skirts from front to rear
Engine	Cosworth DFV
Gearbox	Lotus/Hewland FGA
Front suspension	upper rocking arms, lower wishbones, inboard coil spring/damper units, anti-roll bar
Rear suspension	upper rocking arms, lower wishbones, inboard coil spring/damper units, anti-roll bar
Wheelbase	9ft 0in (2743mm)
Front track	5ft 10in (1778mm)
Rear track	5ft 4in (1625mm)
Weight	11.41 cwt

The idea of the Type 80, intended to supersede the T79 in 1979, was that its under-body aerodynamics would negate the need for wings and aerofoils. Its tub was composed largely of aluminium honeycomb sheet with titanium reinforcement, and, although longer than the T79, it was lighter. The Ford-Cosworth DFV engine was mated to a transverse-mounted Hewland FGA unit, which featured venturii within the casing on either side. At first the upper rocking arms were of welded

Top right: *The tub of the Type 80 was composed of aluminium honeycomb sheet with titanium reinforcement. The side pods were in fibreglass and, although it was longer than the T79, it was actually lighter. (Peter Riches)*

Right: *View of the Type 80's Ford-Cosworth DFV engine mounts and upward-pointing paired exhaust pipes. Fabricated upper rocking arms replaced hard-to-weld titanium. The plug holes in the roll-hoop brace were for pits intercom. (Peter Riches)*

Specifications and Construction of the Types 79 and 80

Peter Riches (left) and Nigel Bennett in a pit-lane discussion with Mario Andretti at Long Beach in 1979. Succeeding Eddie Dennis, Riches was appointed to run the fabrication and assembly process of the Types 79 and 80 at Ketteringham Hall, while Bennett was race engineer. (Peter Riches)

titanium, but the process was problematic and fabricated steel versions were eventually used. Brakes were twin-caliper items, located outboard front and inboard rear, and both front and rear anti-roll bars were driver-adjustable. Initially at least, the side skirts were present beneath the nosecone, and the main skirts extended from behind the front suspension back beyond the rear suspension to the tail of the car. However, when the car was driven in earnest, the front skirts were damaged as the nose pitched, and they were abandoned in favour of regular canard fins. In addition, the curved side-pod skirts were prone to twisting, jamming their slides, which negated the suction effect. When they un-jammed, the driver was caught out by the sudden return of massive grip.

Home Base

By 1979, Peter Riches was in charge of building the Type 80 and running the fabrication and assembly process at Ketteringham Hall, although he did not have quite the same hands-on role as his predecessor Eddie Dennis. Riches joined Lotus Cars in August 1978 and had been running the engine assembly line and the machine shop and fabrication shop at Hethel for a few months when the call came. He recalls the day when Chapman changed his responsibilities:

> Tony Rudd took me down to Kett Hall, and ten minutes later I'd moved jobs. You know what the Old Man was like. He offered you a job and you really didn't have any choice but to take it.

Riches was there for roughly a season and a half before he went back to Lotus Cars to

Specifications and Construction of the Types 79 and 80

work in engineering and then the DeLorean programme:

> My role with the Types 79 and 80 was anything to do with the home base at Kett Hall. We'd take the Old Man's debrief list, or job list, make the parts or procure them, and make sure the parts were with the race team in time to build or uprate the cars. Bob Dance was responsible for the racing team, so between us the cars had to go on time. I was the one at home who got the phone calls: 'We've broken this', 'Can you get someone on an aeroplane with a new one because we haven't got enough of these?', or 'We want this modified'. When we wanted to build a new car, I'd print all the drawings off, because the drawing-office staff were too busy actually drawing. We didn't have a draftsman spare to spend half an hour printing drawings. Then we'd decide whether we'd make it in-house or have it made outside.

By this time there was relatively little in-house capability. Colin Chapman never did what the other teams did, which was to build up this aspect of the business. Before the number of fabricators was reduced, in late 1978, the chassis for the T78 and T79 had been built in-house at Ketteringham Hall. After that, the chassis tubs were made by outside contractors. Much of the suspension was made at the workshop of former Team Lotus mechanic Bob Sparshott, at BS Fabrications, and Hesketh also made suspension parts. BS Fabrications were contracted to make the titanium parts for the Type 80's suspension, but it proved to be too sophisticated for them. It seems that nobody had really researched how titanium had to be handled. They knew it had to be argon-welded, but, instead of being done in an argon tent, the work was carried out in a workshop with a

From 1979, much of the componentry for the Types 79 and 80 was sourced from outside contractors. Originally designed to run without nose fins, the T80's front skirts proved troublesome and the design reverted to canard fins either side of the nosecone, and integral with the car's body top. (Peter Riches)

Specifications and Construction of the Types 79 and 80

normal welding torch. The argon from the welding torch was insufficient to stop the titanium from becoming brittle. Peter Riches talked to Tony Rudd about it because of his aero experience at Rolls-Royce:

> Tony and I went to see Rolls-Royce, but it became obvious that it was going to be just too difficult at that stage to weld all the bits together. When you need a new wishbone by next weekend, it wasn't a practical proposition. So we gave up and went back to using steel again. Overall, the weight factor wasn't that significant.

There was a degree of urgency to build the Type 80, according to Peter Riches:

> The Old Man suddenly rang me up one day and said, 'I've just done a deal with Martini to launch the 80 on such-and-such a date.' I said, 'Well, the programme you and I agreed says it's scheduled for four weeks later.' He said, 'I don't care, we're launching it on the so-and-so. That's what I've just agreed with Martini.' He was ringing from Monaco, or wherever they were based. So we had to make it for that Race of Champions [1979].

Team Lotus did not have the capability to make any fibreglass parts. They employed Lotus Cars tool-room staff to produce what they needed at weekends and nights. It was an arrangement that was officially sanctioned, and they were paid through the Lotus Cars payroll, even though the work was usually carried out at Ketteringham Hall. Otherwise, the home base was very much an assembly operation, as Peter Riches recalls:

> We had suppliers who we could phone on a Monday and say, 'We need this by the end of the week', and they would make it. People like Hesketh made their money like that. We probably paid well over the odds for it.

Apparently Colin Chapman was comfortable with that mode of operation, and had no wish to build up the Team Lotus home base to any greater extent by investing in machines and equipment. Peter Riches describes the set-up:

> There were two machinists and we had two lathes and a mill, and that was it. It was only a small machine, and that was all we had to make any turned or milled component for the car. If those two machine tools couldn't do it, the job had to be farmed out. If you were making racing cars in those days, if there was a drawing for it, the job was generally farmed out. We were down to just four fabricators, whereas at one time we had eight.
>
> Chapman was in dispute with his home-base staff. It appeared, as far as we could tell, to go back to the fact that Ronnie [Peterson] got killed at Monza in 1978 and there were only three Type 79s there and not four as there should have been. The fourth tub was late being finished, and he blamed the home-base fabricators for not getting it finished on time. He wanted to negotiate longer guaranteed working weeks and all sorts of things, and it was all getting very messy. I arrived on the scene just as four of them were made redundant. The Old Man always had to have a scapegoat. That's why not many people ever held grudges against him, because they knew that eventually it would probably be their turn to be the scapegoat.

Bob Dance also remembers a 'them-and-us' division between the people who worked at the Ketteringham Hall home base and those who went to the races:

> Racing people worked all hours and did whatever was necessary to get the cars to the starting grid, whereas the fabricators tended to work more regular hours. Sacking people after Monza was a way of sorting out differences of opinion about the hours they were working.

Opposite: *An unofficial test session finds the Type 80 in the nether regions of the Snetterton paddock, suggesting that the skirts had got stuck or broken. The car was driven by Bob Evans. A T79 is also present in the background. (Peter Riches)*

Specifications and Construction of the Types 79 and 80

In any case, Glenn Waters believes it was unfair to blame the fabricators:

> A couple of points ought to be made about Monza. Two races previously, in Austria, Andretti had a coming-together with Reutemann soon after the start, and went off and ripped the bottom out of the monocoque, plus all the engine gubbins at the back. When we came back to the UK, the fourth Lotus 79 monocoque was just being finished in the jig. I went and helped Roy Franks and Billy Monaghan and the boys finish it off. We finished it off in the weekend between the two race meetings – Austria and Holland. I went in on Saturday morning and helped finish the tub off so that I could get on with putting it back together on Sunday, because we'd be off on the Wednesday to Holland. So the fourth Lotus 79 had been built up, but it was in use because Andretti had crashed his car in Austria. At Monza we did have three 79s, but the third 79 was the original one, with a different dash panel and a smaller fuel tank. The dash panel got modified after the first one because Ronnie couldn't get into it. He was too tall and his knees bashed the dashboard. So it wasn't so much that the car wouldn't finish the race not holding enough fuel, it was that Ronnie was too big for it. It was originally built for Andretti and Nilsson, and Ronnie was at least a couple of inches taller.

Eddie Dennis also confirms that the issue was indeed to do with lengthening the fabricators' working hours, which they resisted. When union involvement to settle the dispute was mentioned, the Lotus hierarchy quickly decided to dispense with their services.

No Lack of Porpoise

The Type 80 suffered from an up-and-down motion described as 'porpoising', set off when the car hit a bump. This made it bounce and pitch in a most disconcerting way until the driver applied the brakes. The harder the springs, the more the car bounced; the front wheels could actually leave the ground. Yet, the harder the springs, the better the ground-effect worked.

Peter Wright attempted to solve the porpoising problem because, in spite of its inherent failings, it proved that there was more downforce available. However, unless it could be controlled, the additional downforce was unusable. Since 1977, Wright had been involved with David Williams, head of Flight Instrumentation at Cranfield College of Aeronautics. When it was clear that data recovery from the Type 78 chassis would be a fundamental part of the development of ground-effect aerodynamics, Williams designed and built a digital data system for Team Lotus. When the Type 80's porpoising character-

The cockpit of the Type 80 includes a Momo steering wheel with ignition cut-off switch, fire extinguisher, adjusters for front and rear anti-roll bars, with tachometer and pressure and temperature gauges in the dash panel. The wiring taped to the scuttle to the right of the picture indicates a test session in progress. (Peter Riches)

istic manifested itself, David Williams offered to model it and validate the results with the data at the team's disposal. This was when the 'flutter' phenomenon was diagnosed, and it was Williams who first suggested computerized active-ride as a possible development route for suspension and chassis technology.

Peter Wright interpreted David Williams' findings:

> On an aircraft wing, flutter is when you get combined bending and twisting in the wings. This was what the Type 80 was generating. Although you'd got a rigid wing in the shape of the chassis, it was on a suspension, so it was the motion of the car on its suspension and tyres that manifested the flutter. It wasn't the chassis itself flexing, but, because it was on springs, it produced a combined up-and-down motion and pitching, which was the same as bending and twisting. That was what was wrong with it, and it was exacerbated by the fact that, as the car moved, if the skirts didn't follow suit, then the skirt gap changed, and that upset the aerodynamics that fed it. So it was a big problem and, ridiculously, it's still around in some of the cars today. It was horrific, and the drivers were having a very hard time. In trying to sort out the T80, we ran it at the end of the year on very stiff springs at Ricard, which is pretty smooth. Once we got the springs up to about 4,000lb, the cars decided to work, but the drivers couldn't cope with it. If they hit a bump they couldn't keep their feet on the pedals. The car was horrid to drive, but it worked.

In the event, both the T79 and T80 were superseded by the Type 81 for the 1980 season.

Stiff Letter

With hindsight, it is possible to determine that many people felt that the Type 80 was never going to work. The driver charged with winning races with it, Mario Andretti, remains critical of the effort:

> We didn't carry on with the 80 because Colin refused to make it stiffer, to do something about it. We went back to the 79s, but in retrospect it was a mistake to do that, and it turned out to be a botched-up situation. I felt we weren't going anywhere with the 80. I knew what it needed and he wasn't about to do it. There were disagreements that took the focus away from the overall effort and we paid for it dearly. That was a year best forgotten.

Glenn Waters is more reflective:

> When you're successful, you end up carrying the weight of success. You're constrained from going too far away from something that works. So they

thought they could get away with using the Type 79 monocoque and building a bigger-wing car on the basis that more wing equals more downforce. They came up with this idea that they wanted to bend the shape of the skirts around the inside of the rear wheels (like the neck of a coke bottle), because it made a better tunnel. But the fundamental problem was that the skirt had an S-bend in it, and because it was a sliding skirt, it was in fact a double S-bend containing the actual skirt. If you put any longitudinal load on this S-bend, it jammed, simply because of the thrust of the car. There was no way they could overcome that fundamental problem. Because you couldn't do the roller film thing with this S-bend, there had to be some other means of pushing the skirt on to the road, and they came up with a spring and a lever. These springs got incrementally stronger and stronger and stronger. I demonstrated it to Mr Chapman. I had the car there just on the wheels, ostensibly finished, and I went and bounced up and down on it, and the car moved up and down. Then I took the bodywork off and showed him that the chassis had no springs or dampers on it at all. It was just the skirt springs holding the car off the road. I asked him, 'Are you aware that this is where we are now?' He went away to think about it.

They were really dangerous things, because there was just so much spring-loading. Interestingly, when Williams produced the FW07, they took a Lotus 79 and made a proper structural job of the monocoque, using a lot of aluminium honeycomb panels, and did a really good job on the skirts. The springs that they used on the skirts were nothing more than the DFV throttle-spring mechanisms – a pair of telescoping, angled, constant-load type springs, so you get the same load all the time. It was all there for Lotus if they'd just continued doing what they were doing. I'm sure they would have maintained their competitiveness. There was always this attitude of 'Oh, we can do it better', instead of 'Let's refine and get what we've done absolutely as good as possible'.

As Eddie Dennis points out,

Historically, the Old Man was a chassis designer, and he wanted all his cars to have free suspension movement, with low friction. He introduced spherical rose joints with needle roller-bearings, rather than have bushes on an anti-roll bar, say, and he liked everything to be as free as possible with no unnecessary stiction. He wouldn't know what to make of modern F1 cars where there's so little suspension movement and it's the carbon-fibre wishbones and tyre side-walls flexing that provide much of the suspension movement. That would be totally alien to him. He was a firm believer in suspension travel, so that in wet conditions you'd remove the roll bars and take the stiffness out of the car so each wheel could get as much grip as possible.

The Type 80's all-enveloping rear bodywork carried twin sideplates. As well as locating the transverse wing, they also provided the housings for the rear 'board-in-a-box' sliding-skirt sections. (Peter Riches)

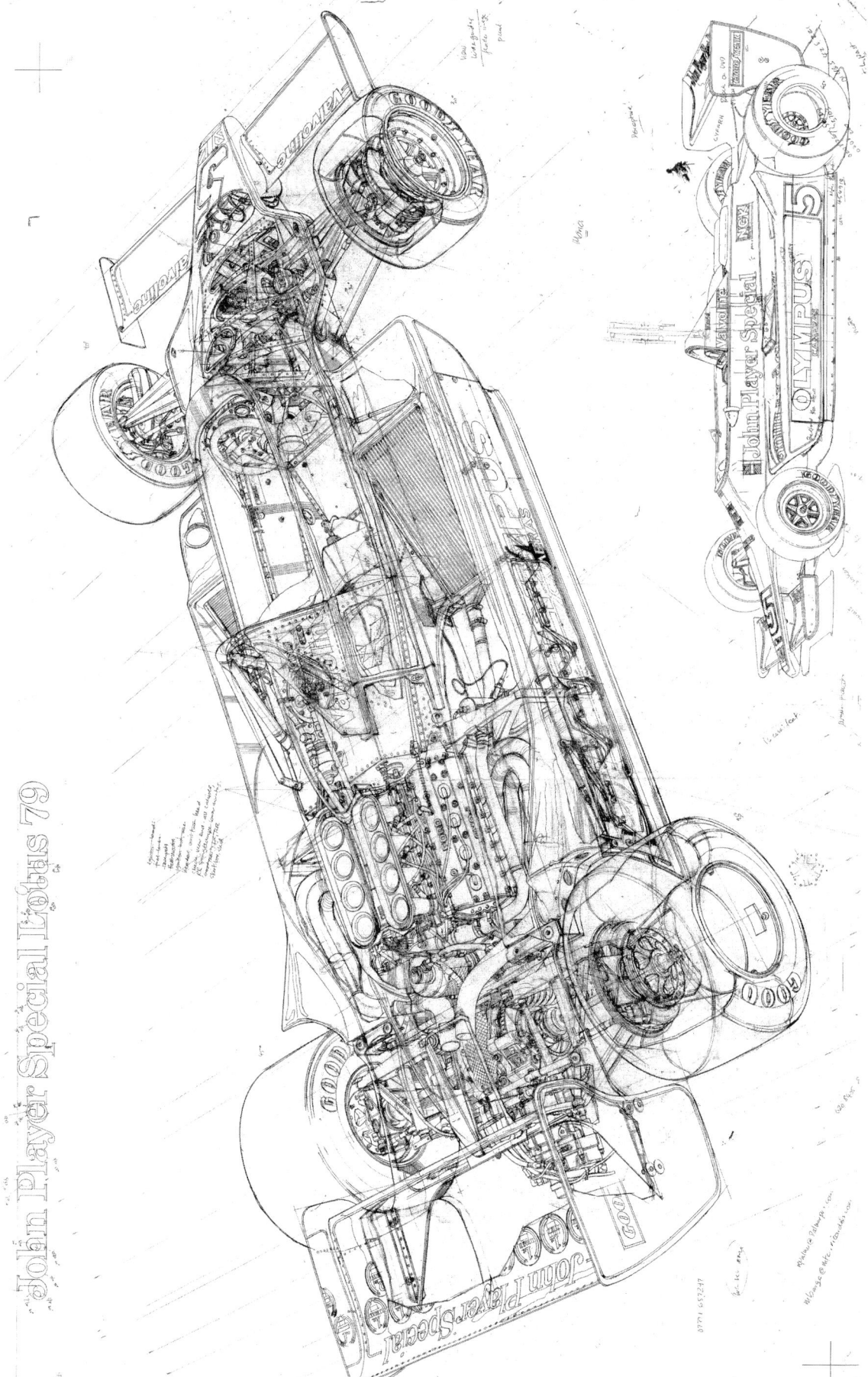

7 Ground-Effect in Action – The 1977 Season

Grand Prix Weekend

On a typical Grand Prix weekend, the Team Lotus crew would arrive at the circuit on the Thursday afternoon before the race and set up its enclave in its designated area in the paddock. In the 1970s, the arrangements were was far less regimented than the rows of colossal identikit transporters and motorhomes that line up today. Normally, a racing car would have its engine installed, either from a test, or the race engine from the previous race. It would do the Friday practice and then the mechanics would change the engine. The engine they put in would run on the Saturday session and also race on the Sunday. The springs were often swapped around, but it was unusual to do much more than just give the driver the feel that he wanted.

The whole team, including the drivers, would very often eat together, although the management would rarely arrive until the

Team Lotus's Dodge 'Travco' hospitality vehicle provided a refuge for mechanics and other JPS personnel in the paddocks at European Grands Prix during the 1970s. (Ian Catt)

Ground-Effect in Action – The 1977 Season

The Race Crew

The Team Lotus race crew never amounted to more than about ten people. With Colin Chapman in overall control, it consisted of team manager Andrew Ferguson, chief mechanic Bob Dance, race engineers Nigel Bennett and Tony Southgate. Southgate was only a short-term presence at Team Lotus; the talented former BRM and Shadow designer left to design the Arrows FA1 (a wing car that was quick on the straights) in 1978. Bennett also became a designer for Ensign (after Bellamy) and Theodore (after Southgate). The core of the race team was Bob Dance, Rex Hart, Bobby Clarke, Glenn Waters and Phil Denney. Mechanics were assigned to particular cars rather than drivers, although the drivers tended to stick with one or two favoured chassis. For example, having done all the testing with the original Lotus 78, Glenn Waters was assigned to that car with Bobby Clarke.

The turnover of personnel was quite regular. When Ian Dawson left the team after Long Beach 1977, Glenn Waters transferred to Andretti's car, and was joined by Mike Truman for a short while. Arthur Burchall looked after the gearboxes. Reg Underhill appeared from time to time but was not a full-time race mechanic. Phil Denney arrived at the British Grand Prix as number two to Glenn Waters, a

combination that endured up to the end of 1979. Tony van Dongen and Trevor Weston – known as the 'two Trevs' – joined up from Surtees just as the Type 79 was being introduced; their first race was the Spanish Grand Prix in 1978. They worked on the spare car with Gilbert Sills, while Rex Hart and Bobby Clarke worked on Gunnar Nilsson's Type 78 and then Ronnie Peterson's T78 and T79.

Above: *Mario Andretti and Colin Chapman debate set-up. The Lotus boss was in control of overall strategy, with input from race engineers Bennett and Southgate, implemented by chief mechanic Bob Dance and his crew. (Ford Photographic Archive)*

Left: *Team Lotus mechanics remained with their allotted car rather than its driver. Here, Nilsson's Type 77 is attended to by Arthur Burchill (briefly chief mechanic) at the rear, with Ian Dawson by Andretti's car. At left, Colin Chapman talks to engineers Tony Southgate and Nigel Bennett. (Ford Photographic Archive)*

Andretti's tyres receive attention from truck driver and spares man John Moses in the Long Beach pit lane during the 1977 US Grand Prix West. Andretti was extremely sensitive about tyres and could tell if one was a fraction larger than its opposite number. Very often, pressures were adjusted in the interests of 'stagger'. (Classic Team Lotus)

Friday morning. The mechanics and drivers (and the drivers' wives) would normally eat together on a Thursday evening in a hotel. Paradoxically, one of the high points of a race weekend as far as the mechanics were concerned was the Thursday evening, because they had a chance to relax before work began in earnest. Once practice had started, anything could happen and they never knew how many hours would pass before they could finish.

JPS caterers Mike and Anne Murphy would also set up in the Team Lotus enclave in paddocks all over Europe, operating a black-and-gold Dodge Travco motorhome. From this team-support vehicle, they would dispense snacks and meals to team members and favoured hangers-on. Their customers were described by erstwhile commercial manager Noel Stanbury as the 'Grease' (mechanics), the 'Techos' (engineers) and the 'Lurkers' (management and PR people). The Travco also served as a conference centre for Chapman, Ferguson and the drivers.

Mix and Match

Clive Hicks was responsible for sorting out tyres and getting them fitted. That was all he did, apart from helping truck driver John Moses with the transporter. A measure of Hicks's responsibility can be gauged by the fact that, in 1978, Team Lotus might have 96 wheel rims for the two race cars at any one event. To manage them, have them fitted to front and rear rims, and get them to the pits in their sets, and back to the Goodyear compound afterwards, was no mean feat. Chapman might dictate all sorts of tyre combinations, front and rear, and Hicks would have to mix and match accordingly. According to Glenn Waters, 'They always had to be ready, because Chapman wouldn't want to wait, would he! When he said, "Get set 27", it had to be ready.'

In 1977, just one Goodyear tyre was used through the whole series, and each team was allocated three sets of tyres for the weekend. Their compound was consistently hard, and teams knew what they were dealing with. But the goalposts shifted in 1978 when Michelin came on the scene with Ferrari. As one of the leading Goodyear runners, Team Lotus was given every available combination of compound to try. Goodyear supplied batches of twenty-four front and rear tyres in different compounds and constructions, including a couple of sets of wets and intermediates. There were four or five specifications of each slick tyre, and they could be mixed and matched with fronts in one spec and rears in another. A different combination of specifications would produce different handling effects. The constitution of qualifying tyres was so soft that they would only last a single lap. Whatever the difficulties and logistics of managing the tyre supply, deployment of the tyres was one of Mario Andretti's secret weapons.

The 1977 World Championship

Argentina

Set against that background, Team Lotus debuted its new Type 78s at the first race on the 1977 calendar, the Argentine Grand Prix. It involved fifty-three laps of the Buenos Aires Autodromo – at 5.968km per lap, a total of 316.314 very hot kilometres. Prospects for Team Lotus were no better than average, as the opposition was potentially still formidable. Most of the teams carried on where they had left off at the end of 1976, with barely time for a few modifications and improvements; however, Team Lotus, Wolf, Ensign and Ligier all had brand-new cars in South America. Mario Andretti and Lotus had won the last race of 1976 at Fuji, while Ferrari had taken the manufacturers' championship, but McLaren had been the undisputed pace-setters. Accordingly, they dispatched their three 1976 cars to South America. Hunt drove his usual M23/8, Mass

Above: *A cloud of spray heralds the rain-drenched start of the 1977 Belgian Grand Prix, with Watson's Brabham Alfa leading the Lotus duo Andretti and Nilsson, Scheckter's Wolf to the left and Reutemann's Ferrari to the right. (Ford Photographic Archive)*

Left: *Andretti's 78/3 leads Hunt's McLaren M26 from Nilsson's 78/2, Watson's Brabham-Alfa Romeo BT46 and Laffite's Ligier Matra JS7 soon after the start of the 1977 French Grand Prix at the Dijon-Prenois autodrome. (Ford Photographic Archive)*

Below: *When it first appeared in September 1975, the Type 77 featured double-wishbone front suspension with inboard brakes and coil spring and damper units, the whole assembly exposed outside the tub. Engine air intakes were part of the cockpit surround. (Classic Team Lotus)*

As the Zolder circuit dried out, Nilsson switched to slicks and drove his T78 to a triumphant win. Sadly, the 1977 Belgian GP was to be his only F1 victory. (Ford Photographic Archive)

Left: *Andretti's cup is filled with Möet, after winning the 1977 French Grand Prix from John Watson. In those days, they were more likely to drink the bubbly than spray it around. (Ford Photographic Archive)*

Below left: *When it looked as if Andretti would win the 1977 Canadian Grand Prix at Mosport Park his T78's Cosworth development engine blew up on the seventy-seventh out of eighty laps. (Ford Photographic Archive)*

Below: *Colin Chapman makes notes on Andretti's performance during practice for the 1978 US Grand Prix West on the Long Beach street circuit. Tyres proved crucial in this race, with Ferrari's Michelins doing better than Lotus's Goodyears. (Classic Team Lotus)*

Left: *In the 1978 Spanish Grand Prix at Jarama, Andretti built up a sizeable lead in 79/3, beating team-mate Peterson in 79/2 by some 16 seconds. (Ford Photographic Archive)*

Below left: *Andretti debuted the T79 prototype at the 1978 Daily Express International Trophy race at Silverstone, but conditions were so bad that he was not alone in going off on the third lap. (Ian Catt)*

Above: *Immaculately turned out, the two works Lotus 79s stand waiting in the Brands Hatch pit lane. Andretti and Peterson were utterly superior during practice, but dramas included Andretti's side skirt being fractured on a manhole cover behind the pits. (Ian Catt)*

Below: *Having got his hands on a Type 79 for the first time at Jarama, Ronnie Peterson returned briefly to the T78/2 for the Friday afternoon practice session at Brands Hatch before the British Grand Prix. (Ian Catt)*

Peterson in discussion with engineer Nigel Bennett at Brands Hatch. The car-to-pits intercom was very much short-range – the wearer's system had to be plugged into the car, so was only usable in the pits. (Ian Catt)

Above: *The privately entered T78/4 of Hector Rebaque qualified well at Hockenheim, started from the ninth row and bested the likes of Watson and Villeneuve and Patrese, finishing sixth and gaining a world championship point. (Ford Photographic Archive)*

A study of ground-effect-induced downforce at work, as Andretti powers 79/3 through the twists and undulations of the Brands Hatch Grand Prix circuit. (Ian Catt)

Below: *Typical Type 79 domination as Andretti and Peterson sweep down the adverse-cambered Paddock Bend soon after the start of the British Grand Prix. Peterson had won pole, but Andretti made the better getaway. (Ian Catt)*

Below: *At Hockenheim during the German Grand Prix, Peterson set fastest lap at 1 min 55.62 secs (211.354 km/h) but, after putting on a show for the lead with Andretti, his transmission failed on lap 37. (Ford Photographic Archive)*

The Type 79 prototype was on hand for the British Grand Prix but was not used. The powertrain consisted of Ford-Cosworth DFV and Hewland gearbox, with oil tank between and insulated water pipe running behind the upswept exhausts. (Ian Catt)

Ronnie Peterson's last outing in 79/2 was in practice for the ill-fated Italian Grand Prix. In fact, he started from the third row in 78/3 with a time set in this car prior to its rear brakes failing at Monza's second chicane during the Sunday morning warm-up. (Ford Photographic Archive)

Left: *Mario Andretti 'won' the re-started Italian Grand Prix from Gilles Villeneuve on the road, but both were penalized a minute for a jumped start, putting the American back in sixth place. It was enough for him to clinch the 1978 World Championship. (Ford Photographic Archive)*

Below: *Depailler and Peterson lead away from Lauda and Laffite at the re-start of the 1978 Austrian Grand Prix; although the rain had stopped, it was still very wet. Peterson eased away to a comfortable win, setting fastest lap on the way. (Ford Photographic Archive)*

Having been recruited from Ferrari to drive the second Lotus 79, Carlos Reutemann leads Mario Andretti in 79/3 during the re-started 1979 Argentine Grand Prix. He finished in second place in 79/2; a first-lap accident meant that Andretti had to switch to the unpractised spare car. (Ford Photographic Archive)

At Monaco in 1979, Andretti practised T79/5 but decided to persevere with T80/1 for the race. (Ford Photographic Archive)

Jubilation after the rain-sodden '78 Austrian Grand Prix, as Ronnie Peterson and Patrick Depailler shake the champers on the Österreichring podium. Gilles Villeneuve, left, has yet to get his fizz open. (Ford Photographic Archive)

The reigning world champion started the 1979 Race of Champions from pole position. He duelled for much of the race in 79/3 with Villeneuve's Ferrari but, by three-quarter distance the Lotus's Goodyears were finished. Andretti did well to come home third. (Ian Catt)

Top left: *Andretti flicks T80/1 into the apex of Loew's hairpin during the 1979 Monaco Grand Prix. He later began to experience rear-wheel steer and pitted on lap 22 to find that the rear suspension had broken. (Ford Photographic Archive)*

Above: *Carlos Reutemann's T79/5 has its fuel topped up while the Goodyears are cooled off in the Silverstone pits, prior to the '79 British Grand Prix. Race engineer Nigel Bennett ticks off the job sheet. (Ian Catt)*

Left: *After trying the Type 80/1 during Friday afternoon's practice session, Andretti was not enthusiastic about racing it. He reports back to Colin Chapman while Bobby Clarke, left, and chief mechanic Bob Dance, right, keep notes. (Ian Catt)*

At half-distance in the British Grand Prix, Reutemann pitted, thinking he had got a puncture. It was discovered that one of the ceramic rubbing strips on the T79's side skirt's had broken up. (Ian Catt)

Andretti raced the Lotus Type 80 at Jarama in the Spanish Grand Prix, staying ahead of Scheckter's Ferrari for third place despite losing a nose fin while lapping Tambay's McLaren. (Ford Photographic Archive)

Classic Team Lotus retains two Type 79s. At the 2002 Goodwood Festival of Speed, former works driver Johnny Dumfries takes one of the world championship-winning T79s up the hill. Clive Chapman prefers to keep the cars as authentic as possible, so any restoration work is sympathetic and incredibly close to the original. (Ian Catt)

Left: *The Type 81, in Essex petroleum livery, in the hands of Mario Andretti at Brands Hatch during the 1980 British Grand Prix. Andretti started from the fifth row, and retired with transmission failure after fifty-seven laps. (Ian Catt)*

Below: *Mario Andretti made a brilliant start at the British Grand Prix, going from the fifth row to sixth place in T79/4. His race lasted only four laps, however, as the Lotus was sidelined by a wheel-bearing failure. (Ian Catt)*

Ground-Effect in Action – The 1977 Season

his M23/9, which had been repaired after its crash in Japan. The Tyrrell team had modified the P34 six-wheelers of Peterson and Depailler over the winter lay-off, with wider front track and longer wheelbase, and a new fibreglass body covering the chassis, engine and rear suspension.

Team Lotus hit problems immediately. During the first tyre change of practice, both cars' front-wheel studs sheered as the wheels were removed. Normally they were not tightened up to the same torque settings as they were for racing, and the heads pinged off the studs, reflecting what was apparently a manufacturing error. That had to be fixed before they could start practising. Subsequently, the front-mounted fire extinguisher on Andretti's 78/2, which was behind the oil cooler, exploded right in front of the pits like a bomb going off. It was because it had been filled

---

Gunnar Nilsson: One of the Boys

Gunnar Nilsson came from the port of Helsingborg in the south-west of Sweden. He graduated to Formula 1 with Team Lotus in 1976 after a relatively brief single-seater grounding in Formula Vee, Formula Atlantic and F2 and F3. Much of his race craft was learned from F3 veteran and fellow Swede, Freddy Kottulinsky, and his first full season in F-Vee was in 1973, so his was a swift rise up the single-seater ladder. A fourth place driving a GRD in an F2 round at the Norisring brought him to the attention of the establishment hierarchy, and he spent 1974 racing in the German Polifac F3 series in a privately entered March. This earned him a works F3 seat for 1975 as team-mate to Alex Dias Ribeiro, and he won the BP F3 Championship. He contested the last few rounds of the Formula Atlantic series, winning five of them in a Chevron B29.

With fellow Swede Ronnie Peterson, Nilsson contrived a swap for the 1976 F1 season, which took him to Team Lotus when it was in the doldrums, while Peterson went back to March. In only his third race in the Type 77, Gunnar was third in the 1976 Spanish Grand Prix. Although most of the season was dogged by retirements, he also posted a fifth at the Nürburgring and a third in Austria.

Nilsson was effectively Mario Andretti's understudy, and a strong rapport built up between the two drivers. In 1977, Nilsson displayed his true colours in the Type 78 by coolly winning the Belgian Grand Prix, which was run in particularly adverse conditions. His other best placing was third in the British GP. All was not well, however. He signed for the new Arrows squad for 1978, but was never fit enough to drive a car. Often spurning painkillers, he underwent an intense course of treatment for cancer, but it proved to be in vain. Tragically, he died in October 1978, at the age of just 29. His lega-

Gunnar Nilsson – very much 'one of the boys'. (Ford Photographic Archive)

cy was the Gunnar Nilsson Cancer Treatment Campaign, for which he lobbied to raise money during his final months. One of the biggest bequests to the fund – £500,000 – came from Bernie Ecclestone.

Friendly and gregarious, Gunnar Nilsson was very popular with fellow drivers and mechanics. As Bob Dance puts it, he was always 'very much one of the boys'.

with the Halon rather than BCF gas, which expanded at different rates and was overheated by the oil cooler and the sweltering temperatures. It destroyed the front of the car, tearing back the aluminium top skin and blowing the throttle pedal out of the car. The anti-roll bar across the front bulkhead saved Andretti's feet, although he later discovered that a bone was broken in one foot.

Glenn Waters remembers the incident:

> The explosion blew the master cylinders off the front bulkhead and bent a three-quarter-inch diameter front anti-roll bar. Andretti was just stunned. Nobody could comprehend what had happened. The front of the car was written off and had to be taken apart. The race took place in a strange atmosphere – Argentina was controlled by the military regime at the time and the whole race circuit was awash with military personnel and guns and regulations. To have a great big bang in the middle of all that, with these military guys running around with their FN rifles, was quite alarming.

Tony Southgate carried the monocoque back to the UK to get it repaired; BOAC was the only airline that would accept it. More to the point, it meant that Team Lotus was left with only one car. Chapman suggested to Nilsson that he offer his car to Andretti as it would come better from him. Indeed, Andretti did drive Nilsson's car (78/1) in the race and he would have finished second, except that one of the wheel-bearings failed. He was left stationary at the hairpin before the pits with only fifty-one laps completed when Scheckter took the chequered flag.

Brazil

After a fortnight of intense activity, the second round of the 1977 World Championship got under way at the sinuous, bumpy 4.946-mile Interlagos track in the suburbs of Sao Paulo on 23 January. Team manager Andrew Ferguson spent much of the interim period persuading Brazilian customs that Andretti's freshly repaired chassis was there to be raced and not sold while in the country. Eventually he prevailed, and the mechanics were able to fettle the car for practice.

Andretti was competitive, but not absolutely on the pace. Then a small but crucial mistake occurred. Tyre man Clive Hicks misassembled a set of rear wheels, and this produced a seminal moment in the development of the car. The wheels were three-piece Speedlines, and the outer rim could be built up with different offsets to suit a variety of tyre widths. Team Lotus had several different offsets and wheel designs and, according to Glenn Waters, Hicks built up a pair of rear rims with the centres further in, which gave the wheels greater offset outside the car:

> When they were fitted they didn't look right because the offset of the wheel was wrong. I called Mr Chapman over and said, 'Look there's a problem here.' There was a discussion between Chapman and Andretti about what he wanted to do. There was no issue about them not being safe to run, they were just different. Time was running out for the practice session, so he said, 'Let's see what they're like.' Andretti went out and, even on full tanks, he immediately jumped right up the running order, and I think we were second in that practice session.

Andretti came straight back into the pits at the end of the session and jumped out of the car and began talking to Chapman. Without further ado, the Lotus boss instructed the mechanics to push it round to the back of the pits and into the garage. Chapman told race engineer Nigel Bennett to gather everyone together and pull the shutters down. He gave strict instructions that no one was to say anything about what had happened. It seemed that, by widening the rear track, the air flow through the venturii had been freed up and, with the wheels out of the way, the ground-

Mechanics Ian Dawson and Darryl Kincaid fettle Andretti's Type 78 in the Kyalami pit lane during practice for the 1977 South African Grand Prix. (Classic Team Lotus)

effect could work much more efficiently. To complement this discovery, the barge boards were taken off and the brush skirts were made solid inside the skirt, using nothing more than tape. The outside of the brush looked the same, so the other teams could not see that anything had been changed. As Glenn Waters recalls:

> That was the incident where we discovered that ground-effect really did play a big part. It changed the emphasis from fiddling with the set-up like a normal racing car to using it as a true ground-effect car.

Gunnar Nilsson had not been to Interlagos before, but posted a respectable time of 2 mins

Ground-Effect in Action – The 1977 Season

Kyalami pit-lane scene in 1977, with Team Lotus personnel at work. From left: Glenn Waters, Bob Dance, Tony Southgate, Ian Dawson. Visible on the pit wall are their toolboxes and basic supplies known as 'pit kit'. (Classic Team Lotus)

Ian Dawson tweaks the throttles on Andretti's T78 while the line from the compressed air bottle is linked to the starter motor. (Classic Team Lotus)

34.37 secs on the first day of practice as he concentrated on learning the circuit before attempting any adjustments to the car. During the final timed session, which counted for grid positions on Saturday morning, Andretti clung on to the inside of the second row with a good 2 mins 30.35 secs. Then, recalling the previous race in Argentina, during the untimed session at the end of Saturday afternoon Andretti 's Lotus burst into flames while negotiating an infield hairpin, the result of a leak somewhere deep in the engine's fuel system. Andretti leapt out hurriedly with only a few superficial burns on his overalls as his car coasted to a halt on the grass, where marshals quickly extinguished the blaze. The driver hitched a ride back to the pits on the side of his Swedish team-mate's car; Nilsson was somewhat apprehensive when he saw the other Lotus in flames because it was clear that he might once again be relegated to the role of spectator. Typically, the Lotus mechanics worked through the night and rebuilt the car so that Andretti did not have to impose on his team-mate for the second successive race.

Andretti was running fifth among the leaders in the early laps and, following a pitstop to change a tyre damaged in a coming-together, Nilsson drove as hard as he could from the rear end of the field. The race then developed into a farce after a small grass fire erupted at one corner. On lap 13, Mass slid off on oil, Regazzoni's Ensign followed him, collecting swathes of catch fencing, which decimated the field as several others ploughed into the turmoil. 'It was just like black ice,' remarked an amazed Lauda after the race was over. Andretti's strong challenge evaporated when a small electrical short circuit in the wires behind the instrument panel of the Lotus caused him to stop out on the circuit, while Nilsson came fourth, a lap down after a second pitstop to take on fuel.

As soon as the team got back to the UK they began to reconfigure the way the skirts worked. Eventually, the brushes were done away with, and the polyethylene trapezoid hinged aluminium skirt and ceramic rubbing strip was introduced. Glenn Waters recalls the process:

> NGK were our very helpful spark plug suppliers. Mr Chapman asked if they would make little ceramic chalks – that's what we used to call them because they looked like little sticks of chalk. They were 10mm diameter by 100mm long. We used an extrusion made by the same company that made the awning for the truck, and we glued the ceramic pencils in as a rubbing strip. They were about the only thing that could endure rubbing on the road. Typically, if the drivers didn't bash them over the kerb they'd last for more than one meeting. The polyethylene hinges used to crack before the aluminium extrusion would rip.

Brushes Off

For the South African GP at Kyalami on 5 March, Mario Andretti lined up sixth on the two-by-two grid, with Gunnar Nilsson tenth-fastest. There was another new car (78/3), so they both had the shorter cars, and a third car in a crate that was never needed. The brushes of the side skirts were replaced with a harder-wearing plastic material. The upper panelling at the rear of the pods rested on the Cosworth cylinder heads and was sealed by brushes of a similar type that had been used for the skirts. When the side-plates were taken off so that the plastic skirting could be replaced, the inverted wing shape of the pod was clearly revealed. At the forward end of the underneath of the side pod were vortex generators in the form of aluminium guide vanes.

It was not a happy race. In a bizarre accident on lap 23, the talented Welshman Tom Pryce was killed when a fire marshal sprinted across the track to Zorzi's car, which had pulled off, on fire, in front of a gaggle of cars travelling at 160mph (over 250km/h) along the top straight. The luckless Pryce was among them.

Ground-Effect in Action – The 1977 Season

Andretti coming up to lap Hans Stuck's brake-less Brabham BT45 on his way to becoming the first American to win a US Grand Prix, at Long Beach. He had the use of the newest chassis, 78/3. (Classic Team Lotus)

He could not avoid the marshal, and took the extinguisher bottle full in the face, continuing at unabated speed to take himself and Laffite into the catch fencing at the end of the pit straight. Pryce and the fire marshal were dead at the point of impact. The fire extinguisher was lofted high in the air and narrowly missed a number of spectators. Nilsson was in the group racing with Pryce, and came into the pits after the accident. His car had no damage, but the wheels were changed. It was clear that he did not want to continue – he had had a close-up view of the tragedy – but he went out again none the less and drove round two seconds off the pace.

At this time, Andretti was running seventh, and was passed by Reutemann's Ferrari 312, which proceeded to block him for several laps. They tangled at the Leeukop hairpin, deranging the Lotus's steering arm and cracking an upright. Nilsson came twelfth, two laps behind.

At the Race of Champions at Brands Hatch on 20 March – the only non-Championship race in 1977 – the leading teams were permitted a single entry. Mario Andretti shared the front row with Watson's Brabham Alfa BT45, holding off Hunt's McLaren M23 for seven hard-fought laps in 78/2, succumbing to bizarre electrical failure on lap 34 of 40. Bob Dance explains what happened:

> A wire connecting the Zenar diode bolted to the bottom of the side pod to prevent the battery overcharging came off and the engine simply stopped working. Vibration had fractured the spade connector right on the Lucas logo.

For the US Grand Prix 'West' at Long Beach, California on 3 April, Andretti had the use of the latest 78 chassis, 78/3, while Nilsson took over 78/2; the original chassis was the spare. Andretti experimented with various front-tyre compounds during first practice, and a smaller rear wing was available, which neither driver wanted to try on the unyielding street circuit – Kyalami might have been more appropriate. As practice drew to an end, Andretti put in a final spurt to claim second-fastest to Lauda's flat-12 Ferrari 312T2, while Nilsson was sixteenth on the grid. He was delayed by brake balance problems and a broken damper, while a bout of over-enthusiasm saw him clip a concrete barrier and break one of the short-wheelbase 78's top links.

As Andretti stole the lead on lap 1, Scheckter put the Wolf ahead almost immediately. Andretti – known as the 'racers' racer' – kept station behind him, just biding his time. For most of the race there was high-speed deadlock, as the South African kept Andretti and Lauda at bay. But as a slow puncture in a front tyre became unmanageable, Andretti was through, along with Lauda, and they finished in that order. Amazingly, Andretti was the first American to win an F1 World Championship GP in his home country. Gunnar Nilsson came eighth, a lap behind.

No Differential

The first race of the European season was the Spanish Grand Prix at Jarama. It was clear from the outset that Mario Andretti was uncatchable; as Denis Jenkinson put it in his *Motor Sport* commentary, it caused March and McLaren personnel 'to appear at the Lotus pit to see if Chapman was cheating in some way'. Indeed, nobody looked like getting anywhere near Andretti in practice, and there was intense speculation over whether it was the 'clever' aerodynamics, the fact that it was running without a differential in the back axle (using the suppleness of the tyres to provide that effect in cornering), or the John Nicholson-built Cosworth DFV engine.

Andretti was on pole in 78/3, with Laffite's Ligier Matra V12 alongside, and Gunnar Nilsson was back on row six with 78/2, nearly two seconds slower. At flag-fall, Andretti was gone into the distance and the rest were also-rans. Jenks remarked that, after the sixth lap, no one tried any longer – virtually all drivers had recorded their fastest laps by then. The main action centred on Scheckter's Wolf battling it out with Mass's McLaren. Nilsson came fifth, the last of the unlapped drivers. In fact, this race was a turning point of sorts for Nilsson, who had received some words of instruction from Chapman before the race. Chapman felt that Nilsson was too intent on emulating Andretti, and that he should back off and concentrate on driving more smoothly. He advised him to stop going

Ground-Effect in Action – The 1977 Season

too quickly into corners, locking up and exiting at full throttle, and Nilsson's technique was indeed smoother and more relaxed from that point.

In the interim, Nilsson tried a transmission with a Salisbury limited slip diff in training at Zolder, instead of the regular ZF unit, but found that it required a different driving technique. While Andretti stuck with the Salisbury item, which had a low-percentage slip setting, Nilsson reverted to the ZF.

For Monaco, Cosworth supplied special 'development' engines with magnesium parts for Lotus, Tyrrell and McLaren. Andretti tried one in his spare car, but the team concentrated on setting up his regular T78/3. Starting from the fifth row of the staggered grid, Andretti drove a gritty race to finish fifth, while Nilsson

In the impromptu paddock at the Monaco Grand Prix, Andretti's tyres have picked up a lot of stones. The chalk inscriptions on the front ones reads 'Fit to other rims'. Andretti would finish the race in fifth place. (Classic Team Lotus)

Nilsson's hour of glory came with his fantastic victory at Zolder in the Belgian Grand Prix, where an astute change to slicks enabled him to pass Lauda's Ferrari and cruise to a comfortable win. Note the steel-shim sprung polythene suck-up skirt. (Classic Team Lotus)

retired on lap 50 with gearbox problems. Victory went to Scheckter's Wolf again.

It was Nilsson's turn to bask in the spotlight after the Belgian Grand Prix on 5 June 1977. After the old Spa-Francorchamps circuit was abandoned, in 1970, the Belgian GP was staged at the new Zolder and Nivelles autodromes. The venue was the relatively slow and twisty Zolder circuit in the Limburg province, and in early practice Andretti was suddenly 2 seconds quicker than anyone else. At first, everyone outside the Lotus pit was incredulous. Then Nilsson clocked third-fastest time, and it began to look as if Lotus had come up with something really special for Zolder. At the end of practice, Andretti was still a second and a half quicker than Watson's Brabham-Alfa BT45, the sort of time lag that would normally cover the top ten runners.

In the paddock, speculation was rife. How had they done it? It could not be down to the Nicholson-built DFVs, because Nilsson was using a regular Cosworth-built one like most other people. The Goodyear tyres were universal at the time, although, with the impend-

105

Ground-Effect in Action – The 1977 Season

ing arrival of Michelin on the scene, maybe Goodyear had slipped something a bit special on to Lotus. Andretti was good, admittedly, but they felt that Chapman must be on to something. It was noticed that both Lotuses were running with their rear wings at a shallower angle than those of most people, giving less downforce and also offering less wind resistance. Maybe it was the air flow under the side pods? Since Andretti was not only fast in a particular long right-hander behind the pits, but looked very stable as well, the inverted aerofoil shapes under the side pods must be working.

When Chapman returned to the circuit on the Sunday morning his pleasure at seeing Mario Andretti on pole and Gunnar Nilsson on the second row was tempered by an anxiety that they had shown their hand too clearly. He would have preferred the gap from Andretti to Watson to have been just a few tenths of a second. Glenn Waters recalls his anger:

> It was Chapman's forty-ninth birthday. He'd been there on the Friday, gone home on the Saturday for his birthday party, then returned on the Sunday morning. On the Saturday, Andretti qualified

At Dijon in the 1977 French Grand Prix, Andretti chased John Watson's Brabham-Alfa with only a slim chance of victory. When Watson's car began to run out of fuel on the last lap, Andretti was through to take the win. Only the left-hand 'suck-up' polythene skirt is visible here, suggesting that the right-hand one has come adrift. (Ford Photographic Archive)

this car something like one and a half seconds quicker than any of the other competitors, which was a huge margin of superiority. And when Chapman found out, there was a serious dressing down. He said, 'Now you've shown them all what you can do! Why did you need to go so quick? You ought to have backed off!'

With the cars assembled on the grid it began to rain. The start was delayed and, when the one-minute signal was finally given, all the teams tried to out-bluff each other as to their tyre choice. At the last minute there was a mass switch to wets – except reigning champion Hunt. Halfway around the first lap, Andretti's pole time counted for nothing as he and Watson tangled at the chicane. Nilsson circulated among the front-runners, pitting for dry tyres on lap 17. It was not a routine pitstop, according to Glenn Waters:

> We had wheel spacers on the front wheels. Once they'd discovered that the wing car worked, there was this big effort to get everything out of the way of the wing, so the front wheels got moved an inch outboard by means of a secondary wheel spacer. During the pitstop, the special nut that this wheel spacer required had baulked going on – and we ended up taking the wheel spacers off during the pit stop and replacing them with some other ones, which required a different nut. He was stuck in the pits for 35 seconds.

During the next ten laps, all other runners came in for drys, in spite of the fact that it was still mighty slippery and rain showers continued to affect parts of the circuit. The race leaders slowly came unstuck – Mass spun off and Scheckter mistakenly pitted for wet tyres again – and a drying wind helped Nilsson close on Lauda's leading Ferrari. Ten laps from the end the Lotus took the lead, outbraking the Austrian at the chicane, and then cruising at 9,500rpm instead of the customary 10,800rpm to a fantastic victory. He crossed the line with both arms raised in salute. Chapman's joyful embrace of the young Swede on the podium spoke volumes about the effect of the win on team morale.

For the first time it became clear that ground-effect had a beneficial effect on the brakes, as Glenn Waters explains:

> These point-and-squirt tracks normally exacted a heavy penalty on the brakes of an F1 car. There was a lot of high-speed running, then you had to slow right down for a low-speed corner, and accelerate up to high speed and then back down again. Every Formula 1 team had a big issue with its brakes. We had enormous brake-cooling scoops fitted. And the brake guys from Ferodo would come up with asbestos pads to put in the back of the brake pistons so that the pads didn't actually touch the pistons, to try and keep some of the heat transfer out of the fluid. But when we ran the 78s there, there wasn't a problem at all with the brakes, because they didn't have to slow down. They could go round the corners without having to kill the speed.

Back home in Helsingborg, Gunnar Nilsson was justifiably feted as the new hero of Sweden, with masses of interviews and adulation. As Bob Dance remembers, 'It was a great win, with a big beer-up on the night ferry home to Felixtowe.'

Injection Malady

Fortune did not favour Gunnar Nilsson in the same way at Anderstorp for his home GP on 19 June. Early on in the race he was shunted from behind by Laffite's Ligier and sufficiently elevated for the Lotus 78/2's nose to be damaged as it landed. He lost a lap for repairs to be carried out and came back out to be towed around by Mario Andretti for many laps, only to retire with suspected wheel-bearing failure on lap 65, close to the finish. Andretti, meanwhile, had gone off into the distance again and had a comfortable lead when he gave Nilsson the tow. However, on lap 69 out of seventy-two, the Lotus spluttered and he had to pit for a splash-and-dash. It transpired that the fuel-injection adjustment had vibrated from weak to rich mixture, affecting fuel consumption but not performance. The battle royal between Watson, Scheckter, Hunt, Depailler, Mass, Reutemann and Laffite passed by as Andretti was in the pits. He was able to manage only sixth, but his earlier performance was enough to demonstrate once again that Chapman's ability to mould all the ingredients of set-up and specification into a homogenous package was unparalleled. Glenn Waters tells what happened:

> In Sweden, the little shuttle in the fuel-metering unit, the little eccentric cam which you could push to one side and rotate to change the fuel mixture, actually rotated during the race from its proper setting, round to full rich. Mario ran out of fuel before the end of the race.

At the tight little Dijon-Prenois circuit for the French Grand Prix the only obvious difference between the performance of the two Lotus 78s was that Andretti was smooth while Nilsson was on the ragged edge, with wheels over kerbs and opposite locking here and there. The upshot was that the American driver was quicker but, by the conclusion of practice, they were split only by Hunt's McLaren. Andretti trumped Hunt's quickest time by half a second with no trouble. His three quick laps were preceded by a cold shower for his tyres to cool them off, a move copied by Lauda and Ferrari to no avail.

At the start, Andretti bogged down with wheelspin and Watson and Hunt got ahead. By lap 17 Andretti had got by Hunt, but catching the 12-cylinder Alfa-powered Brabham proved more difficult as it had more top-end power along the straight, and the rest of the circuit was too tight to allow much in the way of overtaking. Andretti had all but resigned himself to taking second when, on the penultimate corner of the last lap, the Alfa engine coughed with fuel starvation, and Andretti was through to take the victory. The fact that Andretti was in such close proximity to Watson for much of the race paid off; had Andretti backed off, Watson could have just coasted over the line to win.

Pre-race testing at Silverstone suggested that Andretti would once again be fastest in official practice. However, things started going wrong when Andretti was obliged to take avoiding action, as Brambilla's Surtees went awry and the Lotus ended up so far in the infield as to be undriveable. Gunnar Nilsson gave Andretti a lift back to the pits where the new 78/4 (also known as JPS 18) was waiting; all too soon, its Hewland gearbox packed up.

The mechanics recovered 78/3 from the scenery and Andretti began again, but was unable to find a set-up to his liking, despite having Chapman's full attention. Nilsson meanwhile was going very well, pipping his team leader for fifth on the grid. Both Lotuses thus started from the third row. As the race quickly settled down, the order was Watson, Lauda, Scheckter and Hunt, with Andretti having passed Nilsson next up. By three-quarter distance Andretti's engine was tiring; initially, Nilsson was inhibited about passing his team's number-one driver, and hung back. He sailed by on lap 53, pressuring Scheckter into blowing his engine, and then set about Lauda. Andretti's engine went bang under the *Daily Express* bridge on lap 63, but Nilsson set fastest lap and finished third, just a second and a half behind Lauda. As Glenn Waters recalls,

> We just completed a fourth 78 at the time of the British Grand Prix. That car could never make the weight limit because its structure was slightly different; it was built with some thinner-gauge panels. That one was not a terribly well-liked car.

Professional Opinion

Writing in *Motor Sport* magazine (October 1977) just after Mario Andretti's victory in Italy, Denis Jenkinson, also known as 'Jenks', provided a fitting tribute to the American driver:

> He makes it all look so easy, and then floors you by saying that it really is that easy, and he is not boasting, he is being honest. He looks at a race as a team effort, of which he is merely a part, and when he says, 'We are getting it to look good', or, 'We have found a bit of extra speed', you know he is talking about everyone who is working with him, or conversely, everyone he is working with.

There was no better contemporary commentator than Jenks to lionize the true racer – he had no time for the driver who lifted the championship by picking up points at others' expense – and he went on as follows:

> Hunt and Lauda formed a two-man deputation to visit Andretti to reprimand him for the way he drove at Zandvoort [1977], trying to overtake round the outside of the Tarzan hairpin. They suggested that in Formula 1 you did not try to overtake around the outside of a corner (which brings to mind Jacky Ickx's sublime move on Lauda's Ferrari at Brands Hatch's Paddock Bend in the Lotus 72 in the streaming wet 1974 Race of Champions). Andretti's reply was pretty simple. It was to the effect that he was in Europe to win races and he would overtake outside or inside, wherever there was room. Andretti is such a full-time professional racing driver that he makes most of the others in Formula 1 look like a bunch of amateurs.

There is no doubt that much of the credit for the success of the ground-effect Lotuses must go to Mario Andretti. He was able to galvanize the team around him, like Senna and Schumacher would do subsequently, and he was extremely sensitive and mechanically adept. Thus, he could juggle all the finer points of the T78 and T79 and use them to the maximum. He was sensitive to the variables of tyre compound, tyre size and construction, anti-roll bar settings and spring rates, aerofoil loadings, suspension settings and camber angles, and able to achieve a compromise for all of these factors that would add up to consistently quick lap times. From Andretti's point of view, those were good times:

> I cherish the development times, because we were really on to something, and we were working so harmoniously and positively. That's what produces championships.

The European Season Continues

A combination of motor-racing politics and business interests affected the location of the German Grand Prix that season. The ADAC was split as to whether it should be run on the traditional Nürburgring or at Hockenheim. They elected to run it at Hockenheim, where both Lotuses were troubled by inadequate power along the high-speed straights, although they worked well enough in the curving section in the stadium area. They started from the fourth and fifth rows, and both Andretti (78/3) and Nilsson (78/2) retired with blown engines on laps 35 and 32 respectively. The race winner was Niki Lauda, who, just a year earlier, had received the last rights after his fiery crash at the Nürburgring.

At the scenic Österreichring Colin Chapman had a spat with Goodyear concerning the hard, puncture-proof compound that the Wolverhampton company was now providing, because the Type 78 worked better with a grippier, soft-compound tyre. It was somewhat academic in the event as race day was greeted with pouring rain and, initially at least, the entire grid elected to go on wets. Andretti made the second row in 78/3 alongside Stuck in the BT45, with Lauda on pole in the 312T2

Ground-Effect in Action – The 1977 Season

Starting from the second row at Monza, Andretti drove around Scheckter's Wolf at the Parabolica on lap 10 and led thereafter to knotch up the T78's fifth victory. (Ford Picture Archive)

and Hunt's M26 also on the front rank. Nilsson was back on row 8 in 78/2 along with Peterson in the Tyrrell P34, but Nilsson had the advantage of the Cosworth development engine. After the parade lap it was clear that the track was drying, and many teams switched to slicks. Team Lotus put Andretti on slicks and left Nilsson on wets in order to give him a chance to make up ground in the early laps at least. Andretti proved he did not need wets almost immediately by surging into the lead, while by lap 4 Nilsson was running second. This state of affairs lasted for six laps, and then Nilsson pitted for slicks on lap 10, rejoining in thirteenth place.

Andretti's race was run on lap 12 when the Nicholson-McLaren-built DFV blew up. The Swede, however, seemed to be driving at his most inspired, and by lap 32 he was back up to second and in pursuit of Alan Jones's leading Shadow DN8. It was not to last, though, and as he came past the pits on lap 39 the Cosworth engine let go in the biggest possible way.

The Zandvoort circuit really suited the type 78, and it was clear from the outset that the F1 brigade were going to have a hard time catching Andretti. In first practice no one could get within a second of the American driver. Eventually he retained pole, with Laffite's Ligier-Matra V12 alongside, half a second slower. Nilsson in 78/4 and Reutemann in the second Ferrari shared row 3. The Swede had to switch to the spare car when his regular mount failed to run properly. Andretti almost jumped the start, but got away with wheels spinning, with the Ligier of Laffite alongside. As they headed into Tarzan hairpin, Hunt's McLaren was on the inside, and he and Andretti banged wheels all round the turn. Having the inside line meant that the reigning world champion had the advantage as they came out of the turn, and the Lotus driver found himself back in third as the opportunist Laffite slipped by as well.

By lap 3, Andretti was chasing Hunt for the lead, and two laps later the two cars touched as they fought wheel to wheel around the big hairpin. Hunt was launched while Andretti spun; the McLaren was beached and broken on a kerb, but the Lotus escaped unscathed. Hunt stormed into the Lotus pit to let Colin Chapman know what he thought of Andretti, who, meanwhile, was cantering off after the Ligier and two Ferraris that had got by. On lap 15, when he had fought back to second, the engine in T78/3 cried enough. A determined Nilsson had battled vigorously past his countryman Peterson for fourth place, but ran into the back of Reutemann's Ferrari and went off into the sand dunes on lap 35.

Traditionally the last race on the European leg of the World Championship, Monza had only the year before been subject to a range of modifications aimed at slowing the cars. There was no attempt at widening the track as it funnelled away from the pit straight. Instead, there was a new S-bend at the Ascari curve and two chicanes, one before the Curva Grande and the other before Lesmo. These were also the days when a small army of private teams filled the remaining places on the grid. They were sometimes required to pre-qualify, and at Monza they were almost literally camped out on the grass at the far end of the pit lane, because there were not enough pits in the original complex to accommodate everybody. It was far from ideal. One of their number, Arturo Merzario, packed up and left in disgust. Sadly, a young spectator was also killed and many others injured when the advertising hoarding they were using as a vantage point collapsed.

Exercising caution, Team Lotus was running its regular (non-Nicholson spec) 470bhp DFVs in both Andretti's and Nilsson's cars during practice, with a view to fitting a more powerful development engine in Andretti's car for the race. While Andretti logged a respectable 1 min 39.45 secs in first practice, Nilsson bamboozled himself experimenting with tyres and roll-bar settings, and achieved a troubled 1 min 41.22 secs. Even though he improved on the Saturday to 1 min 39.85 secs, he was still down among the privateers such as Lunger, Keegan and Neve. (Interestingly, one of the ten non-qualifiers who did not make the grid was Emerson Fittipaldi, in his family car.)

Andretti fared much better. He was on row 2 alongside Jody Scheckter (with brother Ian Scheckter one row ahead of Nilsson), with Reutemann's Ferrari and Hunt's McLaren on the front rank. The initial scrap for the lead was between Hunt, Reutemann, Scheckter, Andretti and Regazzoni. Andretti passed Hunt on lap 2, then gradually reeled in Scheckter's Wolf, shadowing him for a complete lap before calmly driving around the outside of him at the Parabolica on lap 10. After another lap of weaving to dislodge him from the 78's slipstream, Andretti was home and dry for the day. It was the fifth victory for the Type 78, emphasizing the point that Team Lotus was indeed enjoying a renaissance. For Nilsson it had been a less than illuminating race; he lasted no more than four laps as his suspension was damaged in a nerfing match, probably with Jean-Pierre Jarier's Penske.

Prima Donnas
The US Grand Prix 'East' was held at Watkins Glen on 2 October, and the American Mario Andretti was understandably keen to win the second of the two US races, having won at

Long Beach earlier in the year. It was just before the US Grand Prix that Peterson's manager Staffan Svenby and his private sponsor Count Ghughie Zanon began negotiations with Colin Chapman on Ronnie's return to Team Lotus. No sane driver wanted Super-Swede on his team, such was his outright speed and ability. Unsurprisingly, Andretti was not in the best of humour with Chapman, having learned that his team-mate for 1978 was likely to be Peterson rather than Gunnar Nilsson; Nilsson and he got on extremely well, and Nilsson also fulfilled an unchallenging back-up role. Peterson would present a sterner challenge. Andretti's view was that there was room for 'only one prima donna in this team, and the whole situation is ridiculous'.

As if to demonstrate that, given a decent racing car, he too could be champion, Peterson flung the six-wheeler Tyrrell around as never before, despite Goodyear's failure to supply effective front tyres all seasons, failing to match Andretti's practice time by just 0.5 of a second. Nilsson, meanwhile, was a second slower. It was a wet weekend at Watkins Glen, and, at the green light, Hans Stuck's Brabham-Alfa hurtled off into the lead followed by Hunt, with Andretti close behind in the wall of spray. After fifteen laps Hunt was leading, when Stuck's car jumped out of gear, pitching him into the catch fencing, and the McLaren eased away from the Lotus. That was how they finished, with the Englishman taking the chequered flag just two seconds ahead of the American on a fast-drying track. Nilsson was not the only driver to fall victim to the exuberant driving of his compatriot, Peterson moving over on him as he tried to overtake, just as he apparently did to Jones and Laffite. Afterwards, Peterson was unrepentant, asserting that Nilsson had been following him for enough laps to know how much room and what part of the track the Tyrrell would be occupying. It was the only row that the two Swedes ever had, and it had blown over by the end of the weekend.

The Grand Prix circus then relocated a week later to Mosport Park, Ontario, aboard a fleet of semi-trucks, for the Canadian GP. There was immediate controversy: the track surface was in a rutted state, the Armco was poorly installed, only 95 out of 211 marshals had turned up, and there was no permanent helicopter pad for ferrying injured drivers to hospital. The dissatisfaction with the arrangement set the tone for the weekend, with some drivers threatening not to race at all. First practice was held in bright, but cool, sunny weather. Andretti laid down a marker in 78/3 at 1 min 11.58 secs, and Hunt could not get within a second of this. These two occupied the front row, with the Swedes Peterson and Nilsson behind them.

Andretti swept into an immediate lead of five car lengths, with Nilsson in 78/4 in third place behind Hunt. The Lotus number two was soon displaced by Mass and Depailler, but Andretti and Hunt were in a race of their own. On lap 18, Nilsson lost it and badly damaged the front of the car.

As the race leaders came up to lap Mass on lap 60, the German dutifully played the part of number two, baulking Andretti at the hairpin so that Hunt could get by him. But when Hunt attempted to go by Mass, it all went wrong for them. Mass moved over as if to let Hunt by, but Hunt had already decided to use the bit of road that Mass was moving across to. The collision was inevitable and the lead McLaren was tossed into the retaining wall, while the second one merely spun. In his haste to return to the pits to remonstrate about his team-mate's conduct, Hunt decked a marshal who tried to restrain him from crossing the track, and was later fined $2700. Meanwhile

Tony Matthews' magnificent cutaway illustration reveals the anatomy of the Type 78, first of the ground-effect F1 cars and Team Lotus's weapon for the entire 1977 and start of the 1978 seasons. (Tony Matthews)

Ground-Effect in Action – The 1977 Season

Andretti cruised serenely on, even backing off to 9,500rpm and avoiding the kerbs. However, on his seventy-seventh lap, the Cosworth engine suddenly blew up, and he was forced to coast round to the pits to retire. In the end, he was classified ninth, three laps down on the winning Wolf of Scheckter.

Before flying to Japan for the final round in the championship, Gunnar Nilsson went down to Riverside Raceway in California to drive Chevrolet Z28 Camaros in the IROC race. He finished sixth in the company of all the NASCAR and SCCA greats, including Al Unser, Richard Petty and Cale Yarborough. By now, Nilsson had signed up with what would become the new Arrows F1 squad, born out of the key personnel from the Shadow team. The prospect of being number-one driver at Arrows rather than number two at Team Lotus was sufficiently tempting for him to join Jackie Oliver, Alan Rees, Tony Southgate and Dave Wass in their new venture. What he probably did not know at the time was that the symptoms he was feeling were the beginnings of the cancer from which he would tragically not recover.

The final round of the 1977 championship was staged for the second year running on the Mount Fuji Speedway in Japan. Nilsson's Type 78/4 had been repaired after its Mosport accident, and was now painted crimson and bearing 'Imperial' logos instead of its normal black and gold colour scheme. Nilsson logged 1 min 13.66 secs to put himself on the seventh row of the grid, while Andretti made no mistake about his intentions, clocking 1 min 12.23 secs to claim pole on the track where he had scored his first Lotus win. This time was set on the Friday session, as was Hunt's front-row time, while the Saturday practice was spent running on harder-compound tyres that yielded no benefit.

For once, Andretti was swamped by several other cars as the field swarmed away from the grid, and he was down to eighth at the end of the first lap. In a bid to regain lost places, he surged past Mass and was attempting to go around the outside of Laffite when the Lotus's front wheel clipped the Ligier's rear, sending the American into the guard rail. The Lotus 78's left rear wheel was lost in the impact and ran back on to the track, where it was hit hard by Takahara's Kojima. Further back, Nilsson had been battling away with Laffite and the two Shadows of Jones and Patrese, but his gearbox was gradually packing up. Nilsson was trying to force it to comply, to no avail, even bending the linkage in the cockpit in his efforts. He was forced to retire his bright red T78 on lap 64. Hunt won the race, but upset the establishment by leaving the circuit without even mounting the podium in order to catch a plane back to the UK. Reutemann was not present either, and the rostrum was occupied solely by third-placed Patrick Depailler.

It was not the best way for Team Lotus to end the season, as Glenn Waters recalls:

> Mario's car had a fairly hefty shake in Japan, and I put it on two breeze blocks at the circuit and sawed the suspension off it for it to come home. We put all the suspension into the monocoque and tied it up with a big bow on it for the guys to come along to remove it on a pallet.

The 1977 world title was won by Niki Lauda on 72 points, from Jody Scheckter on 55, and Mario Andretti on 47. Nilsson was eighth on 20 points. However, it was Andretti who came top of the chart of most laps led. He had led 279 laps from seven Grands Prix, to Hunt's 222 laps from 10 GPs, and Scheckter next up with 197 laps led from seven GPs. In the constructors' championship, Team Lotus was second to Ferrari with McLaren third.

8 The World Championship Year – The 1978 Season

The Season Starts

There were four Type 78s at Buenos Aires for the 1978 Argentine Grand prix, held in the Parc Almirante Brown autodrome on 15 January. A delighted Ronnie Peterson enthused about his third-fastest practice time in 78/2, while Mario Andretti was initially slowest of all as the DFV in his 78/3 would not run right. The problem was later traced to a faulty O-ring in the injection system. The spare chassis 78/4 was not used, while the fourth 78 present was that of Hector Rebaque, the Mexican Formula Atlantic graduate. This was

Reunited with his former team, Ronnie Peterson quickly found his old form and was third-quickest in practice at Jacarepagua for the 1978 Brazilian Grand Prix. He retired from the race after a coming-together with Gilles Villeneuve on lap 15. (Ford Photographic Archive)

the original chassis, run for him by ex-Team Lotus mechanic Ian Dawson. In the event, Rebaque failed to qualify (something that would be a fairly regular state of affairs as the season wore on).

By Friday afternoon, Andretti had demonstrated that nothing had gone missing during the winter lay-off, logging second-quickest time, with Reutemann's flat-12 Ferrari top of the sheets on its new Michelin tyres. In order to counter the threat from the rival French tyre maker, Goodyear produced a limited batch of tyres code-numbered 58 front and 59 rear. They were available only to the top teams, who got two sets each and were told to use them sparingly. While Ronnie Peterson's set delaminated on the splice, Andretti made his work to best effect. He felt that it was the comparatively high weight of the F1 tyre that caused the carcass to split, believing that a smaller-gauge USAC-spec tyre would not split and would allow an even softer compound to be used. Many of the other teams were running with rudimentary brush-type skirts now, although they were not as effective as the Lotus 78's set-up.

Team Lotus used the occasion to try out its new, compact Getrag gearbox. It differed from a conventional gearbox and differential in having ratchet-type freewheel mechanisms to be used with a clutchless shift system. Peterson was experiencing selection problems with his Lotus-Getrag gearbox, so that was switched for a Hewland six-speeder for Saturday's practice. Clearly revitalized, SuperSwede was confidently predicting that he would be winning races again. In the final hour of Saturday's practice, Andretti got the pole, with Peterson third-quickest overall.

As the green light came on to signal the start of the race, Andretti made a lightning start and got the jump on Reutemann. Peterson nearly made it through as well, although three laps into the race the American was some 7 seconds ahead. Peterson then appeared to go backwards, with Watson, Lauda and Depailler in the new (four-wheeler) Tyrrell 008 passing him. Andretti was blissfully unaware of his teammate's progress (or lack of it). According to Alan Henry, writing in *Motoring News*:

> His progress was startling even to those accustomed to the winning potential of Colin Chapman's supercar. And all this on a circuit with long, long straights. Even at his 1977 peak we had never seen this sort of domination from Andretti; it was all quite stunning and executed in that smooth, unruffled style which the Italian-born American ace has cultivated to go along with the philosophy of the Lotus 78 design.

Andretti led from start to finish, with no problems apart from a question mark over his left front tyre. After half-distance he could see the inside edge getting blacker from the heat. By maintaining a 10-second gap between himself and Watson he knew he could control the race. Ronnie Peterson was fifth, although he received the chequered flag first from Juan-Manuel Fangio, who mistook his car for Andretti's. The Swede was nursing a difficult understeer, not having had the set-up adjusted to allow for the heavier Hewland gearbox installed after first practice. He was battling against another problem, too: the heat within the cockpit made the accelerator pedal so hot that it was blistering his foot and at times he was obliged to lift off just to let it cool.

Interestingly, *Autocar*'s Peter Windsor quoted James Hunt, the man most fancied for the 1978 championship in his McLaren M26, as saying, 'Give me a Lotus 78 like Hector Rebaque's and I'll be happy to drive that same car for two years. I think the Lotus is that far ahead of us. It's in a class of its own.'

Brazil

The Brazilian round was staged at the Jacarepagua circuit at Rio de Janeiro on 29 January. Although some described it as 'anoth-

The World Championship Year – The 1978 Season

At the start of the South African Grand Prix, Andretti snatched the lead as Lauda missed a gearshift in the Brabham. Next up are Hunt's McLaren and Scheckter's Wolf. (Ford Photographic Archive)

er Lotus circuit', Andretti was more circumspect, observing that many of the corners followed very closely one after the other; it was risky to take the ideal approach into one, for fear of messing up the next. There was never an opportunity to relax between gear changes, either.

Ronnie Peterson was quickest on Saturday's practice session with 1 min 40.45 secs, with Andretti's 1 min 40.62 secs placing him on the inside of the second row. At the start of the race Peterson applied too much power, got bogged down and was overhauled by Reutemann, with Hunt in hot pursuit. After two laps, Reutemann's Michelin radials-shod Ferrari was 6 seconds ahead of Hunt, who had squeezed past Peterson. Soon enough, the Swede's right front tyre was blistered and he fell back behind his team-mate in the other 78. On lap 15, Peterson came under pressure from Villeneuve's Ferrari, and the pair collided at the end of the back straight. Peterson limped back to the pits with a puncture, but his rear suspension was also damaged and he spun out soon after rejoining the race.

Five laps from the finish, Andretti's apparently safe second place was whipped away from him by the dramatically improved Fitti-

The World Championship Year – The 1978 Season

paldi F5 of Emerson. The Lotus had severe gear-selection problems, and by the time the chequered flag came out Andretti had fallen back to fourth.

Glenn Waters recalls the race at Jacarepagua:

It was so hot you could hardly put your feet on the tarmac. It came through the soles of your shoes. We had gearbox problems with third gear there because the gearboxes overheated. They got maximum use on that circuit and that was what shredded third gear. I don't think we could have won at that event with Ferraris on Michelins. But we would have come second but for the fact that Mario had to do the last three or four laps stuck in fourth gear.

South Africa

The escalating costs of staging a Grand Prix meant that the South African Motor Racing Club had to seek outside sponsorship for the 1978 event; fortunately, the national *Citizen* newspaper came to the rescue.

In practice Ronnie Peterson put some more miles on the Lotus/Getrag gearbox, until a crownwheel and pinion broke, and was then obliged to spectate as the spare chassis (78/4) was reserved for Andretti. On Thursday morning's untimed session Andretti needed to use it, a track rod end having sheared off on his regular mount (78/3). Then the Cosworth development engine blew its fuel-injection metering unit in the afternoon session as Andretti

went out in the repaired car. Meanwhile, Peterson was using the Hewland six-speed box again in 78/2 and providing entertainment by using his fine judgement to pass slower cars at 150mph (240km/h).

There was confusion at the start of the race, when Andretti lined up on the right-hand side of the grid although Lauda's Brabham had designated that as pole the night before. A clerical error had identified pole as the left-hand side, which Lauda was obliged to take, but several rows lined up according to the previous day's hand-written grid. Chaos reigned. At flag-fall, Lauda streaked away only to muff his gear change, allowing Andretti to seize the initiative with a vengeance, and disappear into the distance. Twenty laps into the race, the tyres of the Lotus began to overheat, allowing first Scheckter and then newcomer Riccardo Patrese in the Arrows FA/1 to steal the lead. Peterson was quick around the corners but losing out on the straights.

Eventually, attrition found Depailler's Tyrrell in the lead, with Andretti behind him and Peterson dutifully ensconced in third place. The Frenchman's car began to smoke, and Team Lotus was looking set for a one–two finish, but with three laps to go Andretti ran out of fuel. The Tyrrell was faltering, too, and Peterson was alongside him. The former Tyrrell team-mates ran wheel-to-wheel around the circuit for the final half-lap, neither giving an inch, but Peterson had the line out of the final corner and took the win by less than half a second. It was a vintage Peterson performance, and his first win since the 1976 Italian GP for March. He was euphoric about the 78, and was quoted in Fredrik Petersen's *The Viking Drivers* as saying it was 'the best car I've ever driven'. He had had the inner shoul-

Opposite: *For Kyalami Peterson used 78/2, now with a roll-hoop over the front of the cockpit and, after Andretti ran out of fuel, he chased down Depailler's Tyrrell to snatch victory with less than half a lap to go. (Classic Team Lotus)*

> **Out of Gas**
>
> At Kyalami in 1978, Mario Andretti was unlucky to run out of fuel on the last lap. It was actually the fault of team boss Colin Chapman, as Andretti recalls:
>
> > He ran me out of fuel. He had a an imperial gallon of fuel siphoned from the car and poured it on the grid just before the start of the race, because he'd learned the mechanics had put in more fuel than he had requested. I told him, 'If I'm leading at the end of this race and I run out of fuel I'm gonna take it out of your hide.'
>
> It was Chapman's policy always to run tight on fuel so that the car finished the race with no more than a litre in the tank. A similar thing happened at the 1978 Swedish Grand Prix at Anderstorp, where, again, Andretti was leading comfortably. He remembers, 'Suddenly the fuel meter barrel went to full rich about half-way through the race, and I realized I might not have enough fuel to finish.' Every time he passed the pits, Andretti kept indicating that he would have to stop before the end of the race so they would be ready with a gallon of fuel. The inevitable happened – the car began misfiring and, two laps from the end, the driver pulled in for a splash-and-dash. When he went out again, he was classified sixth instead of first.

der of his left-hand front tyre hand-cut for better cooling, and it paid off in the race.

Glenn Waters provides a postscript to Andretti running out of petrol in South Africa:

> We'd been down at Kyalami for a week's testing, using the data-recording equipment. Peter Wright had this panel of gadgets mounted on the sides of the car. In order to make the car more like it would be in race trim, Chapman had us take out the two side fuel tanks, so the car only ran with a central fuel tank, with the data-logging pannier on the side of the car. Then when we came to the race we removed the equipment and put the fuel tanks

The World Championship Year – The 1978 Season

back. They had us remove some fuel from the car to begin with, which was always the Lotus way. Fill right up with fuel and then take so much out to get to the required amount, rather than pour in that specific quantity in the first place. If you were meant to put 10 gallons of fuel in the car, you had first to pump 90 gallons and then take 80 out, which made it easy to introduce errors. If you had 10 gallons in and they wanted full minus 30, you had to fuel it up from 10 to 45, and then pump 35 out, so you ended up pumping 70 gallons of fuel to put 10 in it. Not surprisingly, that led to miscounting. So if we were told to take 3 gallons out, we'd only remove 2 gallons, just to be safe. The one left in was called 'the mechanic's gallon'. But this time we were under Mr Chapman's direct supervision so there was no opportunity to fudge. So the car ran out of fuel while leading the race.'

Bob Dance recalls Andretti's curt comment to the Lotus boss: 'Old Man, you cut it too fine this time.'

The Season Continues

The Type 79 prototype was first tested during the winter, and 79/2 was given its race debut at Silverstone in the rain-drenched forty-lap *Daily Express* International meeting on 19 March. This proved a total debacle, with Ronnie Peterson crunching his T78 on the warm-up and Mario Andretti going off at the fast Abbey Curve in T79/2 on the third lap, skating helplessly into Regazzoni's beached Shadow DN9. Of the fifteen starters, just four finished, and of these, Rosberg and Fittipaldi were three laps ahead of Trimmer and Lunger.

Andretti gives the Type 79 its race debut at the Daily Express International. *The mixture of 79/2 is being adjusted in the Silverstone pits and, over by the T78, Nigel Bennett, Colin Chapman and Phil Denney speak with Peterson. In the waterlogged race the Swede retired in the pits on lap 3, while Andretti skated off on the same lap. (Ian Catt)*

Transport and Sponsorship

Back in the 1960s, racing cars were trailered to circuits or packed into converted coaches or pantechnicons. By the late 1970s, the F1 teams ran state-of-the-art semi-trucks, and Team Lotus's Volvo F89 with its Crane Fruehauf trailer unit was as big as anybody's. The tractor unit was sourced in Sweden, thanks to Gunnar Nilsson's rapport with Volvo Trucks' PRO, while the North Walsham-built Crane Fruehof trailer was fitted out by Smiths of Kettering. It could contain three F1 racing cars and a small Honda pick-up truck. When a second Type 79 was unloaded in the paddock at Jarama, as well as a pair of T78s as back-up cars, the rest of the field probably realized that they had little hope. The Team Lotus domination at Zolder had been so complete, and now Ronnie Peterson also had a T79 at his disposal. He would have 79/2, while Andretti would use the brand-new 79/3.

For the first time, the logos of a new major sponsor adorned the JPS-Lotus's side pods – that of Olympus cameras, which had recently funded Divina Galica and Derek Daly's Hesketh 308E, a budget allegedly worth £250,000. Team Lotus had also attracted two other sponsors not previously seen in F1: Valvoline oil and NGK spark plugs. Being contracted to Valvoline meant they could not use other lubricants, but were free to use whatever five-star pump fuel was available in the paddock. Other teams tended to have fuel contracts, with Tyrrell being committed to Elf, Brabham-Alfa and Ferrari to Agip, and McLaren to Texaco.

Team Lotus's main transporter in 1978 was this Volvo F89 tractor unit coupled to a Crane Fruehauf trailer, which could accommodate three Formula 1 cars and a small Honda pick-up truck. (Peter Riches)

The T79 was badly damaged, losing its left front corner and tearing the right-hand engine mounting out of its socket.

Long Beach street circuit was configured on 2 miles (3km) of the southern Los Angeles waterfront, with the venerable *Queen Mary* ocean liner as a backdrop. The brainchild of Chris Pook and Dan Gurney, the circuit was defined by massive interlocking concrete-block tyre-walls and copious amounts of protective wire netting that were transported to and fro by mobile cranes. The advantage was that the race brought handsome dividends to the city yet did not have to fund itself throughout the year like a regular track. Graduating from a Formula 5000 event to host the second US GP, the other advantage that Long Beach had over its European counterpart at Monte Carlo was that the streets were much wider, enabling overtaking and precluding baulking. Speed traps showed that cars were doing 170mph (270km/h) on the long Shoreline Drive.

Team Lotus had three cars available: 78/2 for Peterson, 78/3 for Andretti and 78/4 as the spare. None of them was fitted with the Lotus/Getrag transmission, using the normal Hewland gearbox instead. There were three incarnations of the Cosworth-Ford DFV engine: the so-called super-screamer, which was Cosworth's own development motor; the

The World Championship Year – The 1978 Season

Mario Andretti (left) and Ronnie Peterson have an informal debriefing with Colin Chapman during practice for the US Grand Prix West at Long Beach in 1978. There were several permutations of tyres and even DFV engines to try, although Hewland gearboxes were used throughout. (Classic Team Lotus)

Peterson describes to Colin Chapman how 78/2 has been going during practice at Long Beach – well enough for him to qualify sixth-fastest. While Andretti came second in an understeering car, Peterson finished fourth, having pitted for fresh tyres. (Classic Team Lotus)

The World Championship Year – The 1978 Season

Nicholson-McLaren-built unit; and the normal Cosworth-assembled version. Goodyear provided five differing front and three rear tyre constructions for Lotus, Brabham and McLaren to play with.

Initially, Andretti was the quicker of the two drivers, until his engine blew, having logged fourth-fastest overall. The Lotus was struggling for rear-end grip, but Andretti remembered that hand-cut tyres built up more temperature through increased tyre movement, and thus provided better grip. He showed the Goodyear technician what he wanted and the car immediately improved. However the new Ferrari 312T3s of Reutemann and Villeneuve proved quickest of all, with Lauda's Brabham-Alfa BT46 next up. Watson's similar car separated Andretti and Peterson, with Hunt following on in the M26. It was Canadian newcomer Gilles Villeneuve who led away at the green light, confidently stealing a march on his more experienced rivals. Alan Jones too made an excellent start to usurp Peterson and then Andretti. On lap 40, Villeneuve was coming up to lap Regazzoni, but tripped over his Shadow and spun into the barriers. Reutemann was challenged by Jones for the lead, but fell back with fuel pick-up problems, demoted by Andretti, Depailler and Peterson.

It finished in that order, with Peterson having had to make a pitstop to change his flat-spotted front tyres and Andretti affirming that it was the worst set-up he had ever raced the T78 with, having to cope with understeer and a too-short top gear. At this point in the season, Andretti and Reutemann led the points table, both on 18 points, with Peterson and Depailler joint second on 14 points.

Failure in Monaco

At Monaco the weeding out of the also-rans began before the Armco barriers were assem-

Andretti drove the rebuilt 79/2 during Thursday afternoon's practice session at Monaco but elected to race his usual 78/3. The T79 looks odd because it is fitted with the T78-style air-box. (Ford Photographic Archive)

The World Championship Year – The 1978 Season

Opposite: *Having tussled with Jody Scheckter, team-mate Peterson and Gilles Villeneuve for fourth place at Monaco, Andretti was forced to pit with a broken fuel-pressure gauge feed pipe. (Ford Photographic Archive)*

bled. FOCA had booked the twenty available grid positions for its members, with eleven cars vying for the four remaining practice slots – twenty-four cars could practise. One of these was Hector Rebaque, in his newly acquired 78/4, but he crashed that car. He still had 78/1 to try, but he was not quick enough to make the cut. Andretti had his usual 78/3 and Peterson had 78/2 as race cars, and Team Lotus also had the rebuilt Type 79/2 on hand as the spare car.

There was much talk about aerodynamics, focusing on Brabham, which favoured a V-shaped skirt under the nose of the car to deflect air sideways. The skirts were designed to prevent air getting under the car, the concept being to achieve downforce from above rather than by suction. The ground-effect

Highlight of the Monaco Grand Prix was the battle between Andretti, Scheckter, Peterson and Villeneuve, hurtling down the hill from Casino Square. (Classic Team Lotus)

The World Championship Year – The 1978 Season

route was favoured by Arrows, Shadow (Southgate's design) and the Harvey Postlethwaite-designed Wolf WR5. Like the Lotus 79, the Wolf had exhaust pipes that were upswept so that they did not impede the air flow. They had the effect of charring the fibreglass of the all-encompassing rear bodywork, however. Whereas the T79 still used flexible skirts, the Wolf had sliding skirts that moved up and down in the boxes along the bottoms of the side pods. They operated by means of thin strip wishbones anchored to the chassis on ball joints, so that the skirt could move up or down or rock fore-and-aft. They were protected from erosion against the track by metal skids, and were held up by locking pins when the car was being moved around in the paddock.

Andretti only drove T79/2 on the Thursday afternoon session at Monaco. Peterson had done a good time in the morning session but stuffed his 78/2 towards the end of it, so he had to sit out the afternoon one. In any case, Andretti abandoned the T79 and carried on with T78/3. On the Saturday afternoon session (Friday being free), Andretti stripped second gear and thus failed to improve on his earlier time. Nevertheless he would race this car, with a Nicholson-built engine, while Peterson used a standard-issue Cosworth-built job.

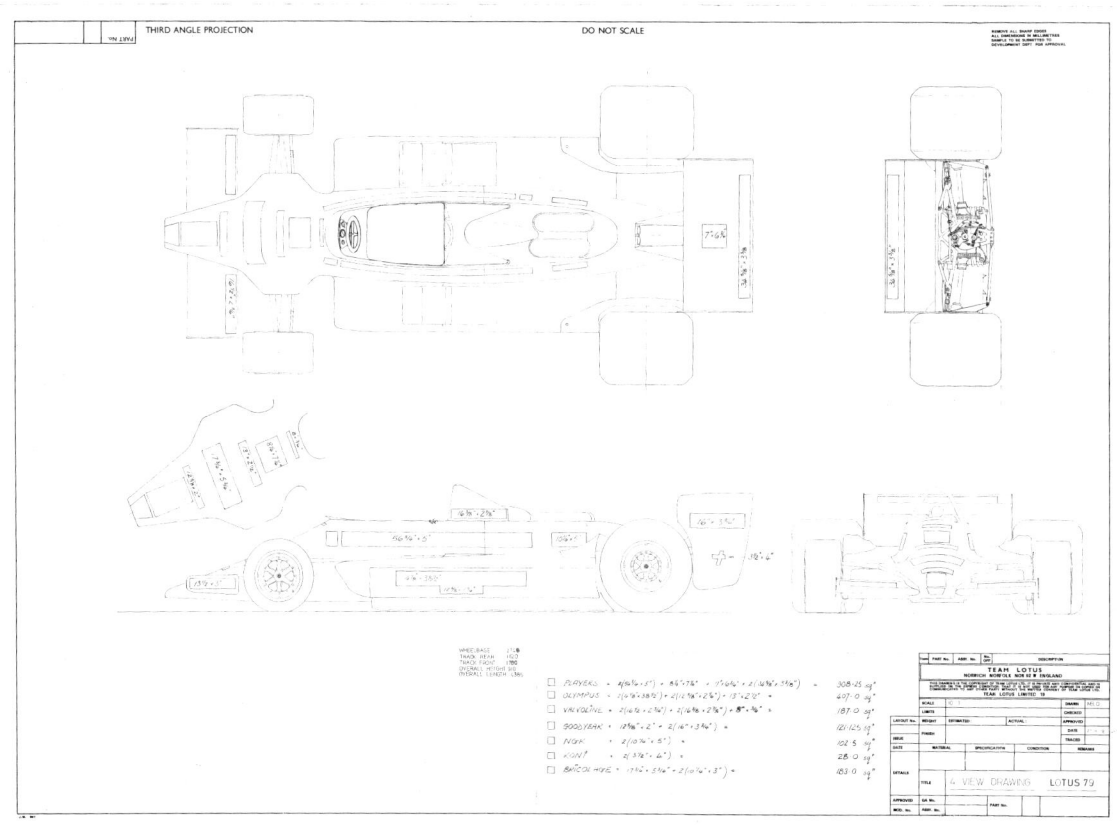

This GA drawing of the Type 79 was used to decide how much space each sponsor would be allocated on the car. (Classic Team Lotus)

Having set up the Type 79/2 to his satisfaction, Andretti annexed pole position and then cruised to an easy victory at Zolder. Team Lotus personnel in the pit lane include Glenn Waters, left, Bob Dance, centre, Gilbert Sills, back to camera, and Colin Chapman. (Ford Photographic Archive)

After the start, Watson led from Depailler, Lauda and Andretti, Hunt and Reutemann having clashed at Ste Devote. Peterson was seventh behind Scheckter and Jones. The battle for fourth place was one of the race highlights, involving Andretti, Scheckter, Peterson and Villeneuve. By lap 45 the Frenchman led in the Tyrrell. Andretti was obliged to pit for the fuel-pressure gauge to be mended – the pipe feeding it had split, spraying fuel around in the cockpit. He was now out of the picture in terms of a result, and on lap 56, Peterson's gearbox packed up when he was running fifth. While Patrick Depailler won his first Grand Prix, Andretti placed eleventh and last, six laps in arrears.

Lotus One-Two

The Belgian GP had provided Gunnar Nilsson with his one and only F1 victory in 1977, and Team Lotus came to Zolder in 1978 with high hopes of a repeat performance. The new weapon would be the Type 79/2, fresh from testing at Anderstorp where Peterson had taken it round a cool 2 seconds faster than the existing lap record. Andretti spent some time – two hours, in fact – having it set up just how he liked it, with a new seat and pedals just so, and

The World Championship Year – The 1978 Season

Andretti and Peterson celebrate a fabulous Lotus one–two in the Belgian Grand Prix on the podium at Zolder. It was a handsome fiftieth birthday present for Colin Chapman. (Ford Photographic Archive)

then ensuring that his T78/3 was just the same. That was typical Andretti, leaving nothing to chance for the weekend he intended to make his own. To the opposition's dismay, he just walked away with a pole-position time, almost a full second faster than Reutemann's Ferrari, and using race tyres rather than qualifiers that, he claimed, were not even good for a whole lap before they went off. The whole package was right – the neutral-steer characteristics of the T79 chassis, engine, gearbox, tyres, and driver. It appeared that Chapman had done it again. In T78/2, Ronnie Peterson was seventh-quickest.

At Zolder, most of the other teams worried about the Lotus advantage rather than concentrating on their own set-up. Andretti recalls that first race with the T79:

> The car was tested by Ronnie Peterson in Anderstorp before the Belgian Grand Prix, and the test car was brought to Zolder. I asked Nigel Bennett how the test went. He said, 'Oh, really quite well. Ronnie might even want to race the car.' I said, 'I don't think so. I want to race the car.' I told Colin, but he said, 'Oh no, no, it will almost certainly break.' I went to Bob Dance, and said, 'The car looks a bit ratty, but can you make it reliable?' He and the boys worked day and night and then I went back to Colin and said, 'I want to race it.' That was the start of a great sequence of events.

The World Championship Year – The 1978 Season

At the start of the Belgian GP there was a huge Formula Ford-style pile-up almost before the field had cleared the pits, caused probably by Reutemann missing a gear and being swamped by all-comers. Of the leading contenders, Lauda and Hunt were eliminated, while Andretti cruised away. He was using parts of the track where no one else could venture, braking much later and even into the first part of the corner; there was so much grip that he could re-define apexes. Meanwhile, Villeneuve was second, and, soon enough, Peterson was up to third. Then, at forty laps, the Canadian's Ferrari got a puncture and Peterson was through to second. On lap 56 he rushed into the pits for a fresh left front tyre, exiting at around 100mph (160km/h). Eleven laps later he had passed Laffite and then Reutemann with a magnificent one-side-then-the-other and outbraking manoeuvre, and was back in second place. It was pure Peterson magic.

Andretti now led the title chase with 27 points to Depailler's 23, Reutemann's 22 and Peterson's 20. The Lotus one–two finish was the perfect present for Colin Chapman, who had celebrated his fiftieth birthday on the Friday. Andretti struck a less celebratory note in the Team Lotus Travco motorhome after the race, dedicating his victory to the increasingly poorly Gunnar Nilsson, and exhorted all present to raise a glass to their Swedish friend.

Spain

In practice, as the season went on, everything went according to the form book. Andretti took pole on the twisty rural circuit north of Madrid, with 1 min 16.39 secs, with Peterson close behind on 1 min 16.68 secs. Carlos Reutemann's Ferrari 312T3 was third-fastest on 1 min 17.40 secs, and James Hunt's McLaren M26 was alongside on 1 min 17.66 secs – each almost a second slower than the Lotus they sat behind on the grid. As it was, the Lotus duo found it difficult to get clear laps on

When a second Type 79 was unloaded from the Team Lotus transporter in the Jarama paddock, rivals feared the worst, since both drivers now had the best equipment. (Classic Team Lotus)

the tight circuit, since even the quickest of the opposition were over a second a lap slower. Andretti might have gone quicker still but was badly baulked when fully wound up on a flyer and ideally placed to go for a time of 1 min 15 secs. Instead, he ran out of fuel trying to get another lap in, which allowed Peterson to take the pole for a time.

Andretti was also getting through his experimental tyre combinations faster than

The World Championship Year – The 1978 Season

Peterson leads John Watson's Brabham-Alfa on his way to second place in another excellent Lotus one–two finish at Jarama in the Spanish Grand Prix. (Ford Photographic Archive)

the Goodyear fitters could mount hem on the Lotus rims. While waiting for tyres, the DFV's injection system developed a vapour lock and the engine would not run. The mechanics tried desperately to cool things down, pouring cold water on to the fuel pump and injection system, expending copious compressed-air bottles on the starter motor and even bump-starting it. Eventually, it had cooled off enough to start, although Andretti had lost quite a lot of the Friday session. It hardly seemed to matter. Andretti still described it as 'the best car I've ever laid my hands on'. So confident was Team Lotus that they did not even bother to run the T78s. Even running full tanks and race-distance tyres, their times were faster than most others could match on qualifiers and tanks that were nearly empty.

The World Championship Year – The 1978 Season

Before the start, all the drivers were presented to Spain's King Juan-Carlos. The red light changed to green too soon for some of them, including Ronnie Peterson, who was impeded by a policeman standing on the track as the race started. Hunt stormed through to get the lead at the first corner, Virage Nuvolari. For five laps Andretti marked time behind the dashing Englishman in his do-or-die extravaganza at the front. Then the American moved ahead with apparent ease when Hunt missed a gear, leaving him to fend off Reutemann, a gap to Watson, Villeneuve, Patrese and Laffite, with another gap to Scheckter, Peterson and Lauda. As the race order sorted itself out, Mario began lapping the tail-enders, with a comfortable 12-second margin over Hunt. Peterson was able to extract himself from the stalemate of his fifth place when this bunch also came upon the stragglers. He then drew them on in pursuit of Hunt.

At the start of lap 53, the number-two Lotus was past the McLaren and into second place, and that was how they finished. Andretti won

Peterson's T79/2 sits in the Team Lotus enclave in the drive-through pits garages at Anderstorp prior to the 1978 Swedish Grand Prix. The red tape visible by the letter 'P' in Olympus shows that the skirt pin is in place, holding up the sliding skirt while the car is off the circuit. (Ford Photographic Archive)

The World Championship Year – The 1978 Season

For a while Andretti was able to hold the Brabham-Alfa BT46 fan car of Lauda at bay, but hopes of a Lotus victory at Anderstorp exploded with the T79's DFV engine. (Ford Photographic Archive)

by some 20 seconds in another Lotus one–two, this time with a couple of Type 79s. Fastest laps in the race were logged by Andretti with 1 min 20.06 secs, Peterson on 1 min 20.40 secs, Hunt extremely close on 1 min 20.44 secs, and Reutemann on 1 min 20.78 secs. Slowest, with 1 min 23.46 secs, was Hector Rebaque in the long-chassis T78/1, which had lost a complete exhaust pipe due to grounding over kerbs. Afterwards, Andretti remarked that he had worn only 1mm off the left front tyre, implying that he could have done another race distance on that set of medium-compound (9 front and 89 rear) Goodyears.

Post-race presentations went awry on account of the winning cars being shepherded into a parking area some distance from the dais and royal box at the control tower at the beginning of the pit lane. Colin Chapman had made his way there to greet his victorious drivers, discovered the slight error in administration, and ran back to the marshalling area to fetch them. Getting back to the control tower involved fighting their way through the race fans, who had by now invaded the track en masse. It was a somewhat dishevelled trio – plus third-placed Laffite – who were greeted by race fan King Juan-Carlos.

Fan Assistance

As Murray Walker would say, 'Formula 1 is full of surprises,' and so it was to prove at Anderstorp, where the Lotus 79 suddenly no longer

The World Championship Year – The 1978 Season

Peterson leads Patrese's Arrows and Watson's Brabham-Alfa fan car. After pitting to change a punctured tyre, the Swede delighted his home crowd with a dazzling display, elevating himself to third place. (Ford Photographic Archive)

looked so invincible. The first real challenge to the T79's superiority was the Brabham-Alfa Romeo BT46-B, known as the fan car. Having experimented with BT46/2, the Brabham team arrived in Sweden with the Gordon Murray-designed BT46/6 for Lauda and BT46/4 for Watson. Both cars had the water radiator positioned above the Alfa Romeo flat-12 engine and the entire rear end of the vehicle was sealed off by rotund bodywork apart from the radiator. At the back of the car was a large fan that was driven off the gearbox main shaft by a system of gears and fitted with a rubberized clutch. Its declared purpose was to draw cooling air down over the radiator, having extracted hot air from around the engine and gearbox, thus provid-

The World Championship Year – The 1978 Season

ing the cooling function. Controversially, the huge fan was also at liberty to suck air from underneath the sides of the car as well and, given the flexible skirts that fringed the underside of the car, the fan was effectively sucking it to the ground – the reverse principle of a hovercraft, in fact.

Naturally, the Brabham fan cars caused consternation in the Lotus enclave, and neither were the McLaren, Tyrrell, Surtees and Williams camps very impressed. The Formula One Constructors' Association was divided, and there were five official protests, submitted and then re-submitted, on the grounds that the Brabhams contravened CSI rules on moveable aerodynamic devices; if fitted, such devices had

---

Engine Supply and Maintenance

At Paul Ricard, the engines of the two drivers differed again. Andretti was using a Cosworth development engine (as did Depailler's Tyrrell, Scheckter's Wolf and Tambay's McLaren), while Peterson's 79/2 was fitted with a John Nicholson-built DFV like Hunt's McLaren. By 1978, Cosworth had made 12 of these 500bhp 'development' engines. In July 1978, a private customer such as Hector Rebaque would have to pay £15,910 plus VAT, ex-factor, for a brand-new DFV (and Rebaque failed to qualify either 78/4 or 78/1 at Ricard). Rebaque's engines were maintained at Nicholson-McLaren engines in Hounslow, where a 120-hour rebuild cost £900, with a replacement cylinder head costing just over £3,000. Here, seven engine-builders looked after 23 Cosworth DFVs, eleven of which were used by McLaren and five by Team Lotus. A powerboat enthusiast, New Zealander John Nicholson was probably better known as a top Formula Atlantic runner with the Lyncar in the early 1970s. Two other engine specialists that supplied Team Lotus were John Dunn's Swindon Racing Engines, which provided three DFVs used in testing and practice only, and Reading-based Euroracing Engines, formerly March Engines, and run by Peter Hass. Peterson's Kyalami-winning engine was a Euroracing-built unit.

Widely regarded as the fastest man in an F1 car at the time, Peterson was as good as his word and dutifully shadowed team leader Andretti during the Lotus clean-up in 1978. (Peter Riches)

to be firmly fixed while the car was in motion. Colin Chapman calculated that the 18in (45cm) diameter fan in the back of the Brabhams was producing ten times more suction than would be required to cool a radiator of the size that would be mounted on the car. It was observed to sink on its rear suspension by at least ¾in (almost 2cm) when the Alfa Romeo engine was fired up. Mario pointed out that, like the Chaparral 2J CanAm car, the

Opposite: *Mario Andretti poses for the camera of John Player's special events executive Ian Catt before the British Grand Prix at Brands Hatch. Behind him in the pits garage are chief mechanic Bob Dance and Colin Chapman. (Ian Catt)*

The World Championship Year – The 1978 Season

Brabham's fans threw grit at the following cars. Despite all this, turning the Brabhams away at scrutineering would have appeared like favouritism on the part of the organizers, so the cars were allowed to race.

At first, the cars did not seem to be that quick – at least as long as the politicking was going on among the constructors in the Marlboro motor home. In the final 30 minutes of qualifying, however, the Brabham duo found another 2 seconds a lap and were suddenly alongside the Lotus 79s at the head of the grid. By that time it was too late to ban them.

Until that time, the Lotus 79s of Mario Andretti and Ronnie Peterson had ruled the roost, with the team leader almost half a second faster than his Swedish team-mate. At the start of the race, Watson got bogged down, while Lauda took advantage of Andretti's efficient getaway to follow him into second place. Patrese too made a good start, with Peterson behind him. Watson spun off trying to make up lost ground, and sucked dirt up into the engine. Up at the front Andretti held Lauda at bay, but they were closely matched, that is, until Andretti came across the oil and debris from Pironi's wrecked Tyrrell that had collided with Brambilla's Surtees. He was obliged to stick to his line, while Lauda was evidently able to place the fan car wherever he liked. No sooner had the Austrian got by the American than the Lotus's DFV went bang, ending any chance of a one–two hat-trick. Meanwhile, Peterson had to stop for a new tyre, having picked up a puncture, and that put him back in seventeenth place. After another display of top-quality Peterson magic, he managed to elevate himself to third place; indeed, it was only the blocking and wheel-banging tactics of Patrese in the Arrows that prevented him from coming in second. Peterson had some uncharacteristically harsh words to say to Patrese on the podium afterwards, along the lines of, 'This is Formula 1, not Formula 3.'

According to those who take the view that Formula 1 should be about innovation and technical excellence, the Brabham should not have been banned. However, although Lauda's Swedish victory was permitted to stand, all fan cars were subsequently declared illegal by the CSI. While Brabham converted its fan cars back to their previous format for the French Grand Prix at Paul Ricard, Team Lotus resumed its confident attitude, billing the Type 78s not merely as spares but exhibition objects. Even when Andretti crashed 79/3 over a kerb at the Esses at 130mph (210km/h) during a practice shower he preferred to carry on with the newer car despite its slightly creased cockpit scuttle panel, rather than resort to the T78.

At Paul Ricard, the fastest cars along Ricard's back straight were the Alfa Romeo-powered Brabhams, at 177.7mph, while the McLaren of Tambay was clocked at 170.9mph, and Laffite's Ligier-Matra V12 could only achieve 167.8mph. Having experimented with tyre combinations again – some ultra-sticky qualifiers only lasted a single lap – Andretti ended up marginally slower than Watson's pole-winning Brabham over a full lap, with just five-hundredths of a second separating them. Behind were Hunt and Lauda, with Tambay and Peterson behind them. An element of farce crept in, as Jackie Stewart headed the field for the warm-up in the spare Renault RS01/03 equipped with a camera, while the V6 turbo engine in Jabouille's RS01/02 began to smoke. It barely lasted a couple of laps, much to the consternation of the Renault chiefs present, still basking in Pironi/Jaussaud's recent Le Mans victory with the A442.

Although Watson made the best start, Andretti had forced his Lotus past to take the lead before they had come to the end of the long back straight – a feat that the T78 would not have managed the year before. At this point, Tambay was third, Lauda fourth and Peterson fifth, the Lotus driver having bent his

In practice for the British Grand Prix at Brands Hatch, Peterson drove 78/2 while a new oil tank was fitted on his 79/2 race car. Since tobacco advertising was banned in the UK (and Germany) at the time, the JPS logos were removed from the car, although ironically the event was sponsored by John Player & Sons. (Ford Photographic Archive)

Also present at Brands Hatch was the refettled prototype, 79/1 (identifiable by its scuttle roll-hoop), now fitted with elliptical-section rear wishbones and revised front brake callipers. (Ian Catt)

The World Championship Year – The 1978 Season

Since the early 1970s, when the JPS promotions agency Stanbury-Foley began producing stickers proclaiming individual race victories, the cars wore them as a talisman on their rear wings. After a dearth of wins mid-decade, they were now back with a vengeance. (Ian Catt)

right front wing in a vain passing manoeuvre on the second Brabham. The French newcomer was soon demoted to fifth while Peterson set about Watson, who had been passed by his team-mate. Having passed the Ulsterman, Peterson was handed second place when Lauda's Alfa Romeo engine blew up, and all he had to do then was protect the Lotus train from attacks by Hunt. Although Andretti controlled the race, Peterson remained relentlessly on his tail, although team orders precluded any overtaking. Late in the race, Hunt made another bid to challenge Peterson, but such was the T79's traction and rear-end grip that he never really got near enough to make any serious moves. Andretti crossed the line a mere 3 seconds to the good, reasserting the superiority of the Lotus 79.

Colin Chapman was understandably jubilant, but there had always been a question mark over Andretti's chassis alignment following his practice off. Until the car was placed on a jig at Hethel there was no knowing how straight it was. Suspension adjustments compensated for any out-of-trueness, but, apart from trying different tyres in practice, he had also been playing with wing settings, trading a little downforce against straight-line speed. The team had confused itself with positive and negative adjustments to the trimming of the front and rear wings when applying Andretti's requests, and it was not until the pre-race warm-up lap that Andretti elected to go with more front wing.

Completely Staggered

Mario Andretti was extraordinarily sensitive when it came to the diameters of his rear tyres. When they were slightly different, this was something called 'stagger', and Andretti was quite the expert on it. He explains what it involved:

> One thing that I had learned from oval racing was how important it was to pay attention to stagger, especially in those days when the cross-ply tyre was very inconsistent. You could have ten sets of tyres, and if you measured the circumference, there would be some differences. Until I started measuring this, few people were aware of it. They would go from one set to another, saying, 'This is good, this is bad.' They didn't know that it could be fixed just by playing with tyre pressures. That's one thing that I kept to myself and I appointed one man to have sole responsibility of my tyres, an American named Kenny Szymanski. I used to have him measure tyres, keep records and give me sizes. There was more to the trick that I never explained, even to Colin. He would trust my judgement because I would make a change and go quicker. I didn't want to explain, because it was my knowledge and experience that gave me that and I wasn't going to give it away.

It was not just a matter of applying stagger the right way to maximize the set-up. If the left rear tyre was bigger than the right one, it had to be compensated for on the chassis, because if the car was placed on the scales, it would show cross weight. According to Andretti, that would eliminate the benefit gained from the stagger:

> It wasn't just a matter of copying what I did, and putting the same tyres on another car. You had to know what to do. I used to go by feel. I would go out in the car and come in again, and tell them to adjust the springs or the damper or the track-rod end. Either go up on the right side and down on the left by, say, a quarter-turn or a half a turn, and I used to drive them crazy doing that. But once I got it perfect the car was just awesome. I really fine-tuned those chassis in that way and that worked for me. I'd play with that everywhere. Every circuit I went to, I would analyse in my own way the important corners. If you have fourteen turns in one circuit, not all of them can be equally important. So what I would do is say, OK, I must set the car up for the six main corners and give away some of the others, or maybe ten and give away four.

Andretti always wanted the car to be set up totally square, and then he would take off on his personal set-up from there. However, to begin with, his methodology was not fully appreciated:

> The first couple of times after practice, they would put the car on the scale, and one morning Nigel Bennett said, 'I can't believe you went that quick. The car was all screwed up, the weights were off, so we put it right back correct.' I went out and it was a disaster. I had to start all over again. I said, 'Did you write down what we did? Because you blew away a whole day's work and we'll have to start all over again.' I told them, 'Whenever we come back from practice, I want the car to be blueprinted exactly the way you found it after I messed with it. Then I want to evaluate what I did and keep that as a record, so the following day I can make corrections. But don't ever think that the car was all messed up because I was jacking up and down with the springs, because that was the whole purpose of it!' He learned to understand how I wanted to operate.

Andretti's technique was not appropriate for his team-mate, however:

> The guys on Ronnie's car would have a tough time keeping up with me, because they would try to copy what I'd got. Rex [Hart] and Bobby [Clarke] would put the same set-ups for Ronnie on his 79, but he wouldn't always understand what was being done. And I would change things around and go round, and they'd put my car on the scales, and his, and they'd be so different. Ronnie was often confused, because he didn't understand the process. If I

The World Championship Year – The 1978 Season

> **Completely Staggered** *continued*
>
> was going really well, Nigel [Bennett] thought he had to copy the set-up, but he didn't know why I was doing what I was doing.
>
> Andretti did not just experiment with the tyres and dampers:
>
> I was playing with toe-ins quite a bit. Sometimes I would run just a toe-in on one side and straight on the other side. Sometimes if I could get rid of the toe-in on one side and only need it on the other side, I not only gained big time on certain corners, but also gained straight-line speed, because I freed up at least one side. When we'd get to Paul Ricard and other places with a really long straight, I used to really play with toe-ins, and that was another thing they didn't understand. It fascinated me to be able to do that, because the car was really responding to everything that I was doing. I don't think I was ever at a loss with the set-up of that car, in either year.

Brands Hatchings

Straight after the French GP, Peterson's car was dispatched to the Österreichring for tyre testing, which Andretti conducted. After a quick stopover at Hethel for its leaking oil tank to be welded up, it was down at Brands Hatch for Peterson to use in the Friday morning practice session for the British Grand Prix. Andretti's own car (79/3) went straight back to base from Le Castellet for its chassis to be fitted with a new front bulkhead and for panel-beating of the dented and rippled scuttle panel. Its Cosworth development engine was left in situ, to be used for first practice and then swapped for a rebuilt unit.

Having lapped Brands Hatch fastest of all in a recent tyre test in his old 78/2, Peterson was in fine form for Grand Prix practice. He was quickly down to 1 min 17.16 secs, while everyone else struggled to break 1 min 20 secs, although Andretti soon managed 1 min 17.83 secs after judicious adjustments to the handling set-up. Peterson's mechanics Rex Hart and Bobby Clarke then set about dismantling 79/2 to fit a new oil tank between engine and gearbox, and the Swede took over 78/2 for the afternoon session. Andretti, meanwhile, was not having the best of luck. A few laps into the session his Hewland gearbox began playing up, and he had to stop to have it checked. The internals were replaced in short order, but the engine refused to start due to fuel vaporization. A push start down the pits access road got him going, only for the T79 to rip one of its side skirts to bits on a manhole cover.

In spite of hardly any running by the Lotus drivers, no one else had come close to matching their morning times. On the second day of practice another 79 was present – the refettled 79/1 prototype – complete with elliptical-section rear wishbones similar to those fitted to 79/3, and a revised front brake caliper. A Hewland transmission was fitted, since the Lotus/Getrag project had been shelved for the time being. Now it was Peterson's turn to be in a class of his own, getting swiftly down to 1 min 16.80 secs, and calling it a day at that. Peterson certainly knew Brands Hatch like the back of his hand.

For the race, Peterson elected to start on the higher left-hand side of the grid, to avoid the steep camber on the inside line. At 3.00pm, the awesome cacophony of massed racing engines at full revs began in the confines of the Brands Hatch amphitheatre, and the grid was unleashed. It was Andretti who led out of Paddock Bend, and he and Peterson inexorably built up a commanding lead over Scheckter, Jones, Lauda, Patrese, Reutemann, Depailler, Watson and Hunt. The T79s looked sublime, while most others scrabbled for traction in their wake. It was the sort of demonstration to which race fans became accustomed with Michael Schumacher and Rubens Barrichello. Suddenly, on lap 6, Peterson stopped on the exit of Druids, his engine-driven fuel pump having failed. As the battle raged behind him, Andretti motored on, but on lap 19 it appeared that he had backed off. In fact he had got a puncture, and had to head for the pits. Despite a rapid stop, he was back in twelfth place. On lap 29, his DFV engine gave up, and that was the end of Lotus's British Grand prix. Victory went to Reutemann's Ferrari in what he described as the best drive of his career, with the Brabhams of Lauda and Watson next up.

Germany

By the time the F1 circus arrived at Hockenheim for the German Grand Prix on 30 July, there had already been speculation that Peterson would switch teams the following season. He was clearly a potential champion, and always had been, given the right equipment, but if Andretti stayed at Team Lotus in 1979, Peterson would only be able to beat him through better reliability, since Andretti would insist on keeping number-one status. Given the American's attention to detail, mechanical mishap seemed pretty unlikely. On the other hand, Andretti, according to the pundits, now needed to prove a point, since Peterson was

Andretti leads Watson's Brabham-Alfa Romeo in the German Grand Prix at Hockenheim. At first the two works Lotus 79s vied with each other for the lead; when Peterson's transmission failed, Andretti took a clear win. (Ford Photographic Archive)

Ronnie Peterson: SuperSwede

Known affectionately as 'SuperSwede', Ronnie Peterson was one of Sweden's greatest sporting heroes, ranked alongside boxer Ingmar Johansson and tennis star Bjorn Borg. His driving career took off in the early 1960s in karts, where he won the Swedish title from 1963 to 1966, and he graduated to Formula 3 in a car called the Svebe, built by his father Bengt, a bakery technician and former F3 driver in the 1950s. Peterson's home was Örebro in central Sweden. Working as a lift installer to earn an income, he bought an F3 Brabham BT18 from Kurt Ahrens for 1967 and competed in a combined F2/F3 race at Keimola in Finland against stars such as Clark, Hill, Brabham and Rindt. His pace impressed Alan Rees, co-founder of March, who ran the Winkelmann-Lotus F2 team at the time.

Peterson's greatest rival was fellow countryman Reine Wisell, and the two up-and-coming F3 drivers travelled to Bologna together to buy a pair of Tecnos. While Wisell concentrated on the 1968 European F3 season, Peterson spent more time contesting the Swedish series, emerging with the national championship title.

The curtain-raising F3 race prior to the 1969 Monaco Grand Prix set Peterson up for his break into Formula 1. Both Swedes won their heats, and the final proved to be a tussle of epic proportions. Peterson's Vicks-sponsored Tecno eventually beat Wisell's works Chevron after a wheel-banging, kerb-crossing battle, which ended when the Chevron took to the escape road at the chicane. Peterson signed to March for 1970, but the fledgling firm was spoilt for talent, with Amon, Siffert and Andretti taking precedence in the F1 team. Peterson was allotted the privately entered 701 run by Colin Crabbe's Antique Automobiles operation, and made his Grand Prix debut at Monaco, finishing seventh. That year he drove a Ferrari 512 prototype at Le Mans, paired with Derek Bell, but the engine failed. A full season with the all-conquering Ferrari 312P sportscar team followed in 1972, with Peterson scoring several endurance victories partnered by his friend Tim Schenken. Meanwhile, SuperSwede was unstoppable in Formula 2 with the March 712, taking over the mantle of F2 Champion from Jochen Rindt in 1971.

A string of podium finishes and high placings in the STP March 711 saw Peterson come in as runner-up to Jackie Stewart in the 1971 Formula 1 World Championship. However, he had to wait until 1973 with Team Lotus to score his first GP victory, at Paul Ricard. He

Ronnie Peterson – known affectionately as 'SuperSwede'. (Peter Riches)

took three more wins that season, in Austria, Italy and the USA, helping the team to another constructors' championship title. With Jacky Ickx as team-mate for 1974, Peterson did well to win at Monaco, Dijon and Monza with the outdated Type 72. There was no success in 1975 and, disenchanted with Team Lotus, Peterson switched to March for most of 1976, scooping the honours at Monza with an uncompetitive car. Tempted by the novel engineering of the six-wheeler Tyrrell P34, Peterson spent 1977 with Tyrrell, but third at Zolder was poor reward for a lot of effort.

Widely regarded as the fastest man in an F1 car in that era, Ronnie Peterson rejoined Team Lotus for 1978 on the understanding that Mario Andretti would be team leader. He reasoned that Andretti was unlikely to have all the luck, and that he would at least win some races. So it proved but, tragically, his second place in the 1978 World Championship was a posthumous honour, the universally popular 34-year-old Swede succumbing to his injuries after the Italian Grand Prix.

only nine points behind him in the championship table. SuperSwede had been quicker at Brands Hatch, and Andretti needed to reassert his position as number-one driver.

Even running full tanks and harder race tyres at Hockenheim, Peterson set provisional pole time. Andretti had broken down while warming the car up because the fuel system dried up: the one-way valves from the fuel tank that topped up the collector tank that supplied the injection pump relied on acceleration and braking forces to activate them. As a temporary measure, Andretti tried 79/1, but to no avail. The doubters were silenced when the American, satisfied with his set-up in the recovered 79/3, went out and, in just a few laps, had beaten the Swede's time by one-hundredth of a second. A fresh engine may have helped, giving him another 600rpm down the long straights. Afterwards, mechanic Glenn Waters doused the tyres with water to cool them – they had got up to 250 degrees – and, since Andretti declared them to be in good shape to race on, the words 'Race Mario' were inscribed in yellow chalk on their treads and they were removed and placed in the shade.

On the whole, Andretti hated the tyre wars:

> When Michelin came on the scene in 1978, that was a huge disruption, because with the tyres come many variables, and so little time to sort everything out. It made the job quite a bit tougher in that respect. Whenever you have a tyre war, it almost takes you away from the fine-tuning that you would do if everyone were on a mono-tyre. All of a sudden you start to see throwing stuff at it and really going all out. I always despised that side of it because if you are on the wrong tyre on any particular day, I don't care what you are going to do with the car, it isn't going to make up the difference. So, even today it disrupts the competition, it sets performances apart. If it's a Bridgestone day the Michelin boys can just about settle for second. No chance of winning unless the cars break. And vice versa. For me, as far as racing is concerned, it's mono-tyre. Its fine for the tyre companies but not for the competition.

Glenn Waters has his own perspective on the driver line-up:

> The big difference between Ronnie and Mario's cars was that Ronnie could normally be quicker than Mario. And Chapman would try to slow him down by putting more fuel in the car. Interestingly, and this didn't really come out until afterwards, because Ronnie was quick, they would often not let him use the qualifying tyres and Mario would use them. When people learned more about ground-effect they realized it was probably overcoming the soft tyres. Hard tyres were probably the way to go with ground-effect cars that year. So, although we all imagined that Ronnie would have to use the race tyres, and they would be a second a lap slower, in some ways that wasn't the disadvantage we all believed it might be at the time. In some circumstances it might actually have been an advantage.

In final practice in Germany, Peterson became the first driver to lap Hockenheim in under 1 min 52 secs, posting 1 min 51.99 secs before spinning on the pit straight when a rear top-link broke. There was no time for him to have another go in his T78, and Andretti snatched the pole with 1 min 52.90 secs. Once again, they were way quicker than everyone else and Scheckter's pole-winning time from the previous year – 1 min 53.07 secs – was put into perspective. When Andretti overdid his braking at the first chicane it was Peterson who led away into the forests, getting a better run on to the 180-mph (290-km/h) straight than Andretti. The two Lotuses vied with one another through the chicanes, kicking up the dust as wheels went over the edge of the track. They circulated nose to tail. Then on lap 5, as they entered the stadium, Andretti out-braked Peterson down the inside to take the lead.

The World Championship Year – The 1978 Season

With rain falling on the Österreichring, Peterson built up a massive lead, but the race was stopped after seven laps. He went on to dominate the re-started race in an equally formidable display. (Classic Team Lotus)

Peterson had not exactly capitulated, but he had made Andretti work for it. Behind them there developed a race of attrition, with most of the leading contenders falling by the wayside with mechanical failure. Alan Jones's Williams FW06 had fought its way past Lauda for third, but he too soon fell prey to fuel-pump failure.

Peterson was not going to let Andretti get away, and at times the two Lotuses were side by side. Cooling is an issue in such a situation, which was one reason why Andretti was determined to overtake. When Peterson's engine

Opposite: Midway through the Austrian Grand Prix, Peterson has built up a substantial margin over Reutemann and Scheckter. He had made a blistering getaway on the first lap. The heavens were about to open. (Ford Photographic Archive)

made noises indicating the onset of fuel vaporization he determined to overtake his team leader and for several laps the race was on again. His plan was to pull out enough distance between himself and Andretti to pit for a splash-and-dash, emerging with both drivers' honour intact. Andretti was having none of it. In the end, it was not overheating that ended Peterson's challenge, but the crownwheel and pinion breaking up. In desperation, the Swede completed a few more laps with just fourth gear (out of five), running 11,000rpm along the straights, before giving up. With Scheckter second and Laffite third, it was a clear win for Andretti, leaving him with a much clearer margin at the top of the points table. For the first time, the game Hector Rebaque scored a point for sixth place in 78/4.

Curved Balls

For the Austrian Grand Prix, Andretti's 79/3 was fitted with revised elliptical-section lower wishbones front and rear, although Peterson's retained its round-section ones. The scenario was similar to previous races, in that the Swede went out and set the pace while the American bided his time, making careful adjustments to all the variables, such as tyres, roll-bars and aerodynamic settings. At first, Andretti was unable to match Peterson's best time, and Reutemann was closest. A conference with Chapman suggested that maybe the problem lay in the way the aerodynamics of Andretti's car were affected by the elliptical wishbones, which upset the way the vortex was generated under the car. Rather than give it a try in the spare 79/1, the elliptical wishbones had split plastic hosepipe taped on to them to render them circular in section. Andretti's times suddenly matched those of his team-mate, who was unable to make any counter-claim since his Nicholson DFV had broken a conrod.

As if to confirm that it really was the round-section wishbones that made the difference, 79/3 was thus equipped for Saturday morning's unofficial practice. The timed session in the afternoon was halted by a mistimed demonstration parachute drop, and then the circuit became awash with a rainstorm, putting paid to any further qualifying times. That left Peterson on pole with his Friday morning best of 1 min 37.71 secs, and Andretti alongside with 1 min 37.76 secs from Friday afternoon. Behind them on the grid sat Reutemann's Ferrari and Jabouille's Renault RS01 V6 turbo. A steady drizzle meant that all runners wore wet-weather tyres.

At the start Peterson made a good getaway but Andretti was passed by Reutemann. When he tried to go around the outside of the Ferrari at the third turn, Reutemann did not see him, being more intent on Scheckter on the inside, and Andretti spun off and into the barriers. It would prove to be a critical moment in the fortunes of Team Lotus, since the bottom of the chassis was ripped out on a tree stump, and Scheckter cannoned into it next time round. Peterson had built up a massive lead even on the first lap, leaving the rest to flounder round in the murk and spray, but after he had completed seven laps the officials decided it was too wet to carry on and the red and black flags were held out to stop the the race. It was a lucky break for Peterson, because he spun off after that.

The race was re-started in the order in which competitors had completed the first seven laps. Andretti obviously could not join in because his race car was wrecked. Fortunately, Peterson was able to drive his stranded car back to the pits once it had been extricated by the marshals, and the Swede now had Depailler alongside him for the re-start. Watson's Brabham stalled, delaying his side of the field, while Peterson staged a repeat of the first attempt, forging a huge lead from Depailler almost immediately. By lap 11 it was time to go for dry tyres, and the Lotus pitted. This allowed Reutemann into the lead on the road, although he was actually two laps in arrears, having spun off in the first part of the race a couple of laps before it was terminated. Peterson was now sixth, moving quickly up the field as Depailler, Fittipaldi and Pironi also came in for slicks. Villeneuve hung on for as long as possible on his wets, but after twenty-one laps he too had to go in, and, with Reutemann now spun off, Peterson regained the lead. Whereas his driving style was often wild and exuberant, especially if he was on a mission, now it was tidy and controlled; he lapped his former team-mate Emerson on lap 30 and set fastest lap just before the finish. Despite the untidy circumstances of the race as a whole, it had been one of Ronnie's best drives ever, and he was not short of offers for the forthcoming season.

By now a pattern had emerged: Peterson would simply get into his car when first practice began, drive it as fast as possible and leave everyone else to try and catch up. Not for him the juggling with technical niceties. However,

The World Championship Year – The 1978 Season

A practice shot of Mario Andretti at Zandvoort. Having honed the T79's pitch and ride to perfection, he set pole position before going on to win the race. (Ford Photographic Archive)

it was largely thanks to the diligent Andretti that the Swede had the very best equipment available, since it was the American who, along with Chapman, had honed the T79 to its dominant specification.

Glenn Waters recalls Andretti's contribution:

> The whole programme was Andretti's, right from when he'd joined the company in 1976. The incremental engineering decisions confirmed or requested by Andretti made the cars better. Then of course Ronnie came along, a really quick racing driver, and in the same car on the same day, with the same settings and the same set of tyres, there would be no question – Mario will tell you – Ronnie was the quicker of the two drivers. But Ronnie had difficulty doing what Andretti could do, which was bring it all together, make it focused, incrementally improving the car. He couldn't engineer himself out of a problem, whereas Andretti could.

Dutch Grand Prix

At sand-blown Zandvoort for the Dutch Grand Prix on 28 August, Andretti had 79/4 at his disposal, fitted with some componentry from his damaged Austrian GP car, with 79/1 as back-up Peterson had 79/2 and 78/3 was the spare. Sure enough, Peterson set fastest time of day on the Friday morning, and then,

The World Championship Year – The 1978 Season

Peterson and Andretti taste the champagne as they top the Zandvoort podium, with Lauda in third spot; the Lotus duo had roundly beaten the opposition once again. (Ford Photographic Archive)

with new rear springs fitted, Andretti bettered that by one-hundredth of a second in the afternoon. By then Peterson had a fuel-pressure relief valve stuck, and could not respond. On the Saturday session he had a sticking left-front brake, and a slight leak from the water radiator. Andretti honed the T79's pitch and ride to suit the crucial hill after Hunze Rug and following corner on to the main straight,

fitted a demon set of soft 43 and 91 qualifiers, and knocked out a stunning 1 min 16.36 secs pole time. Unsurprisingly, the Lotus pair were once again in the position of being almost a full second a lap quicker around the sand dunes than Lauda's Brabham-Alfa and Reutemann's Ferrari. The prospect of achieving anything higher than third place looked bleak for everyone except Team Lotus.

As might have been predicted, Andretti led Peterson from a rather hastily shown green light, followed by Lauda, Laffite and Reutemann. Further back, mayhem erupted as Stuck took out Pironi, who struck Patrese, with Daly,

Jones, Scheckter and Rosberg involved in a separate fracas. The midfield runners were headed by Watson, Fittipaldi, Villeneuve, Hunt and Depailler. Ten laps into the race, the Lotuses enjoyed a 4-second lead. By lap 37 it seemed that Lauda was gaining on them, and Peterson began to follow Andretti through ever-smaller gaps as they lapped the back-markers. This so alarmed Chapman that Peterson was told by pit signals to ease off. While he kept watch in his mirrors for the red Brabham-Alfa, Andretti monitored its progress via the pit signals. When Lauda had closed to within 3 seconds of Peterson, the Swede began to hassle Andretti, conscious that his own rear brakes were not fully efficient. With nineteen laps remaining, 79/4 suffered a broken exhaust manifold, prompting the possibility of another Peterson win. Andretti hung on. On lap 67 the threat of the Brabham-Alfa abated, its hard-pressed transmission suddenly vibrating. When it seemed to be OK, Lauda resumed his efforts, but by then it was too late; the Lotuses were uncatchable. Andretti led home another Lotus one–two, with Lauda third, Watson fourth and a much-recovered Fittipaldi fifth. In eleventh place came Hector Rebaque in 78/4, only a lap behind.

It was in Zandvoort at the Bouwes Hotel, that hotbed of political intrigue and manoeuvring, that Ronnie Peterson made his decision to drive for McLaren in 1979. Coincidentally, the CSI also decided that they would ban skirts, a move fiercely resisted by Colin Chapman and Bernie Ecclestone representing FOCA.

Monza Catastrophe
There was every possibility that Andretti could clinch the title at Monza, although Peterson was still in with a chance of it, given the three remaining races on the calendar. The main innovation on 79/4 (Andretti's car) was the cable control for the brake-balance bar, operated by a knob on the right of the scuttle, to the bar down by the pedals. With this he could vary the stopping power between front and rear brakes. It was not a new idea – the Tyrrells had used it previously – but it did mean that Andretti had an awful lot to think about in the cockpit apart from the conventional controls, what with front and rear roll-bar controls and now brake-balance options.

This time it was Andretti who set a commanding pace from the outset rather than Peterson, whose engine blew almost immediately. This meant that he had to use 78/3 for Friday afternoon's qualifying while the engine was swapped on 79/2. Andretti had already done a 1 min 37.780 secs in the morning to Peterson's 1 min 38.256 secs, and, like the two Lotus drivers, hardly anybody improved their times in the afternoon. Peterson was two seconds slower than Andretti, as if to demonstrate the obsolescence of the Type 78, although, by way of a yardstick, Andretti's grid time in his winning 78/3 the previous year had been 1 min 38.37 secs.

At the other end of the pits, meanwhile, Hector Rebaque changed from his 78/4 to 78/2 when a wheel-bearing seized, and then creased the front of that at a chicane excursion. He was lapping consistently in the low 1 min 41 secs bracket, which was not good enough for him to qualify.

Team Lotus had 79/1 present as a spare for Andretti, but this was not much good to Peterson, mainly because, uniquely, it had a roll-hoop within the scuttle bulkhead and the tall Swede found it very difficult to get his legs under this. Being of somewhat smaller build, Andretti was not troubled by it. He tried the car briefly during the unofficial Saturday morning session, when Peterson was reunited with 79/2, only to find his rear brakes overheating. His troubles were magnified when the clutch began slipping due to an oil leak from the main gearbox oil seal, which allowed the lubricant to seep on to the primary shaft. In the timed Saturday afternoon qualifying session, Andretti was once again fastest with 1 min 37.520 secs, followed first by Jabouille's turbocharged Renault and then Villeneuve's Ferrari; these two were the only drivers to break the 1 min 38 secs barrier.

Although Peterson's T79 was ready he could only make 1 min 38.634 secs, so in fact his best time was done on the Friday. His woes were hardly over. In the Sunday morning's half-hour warm-up session, he experienced brake failure at the second chicane and 79/2 went through the catch fencing amid plumes of tyre smoke, ending up with a crumpled front end against the barriers. It was back to 78/3 for him. Glenn Waters explains the reason for Ronnie's brake failure:

> On the Lotus 79 there were two calipers on each disc, and at the rear they formed part of the structure of the gearbox, and the bottom one only had one pin holding the pads in. It was obvious that this pin was a critical component to the safety of the brakes. So we always paid particular attention to installing it. It had a little R-clip to hold it in position but I always lock-wired it for safety's sake. But at the top it wasn't so obvious that this was a big issue. The pad would fit in; the pin would go in, then the R-clip. Anyway, come the morning warm-up, what occurred with Peterson's car was that, for one reason or another, one of the pads on the top calliper came out because the R-clip had failed and the pin had come out. Anyway he put his foot on the brake and obviously the brake pedal went to the floor, and he bashed the front of the monocoque into the Armco, and apparently there was a tree behind it. The car was heavily damaged and unusable for the Grand Prix. He hadn't injured himself. But the other 79 was the original one with the different dashboard bulkhead. He couldn't sit in it very well, and the conclusion was that he was better off in the 78.

Peterson's had to resort to 78/3 for the Italian Grand Prix after his T79 was badly damaged when the brakes failed in practice. This was to be his last race. (Ford Photographic Archive)

The World Championship Year – The 1978 Season

Villeneuve leads Andretti in the gathering gloom at Monza, with Jabouille, Lauda and Reutemann in pursuit in the restarted Italian Grand Prix. The Lotus driver won 'on the road' but both he and Villeneuve were penalized for jumping the start. The Italian starter was subsequently blamed for causing the original accident that cost Peterson his life. (Ford Photographic Archive)

As the cars left the pit lane the drivers were greeted with differing levels of acclaim from the tifosi in the stands: wild cheers for Andretti and Villeneuve, enthusiastic clapping for others, and virtually no reaction for a few. At the end of the warm-up, both Peterson and Reutemann nipped into their respective pits for aerodynamic tweaks. It was by now established in people's minds that Peterson would be going to McLaren, Reutemann to Lotus, and Hunt to Wolf. The number-two Lotus and the out-going Ferrari did another lap and rejoined their grid positions. Peterson was on the third row with Jones alongside in the Williams, while Reutemann was back on row six with Patrese's Arrows beside him. Then there was the formation lap, and as the Lotus and Ferrari that occupied the front row arrived at the start line, the starter raised his flag – long before the tail-enders had even arrived at the Parabolica corner. Without reference to what might have been going on at the back of the grid the starter dropped the flag, and Villeneuve judged it well, while Andretti got bogged down a bit. Peterson also hesitated and was engulfed by cars behind him, including

151

some of those bringing up the rear who had not even come to a standstill on he grid. For them, it was a rolling start and they were already going quite fast.

Patrese had made a good start and came down the outside of Hunt as the pack funnelled out of the abnormally broad pit straight on to the road circuit, hurtling down to the first chicane, which had a single-car entry line. Braking from 170mph (270km/h) to 60mph (100km/h) is hard enough to achieve for a driver out on his own, let alone amongst twenty-four other cars. Peterson was caught in the middle of the pack as quicker cars cut in. There was contact, and the McLaren shunted the Lotus, which cannoned off the inner guard-rail at 120mph (190km/h), tearing the front off and causing fuel to ignite. He collected Brambilla's Surtees, and shot across the track into the other barrier before coming to rest in flames in the middle of the road. Also involved in the horrendous mêlée were Reutemann, Pironi, Regazzoni, Depailler, Daly, Stuck and Lunger. Before the fire marshals were on the spot, Hunt dived into the Lotus cockpit and began hauling the stricken Peterson out of it. His ankle was caught in the bent front bulkhead. Regazzoni and Depailler came quickly to his assistance, bending the steering column. They got him out and, for the moment, the Swede was out of danger. He was conscious and talking. It looked worse for Brambilla, who had sustained a fractured skull. A fire marshal put the flames out.

While all this was going on, the race leaders had completed almost a full lap before the red flags were frantically waved and they came to a halt on the start line. There was mayhem, anger and confusion for a while, with officialdom in chaos as the wrecked cars were cleared away one by one, and eventually Peterson was taken off to Milan's Niguardia hospital by helicopter with serious leg injuries and slight burns. Stuck was concussed, having caught a stray wheel on the head. None of the cars involved was driveable and most were severely damaged. Some of the drivers had spare cars. An hour and a half later, the circuit was clear, and nineteen cars set off on another warming-up lap. Scheckter failed to make it round, the steering on his Wolf not responding through the 130mph (210km/h) Lesmo turns. He was lucky to step out of the ensuing wreck unharmed, and fortunate that he too had a spare car to take part in. However, many drivers had no stomach for a race, having either witnessed or been involved in the Peterson accident. Depailler, who was physically sick afterwards, was quoted later in Fredrik Petersen's *The Viking Drivers*:

> I didn't want to drive in the re-start. I was driving like a robot and could not understand what I was doing in the car. There were others who were not capable of driving either and we did some crazy things, so crazy that I can't even talk about them.

Among those who also wished to terminate proceedings were Hunt, Fittipaldi, Lauda and Reutemann, but, with the GPDA defunct, the drivers no longer had a voice. They were obliged to get into their cockpits and buckle down. The authorities now had to fix the Armco where Scheckter's Wolf had gone off, and another half-hour went by. The crowd became impatient, whistling and jeering, not knowing what was going on. The 49th Italian Grand Prix finally got going just after 6.15pm, the race distance shortened to forty laps instead of fifty-two. This time the starter held on too long, and Villeneuve and Andretti grew restless at the front. Villeneuve went for it, long before the green, and Andretti followed suit. The starter took their departure to be the signal to drop the flag, and the rest of the grid got moving. His Michelins working well and the Ferrari set up perfectly for the circuit, Villeneuve allowed Andretti no leeway, and the Ferrari stayed ahead for thirty laps. The Lotus eased back a bit as its rear brakes began to fade.

The World Championship Year – The 1978 Season

The real race leader was in fact Lauda, with Reutemann second and Watson third, as the two cars that were out in front had been docked a minute's penalty each for jumping the start. Most people thought a minute was far too severe given the bizarre circumstances of the race and the fact that they were uncatchable anyway. With ten laps to go, and dusk falling, the Ferrari's Michelins started to go off, and Andretti passed Villeneuve to take the lead on the road, and Watson took Reutemann. The reception for the winners was decidedly muted, as the *tifosi* really only wanted the Italian-American and the Ferrari driver on the podium. Their one-minute penalties put them back in sixth and seventh places, and this earned Andretti a single point. It was enough for him to be declared World Champion for 1978.

It seemed there was something to celebrate after all, but bulletins from the hospital in Milan spoke of Ronnie Peterson requiring an operation on one of his legs, with the gloomy possibility that he might actually lose it. It was a complicated injury, with multiple fractures and during the night bone marrow embolisms got into his bloodstream. He lapsed into a coma, and died in the early morning. He was 34.

Postscript to the Season

After the race, Team Lotus removed their cars across the border to preclude Ronnie's wreck being impounded. Back at Hethel, Rex Hart was ordered to cut the remains of the chassis up into small segments. These were acquired by Clive Chapman in 2003 and completely destroyed to forestall mawkish souvenir hunters. Back in 1979, the car was rebuilt around a new tub and took part in the Team Lotus World Championship celebratory parade around the streets of Norwich.

The final two races in the 1978 World Championship were virtually a postscript to everything that had happened before. The US Grand Prix 'East' was staged as usual at Watkins

> **Brake Trouble**
>
> The Achilles heel of the Type 79 was its back brakes; indeed, Mario Andretti won races in 1978 with only the front brakes operational. As he recalls, 'I just could not convince Colin what was happening.' The Type 79's inboard rear brakes were designed to make the air flow cleaner. Half the caliper was magnesium and was cast into the gearbox casing. Magnesium was not an appropriate metal for brakes because it was porous, and once heated up it would expand too much. Andretti discovered that at any track involving an excessive use of brakes, his pedal would go right to the floor under hard braking.
>
> After the race Andretti would complain to Chapman about not having any brakes, but when the car went back to the paddock and the brakes had cooled down, the mechanics would say that the brakes were working perfectly. 'Colin never believed me,' says Andretti. 'We had a perennial fight about that and never got it solved.'

Glen, on 1 October. In the stands the mood was upbeat, with the US fans seeing the race as an opportunity to acclaim Mario Andretti as their champion. In the paddock, the mood was more sombre. The newly formed Formula One Drivers Safety Committee was lobbying to get Riccardo Patrese excluded from the race, claiming that he had been responsible for causing the accident at the start of the Italian Grand Prix. Representing this body were Andretti, Fittipaldi, Lauda and Hunt, who threatened to boycott the race if Patrese was admitted. While it was hardly a unanimous opinion, they did represent the view of the senior drivers, and, despite meetings and appeals to the local judge, Arrows withdrew the Italian's entry.

Viewers of the BBC television coverage of F1 during the 1980s will recall that James Hunt never forgave Patrese for the Monza crash. Whether it was correct to scapegoat him, or whether a disciplinary precedent for irresponsible driving in the wake of the tragedy was necessary or a good thing is debatable. In fact,

153

hindsight largely exonerates Patrese from blame at Monza. According to Glenn Waters,

> Although a lot of people point the finger at Patrese, it might be well worth watching what Scheckter does and make your own decision. The video isn't enough to make a proper value judgement about it. It was Hunt that actually touched Ronnie, but what caused him to do it was something between Scheckter and Patrese. One of the reasons why the thing with Patrese became such an issue is that Patrese had banged wheels with Ronnie in Sweden, really for no reason.

In the Team Lotus camp, Colin Chapman had wished to enter just the one car for Andretti out of respect for Ronnie Peterson, but the FOCA rules insisted on two. The second Lotus seat was offered first to Nelson Piquet, who was contracted to Brabham, and then to former F2 Champion and Shadow driver Jean-Pierre Jarier. He was given race number 55, again out of deference to Peterson, who had worn number 6.

Practice was again dominated by Andretti in 79/4, with Jarier performing well enough to earn himself a place on the fourth row alongside Watson's Brabham-Alfa. Those were the bare facts, but qualifying was not without dramas. Glenn Waters recalls events at Watkins Glen:

> We took only three cars, because Ronnie's 79 was now severely damaged. The 79 [79/4] that got damaged in Austria was by now repaired, so we took that. There was also one for Jarier - 79/3 – and we also took the original one that only Andretti could get in, which had a small fuel tank and the small dashboard [79/1]. Andretti put his car [79/4] on pole position, and in the morning warm-up the right-hand rear wheel came off. It had never been done up because, as I was doing it up, Chapman got hold of me by the scruff of the neck, pulled me up and told me to adjust the dampers. Nobody thought to do the wheel up because they could see the pin and thought it was OK. Anyway Mario went out, did a couple of laps and the wheel came off. He spun round, dinged the front of the car and it buckled the little cross bead that goes along underneath the car. So he had to use the car that Jarier was using [79/3] because that was the only one that was going to finish the race without stopping for fuel. Jarier had to jump in the one with the low dashboard and the small fuel tank [79/1].

Andretti's settings were applied to Jarier's car, but there was no time for him to become acclimatized to it. Only on the warm-up lap before the race could he throw it around to see what it might do. Although he led away at the start, it was immediately clear that the brake-pedal pressure was fluctuating, so he could hardly commit as he would normally have done. By the third lap both Reutemann and Villeneuve were through, and the Lotus's handling became more precarious. Before long, Jones's Williams moved ahead. The track surface was taking its toll on tyres, and Jarier was by no means the only driver forced to pit for fresh rubber. He worked his way up from twenty-second to third, duelling impressively with Scheckter and Jabouille on the way. Then Andretti's engine went bang and what had been a less than satisfactory homecoming event came to an end.

It was looking as though Jarier might restore some cheer in the Lotus enclave, since he was now closing on Jones's second-placed Williams. However, with just three laps to go, the Lotus 79 prototype coughed to a halt, the victim of its own inadequate fuel capacity in a race that was 200 miles (320km long). Reutemann was the winner, consolidating the view that he was the right man to fill the Lotus number-two seat for 1979. Said Glenn Waters,

Opposite: *At Watkins Glen for the US Grand Prix East, Andretti leads Jody Scheckter's Wolf. Andretti had to use 79/3 for the race (although it had been allocated to Jean-Pierre Jarier), after a wheel came off his own car in practice. Its engine failed later in the race. (Ford Photographic Archive)*

The World Championship Year – The 1978 Season

In a wet practice session for the Canadian Grand Prix on Montreal's Circuit Notre Dame, Andretti was troubled by an imbalance caused by incorrect camber settings. (Ford Photographic Archive)

Jean-Pierre Jarier gave a good account of himself, leading the Canadian Grand Prix by 30 seconds for all but twenty laps until sidelined by a split oil radiator. (Ford Photographic Archive)

The World Championship Year – The 1978 Season

Jean-Pierre Jarier: The French Connection

Born in 1946, Jean-Pierre Jarier's racing career began in saloons and the junior Formule France series. He moved into Formula 3 in 1970 with a Tecno and finished third in the French national series. In 1971 he competed in the European F2 Championship with a March, and hired Hubert Hahne's March 701 for a crack at the Italian GP, placing twelfth. Lack of funds found him back in F3 for 1972, but he was hired by March to lead its Formula 2 squad for 1973. Nicknamed 'Jumper' because of a tendency to jump starts, he won eight out of thirteen rounds in that year's European series; these wins really made his reputation. By contrast, he drove for March in ten Grands Prix in 1973 with no success whatsoever.

Jarier signed to Shadow for 1974 and became team leader when Peter Revson was killed at Kyalami. Among the high points of his career were wins in long-distance sports-car races driving for Matra, partnering Jacky Ickx at Spa, and Jean-Pierre Beltoise at the Nürburgring, Watkins Glen, Paul Ricard and Brands Hatch.

Jarier spent the next three seasons with Shadow, but despite leading a number of Grands Prix, he never reached the podium. He joined the ATS team to drive Penske PC4s in 1977, and ATS's own cars for 1978. After the death of Ronnie Peterson, he was drafted into Team Lotus for the US and Canadian Grands Prix where, at Watkins Glen, he ran third and set fastest lap before running out of fuel near the end. Then, in a show of his old brilliance, he put the Lotus 79 on pole at Montreal and led the race, until an oil leak ended his run. With Reutemann signed by Team Lotus for 1979,

Jean-Pierre Jarier is remembered as much as anything as the whirlwind Formula 2 champion of 1972. (Ford Photographic Archive)

Jarier found a seat at Tyrrell in the 009 and 010, where he stayed for two years. Inclined to lose interest in uncompetitive machinery, his sojourn in F1 ended in 1983, after a couple of seasons with Osella and one with Ligier. Jarier continued to race touring cars and Porsches in the Global GT series into the 1990s.

Andretti was in a car that he'd never driven before. He was pretty subdued. And then the engine blew up. Jarier came from nowhere in the original car and got right up almost to leading the race. He ended up having to come into the pits for a fresh left front tyre. While I changed it, I think they put five gallons in. But he still didn't have enough to finish the race! After all his trials and tribulations, he'd caught back up to about third place, and the car was really dominant. If he hadn't had any more problems he could have possibly gone on to win the race.

The Canadian Grand Prix was the last race for the works Type 79s in their JPS colours. It was also the first time the event was held on the 2.7-mile (4.35-km) Circuit Notre Dame on the man-made island in Montreal's St Laurence river. Andretti began practice using 79/1, which had had such a good run at Watkins Glen in Jarier's hands. His regular mount, 79/4, had been repaired and was available, while the Frenchman used 79/3. Friday's practice times were unremarkable. On the Saturday afternoon Andretti improved from 1 min 59.071 secs to 1 min 39.236 secs, while Jarier astonished everyone by going even more quickly, logging a pole-winning 1 min 38.015 secs. Troubled by a serious balance problem,

157

The World Championship Year – The 1978 Season

Opposite: *The privately entered T78/2 of Hector Rebaque leads Keke Rosberg's ATS D1 during practice for the Canadian Grand Prix. Rebaque failed to qualify, while Rosberg made the last row of the grid. (Ford Photographic Archive)*

caused by incorrect camber settings, Andretti was no better than fifth row on the grid.

Jarier made the best start, and led from Jones, Scheckter, Villeneuve, Watson, Andretti, Depailler, Lauda and Reutemann. On lap 7, Andretti made a bold attempt to get by Watson on the narrow, sinuous circuit's hairpin, but the two cars collided, spinning both off. Marshals gave them each a push start and, although Watson subsequently retired, Andretti carried on, a lap down. Jarier's comfortable 30-second lead lasted until lap 46, when he sensed that the brakes were not as effective as they should have been. Oil was leaking on to the rear brakes and tyres, and the oil pressure was falling, because of a stone or balance weight perforating the oil cooler. Jarier coasted into the pits on lap 49 to be congratulated by Chapman on a fine drive, while Andretti went on to be classified tenth, a lap in arrears and with badly faded brakes. Glenn Waters recalls what happened in Montreal:

> Up in Canada, they brought out some bits from the UK which we spent all night the night before first practice putting in Andretti's car. But it had been more damaged than we thought and he was never happy with it in qualifying. He didn't qualify well with it, and I think he was still a bit subdued. Jarier was now back in the one he'd qualified in at Watkins Glen. He put it on pole, and he tore off and was miles in the lead. He ended up breaking the oil cooler.

While Gilles Villeneuve, very much a driver in the same mould as Ronnie Peterson, had won his first Grand Prix, Team Lotus, and indeed the rest of the motor-racing fraternity, was not yet done with tragedy. A fortnight later, on 20 October, Gunnar Nilsson lost his brave battle with cancer, having days earlier launched a campaign to raise £350,000 for cancer treatment at the new Charing Cross Hospital in Fulham, in west London.

The world championship points table concluded with Andretti at the top on 64 points, Peterson second on 51, Reutemann third on 48, Lauda on 44, Depailler on 34, Watson on 25, and Scheckter on 24. The constructors' world championship tally reflected Team Lotus's domination; they were way ahead with 86 points, followed by Ferrari on 58, Brabham-Alfa Romeo on 53, Tyrrell on 38, and Wolf on 24.

The high-speed Lotus 79 train of Andretti and Peterson was unstoppable at Zandvoort (Ford Photographic Archive)

9 Soldiering On – The 1979 Season

The Season Begins

Colour Change

For the 1979 season, most other teams attempted to copy the principles of the Type 79 with what was being called the 'Lotus air-flow' system. 'What else could they do?' said Colin Chapman to Denis Jenkinson of *Motor Sport* magazine. Team Lotus had lost its Olympus and John Player sponsorship, with funding coming instead from the Martini and Rossi drinks concern. Count Rossi was a Jim Clark fan, and asked for the Lotuses to be painted in something approximating their traditional colour scheme. The result was a dark green body

Soldiering On – The 1979 Season

Carlos Reutemann: Still Waters Run Deep

Carlos 'Lolé' Reutemann was born in 1942 on an Argentinian cattle ranch, and began racing in 1965, enjoying some success in saloon-car events with a Ford Torino. His first taste of international single-seater racing was in the 1968 South American Temporada series, entered by a number of F1 stars who had come to escape the winter of the northern hemisphere. In 1970 the Automovil Club Argentino sponsored Reutemann for a season in the European F2 series, driving a Brabham BT30, which he repaid by some top-six finishes. The following year he was back in Europe and a win at Hockenheim and several high placings made him runner-up to Ronnie Peterson in the F2 championship.

In his first Grand Prix, driving for Bernie Ecclestone's Brabham team, Reutemann put the BT34 on pole at the Argentine GP, finishing seventh. However, driving the Rondel Racing Brabham in an F2 round at Thruxton, he sustained an ankle injury, which affected his performance during the rest of the season. He bounced back in 1973 with good races at Anderstorp, Ricard, the Österreichring and Watkins Glen in the new BT42. The next year he began confidently, taking wins at Kyalami and, later, in Austria and Watkins Glen, but consistency seemed to be lacking.

After an abortive season in 1976 with the BT45, powered by the Alfa Romeo flat-12, Reutemann extricated himself from his Brabham contract and joined Ferrari. Here, despite winning at Interlagos, he was overshadowed by the recovered Lauda who maintained a dominant presence in the team. In 1978 there were more wins, at Jacarepagua, Long Beach, Brands Hatch and Watkins Glen, but only when the Lotus 78s and 79s failed.

Reutemann joined Mario Andretti at Team Lotus for 1979 and it was a very mature driver line-up that faced the challenge from the incoming noviciate ground-effect brigade. As it turned out, Reutemann had better fortune than Mario, coming sixth in the drivers' points table to Andretti's tenth. Notably, Reutemann preferred to stick with the Type 79 rather than race the unproven

Noted as a deep-thinking perfectionist, Carlos Reutemann joined Mario Andretti at Team Lotus for 1979, creating a very mature driver line-up. (Peter Riches)

Type 80. Reutemann's last couple of seasons were spent with Williams, driving the FW07 ground-effect car, and he scored a number of podiums both years, with wins at Monaco, Jacarepagua and Zolder.

Noted as a deep-thinking perfectionist, Carlos Reutemann was always reckoned to be world championship material, but the necessary consistency eluded him. He retired a couple of races into the 1982 season to concentrate on a career in politics.

Opposite: *All smiles at the press conference to announce plans for the 1979 season. The World Champion has cracked a joke, which his new team-mate Carlos Reutemann and the Lotus boss applaud. The future looks bright once more with fresh Martini, Valvoline and Tissot sponsorship. (Classic Team Lotus)*

colour emblazoned with Martini's red and blue stripes. At this early stage in the season the second major sponsor was Tissot watches. Drivers were to be Mario Andretti and Carlos Reutemann, who did not appear to be overly bothered about who was number one or number

To the rapturous applause of his home crowd, Reutemann came second at Buenos Aires driving 79/2, although the Ligiers were supreme. (Ford Photographic Archive)

Andretti and Reutemann started the Brazilian Grand Prix from the second row of the grid, but Andretti's race ended with a fuel leak on lap 3. (Ford Photographic Archive)

Reutemann pictured during practice for the South African Grand Prix at Kyalami driving 79/2. He finished fifth in the race, troubled by brake fade that meant he had to pump the pedal before every corner. (Ford Photographic Archive)

two. Reutemann was the sort of driver who concentrated on the job in hand and, if circumstances and equipment were favourable, as they had been for his four GP wins in 1978, he was a hard man to beat. His method was more akin to Ronnie Peterson's in that he was not inclined to spend a great deal of time trying compromises on settings. For that reason an intensive winter testing programme was not on his agenda – a surprising attitude, perhaps given Colin Chapman's preference for complete commitment. Andretti's view was that 'the rapport with Carlos was fine. He was very moody, difficult to understand as a person, but that was Carlos.' Team Lotus mechanic Rex Hart was more forthright. 'I worked with Reutemann all that year, and he was a good bloke, but he never though much of Andretti. They didn't get on, end of story.'

Meanwhile, in Leamington Spa, Warwickshire, Team Rebaque mustered its complement of T78/4 and T79/1 chassis, ministered by former Team Lotus mechanics and funded by Hector Rebaque's father. The original 79 was sold to Team Rebaque on condition that Team Lotus could borrow it back if necessary – shades of Jo Bonnier and the Lotus 49 at the 1969 British Grand Prix. Rebaque's move into F1 was something of a leap in the dark; he was coming from Formula Atlantic and F2, where he drove Fred Opert's Chevron against vastly more experienced talents. After a season mostly spent non-qualifying the Hesketh 308 in 1977, he drove the ex-Team Lotus 78 and 79 as a privateer during 1978 and 1979.

Southern Hemisphere

The season began well enough for Carlos Reutemann, who came second in 79/2 at Buenos Aires in his home Grand Prix to Laffite. Andretti, on the other hand, was disgrun-

Soldiering On – The 1979 Season

Privateer Hector Rebaque started the South African Grand Prix from the back row of the grid in 79/1, retiring with nine laps to go with engine failure. (Ford Photographic Archive)

tled at the team's inability to find some extra speed in his 79/4. As it was, the two Ligier JS11s led as they pleased, with Reutemann taking second as Depailler's DFV went off song. Having opted to race the spare 79/3, Andretti was running a distant fifth, delayed by a flapping engine cover that caused a handling imbalance. Neither car felt as balanced as it might have been, and the cause was thought to be the compounds of the new season's Goodyears.

There was start-line drama in Brazil when Andretti's car (79/4) caught fire prior to going out on its warming-up lap due to a perforated metering-unit diaphragm, and again on the Interlagos grid, while Reutemann's car (79/2) would not start. There were extinguishers to one side attending to Andretti and compressed-air bottles on the other for Reutemann. The Argentinian got a push start and overtook a lot of cars on the warming-up lap; controversially, he was not penalized for either 'offence', despite a protest from Ferrari after the race. While the Ducarouge-designed Ligiers of Laffite and Depailler were the class of the field, both Lotus 79s occupied the second row of the Interlagos grid, so they could hardly be considered obsolete. The Ligiers were once again supreme, however, and Reutemann finished some 39 seconds behind them in third place. Andretti's race had lasted but three laps, his Lotus being sidelined by a leaking fuel-injection unit. Bob Dance recalls that they knew it would not last long because of the perforated

At the start of the 1979 South African Grand Prix, Laffite's Ligier JS11 leads Pironi's Tyrrell 009, Lauda's V12 Brabham-Alfa BT48, Jabouille's RS01, Jarier's Tyrrell 009, and the Lotus 79s of Andretti and Reutemann. The Ferraris of Villeneuve and Scheckter came first and second; it was clear that the opposition had finally caught up with Team Lotus. (Ford Photographic Archive)

Soldiering On – The 1979 Season

metering-unit diaphragm, but that Chapman had insisted that the car start the race in order to collect the start money.

For the South African GP at Kyalami on 3 March, Andretti had a new chassis, 79/5, at his disposal, while Reutemann had 79/2, and 79/4 was the spare. The side pods on the cars now sported the Essex logo of the independent fuel company owned by David Thieme. At the time, Essex Petroleum supplied most of the petrol companies that were not in the big league.

Atmospheric conditions often played a part in the performance of race engines at Kyalami, and the cool conditions on Thursday's timed practice proved favourable for the 1.5-litre turbocharged Renault RS01 of Jabouille, who managed to go a second faster than anyone else. Other teams were forced to experiment with no nose fins and minimal rear wing during Friday's untimed session, to try and find a way to jump the yellow Renault. As it was, Andretti started from row four and Reutemann from row six. Apart from the Ligiers, their main competition came from the flat-12-powered Ferraris and V12 Brabham-Alfas. Also quick were the Maurice Phillippe-designed Tyrrell 009s of Pironi and Jarier. But the weather played its part once again, and tyres told at the start; the Renault and both Ferraris were Michelin-shod, and romped away on a damp track. Their lead was such after just three laps that the organizers decided to stop the race. At the re-start, the Ferrari 312T4s of Villeneuve and Scheckter made the best of their wet tyres, and after about thirteen laps cars began to pit for dry tyres as conditions

Above: *Its tyres still wet with melted snow, Chapman and Reutemann show the Type 80 to the press in the Brands Hatch 'Kentagon' at the cancelled Race of Champions meeting in 1979. At the rear, Bob Dance talks to journalist Alan Henry while he waits to take the car to Paul Ricard for testing. (Peter Riches)*

For much of the Race of Champions at Brands Hatch, the Ferrari 312T3 of Gilles Villeneuve was never much further away from the back of the Andretti's Lotus than here at Druid's hairpin. As the world champion's brakes faded and his front tyres disintegrated, Villeneuve took the win, while Mario limped home third behind Piquet's Brabham BT48. *(Peter Riches)*

Soldiering On – The 1979 Season

improved. In the end it was the kind of Ferrari demonstration that race-goers have become used to in recent years; Jarier's Tyrrell was 41 seconds in arrears for third place, closely followed by Andretti's T79. Reutemann was fifth, another 40 seconds behind.

Enter the 80

Snow Tyres

The Race of Champions was postponed due to the circuit being covered in snow, but Team Lotus used the occasion to show the brand-new Type 80 to the press, as scheduled, in the Brands Hatch reception centre known as the 'Kentagon'. JPS-Lotus presentations in the past had been impressively slick, but this time the car was simply wheeled on to the dais with snow melting off its tyres. Tongues wagged more than ever at the prospect of the fin-less wing car. The first public viewing of the T80 was at the re-scheduled Race of Champions on Easter Sunday, 15 April, but Mario Andretti drove it only in practice; it was now sporting nose fins and a second wing between the tailplates at the back. Team Lotus sent just one T79 for Andretti, since this was a non-championship race.

The crowd was treated to a cracking display of racing as Lauda led in a Brabham BT48, with Andretti in 79/3 and Villeneuve in 312T3 jostling for second place, passing and re-passing each other on the excellent Brands Hatch long circuit. The Austrian's Goodyears were finished after just eight laps and, by lap 10, Andretti had the lead. On lap 28, the world champion's Lotus succumbed to brake fade, and the Ferrari took him on the apex of Paddock Bend, a move that further consolidated the French-Canadian's burgeoning reputation as a champion in the making. Andretti finished third, having lost another place to Piquet's Brabham-Alfa V12.

Neither Andretti nor Reutemann had driven Type 79s at Long Beach – the T78s had been used the previous year by Andretti and Peterson – and Andretti tried both 79/5 and, briefly, 79/4, while Reutemann set the pace on Friday's qualifying with 79/2. The Ameri-

Street fighter: Andretti started the 1979 US Grand Prix West at Long Beach from the third row in 79/5, finishing fourth after a battle with Depailler's Ligier. It was another race dominated by the Ferraris of Villeneuve and Scheckter. (Ford Photographic Archive)

167

Soldiering On – The 1979 Season

At Jarama for the Spanish Grand Prix, Carlos Reutemann drove 79/2, starting from the fourth row and finishing second behind Depailler's Ligier JS11. (Ford Photographic Archive)

Starting from the second row of the grid in T80/1 at Jarama, Andretti brought the new design home in third place, having knocked off the right-hand nose fin while lapping Tambay's McLaren. (Ford Photographic Archive)

can fiddled with adjustments to suspension and wings in a bid to match the Argentinian's times, ending up fifth-fastest. Different sizes of Girling master cylinder were also tried in an attempt to improve the braking abilities of the T79s. They were fitted with the ubiquitous Ford-Cosworth DFV engines, their transmissions were Hewland and the tyres were by Goodyear. The brakes were certainly taking a hammering but, for the first time on a T79, a driveshaft failed on Reutemann's car during Saturday's practice. it was thought that the bumpy surface of the street circuit might have been responsible, as Renault, Copersucar and Wolf also suffered similar failures.

Having set a blistering time that was bettered only by Villeneuve, Reutemann got into trouble on the race's warm-up lap when his engine died and he appeared on the end of a tow rope as the rest of the grid assembled. His electrics were changed in the pit lane and a push start got him going; he forced his way out of the supposedly closed pit lane in an attempt to join the grid that, peculiar to Long Beach, was flagged off halfway around the lap. Villeneuve missed the designated 'start line' and they had to go round again, by which time Reutemann was directed back into the pit lane, destined to get going only after the field had passed by. After the race he was penalized 10,000 Swiss francs (about £3,000) for the infringement.

Lotus interest in the race centred on Andretti's battles with Depailler and Jones for fourth place behind Jarier, while the Ferraris of Villeneuve and Scheckter dominated yet again. Andretti eventually took fourth behind Jones, while Reutemann, who had been moving steadily up the field, retired with a broken driveshaft on lap 22. Hector Rebaque's chocolate brown-liveried T79/1 now sported sponsorship from the Mexican Carta Blanca brewery, and he started from the back of the grid, retiring with nine laps to go after a collision when lapping Derek Daly's Ensign.

Unaccustomed Hold-Up
The hard-pressed mechanics were often expected to contend with some difficult situations. Prior to the Spanish Grand Prix, the T80 was dispatched to Paul Ricard for testing, while the three T79s were transported direct to Jarama. The big transporter passed through Franco-Spanish customs on the west of the Pyrenees at Hendaye without incident. However, when the smaller transporter carrying the T80 arrived at Figueras on the east of the Pyrenees, the customs officials demanded that all documentation be translated from English and presented in Spanish. This was extremely time-consuming, relating to every item on board the transporter, including spares. Consequently, the shattered mechanics arrived at the circuit at 3.30am, with the gear ratios to change before unofficial practice at 10am. Andretti told them he was happy to wait and, in the event, practice was delayed by two hours so there was at least some respite.

Timed practice sessions for the Grands Prix now lasted for an hour and a half on the Friday afternoon, and again on the Saturday afternoon, with untimed sessions in the mornings. At Jarama on 29 April, Chapman, Andretti and the mechanics worked away on the 180/1 smoothing out all the rough edges, and the driver put it on the second row, fourth-fastest. He was using nose fins on the T80, which were absent on the Brabham-Alfas. Reutemann was delayed by a split water radiator pipe, taking the start from row four. However, he set off brilliantly and lay third behind the Ligiers almost from the outset, leading his Lotus team-mate. Andretti was only a couple of places behind, but smote Tambay's McLaren while lapping it, damaging the right-hand nose fin of the T80. He was able to compensate to an extent using the cockpit roll-bar adjusters, but was passed by Lauda as he did so. When the Brabham's Alfa Romeo engine expired, the lead Lotus was able to pass Scheckter's Ferrari for third place behind Reutemann's T79 and, in the best result

Soldiering On – The 1979 Season

After a collision with Mass's Arrows A1 in practice for the Belgian Grand Prix at Zolder, Andretti elected not to race his T80/1, even when it was repaired. Here, the car demonstrates full-on ground-effect. (Ford Photographic Archive)

of the season, Team Lotus finished second and third behind Depailler's Ligier.

Belgium and Monaco

Team Lotus arrived at Zolder for the Belgian Grand Prix on 13 May with the T80/1 and three T79s. The T80 had a shorter nosecone with no skirts under it, due to problems of keeping the nose cowling parallel to the ground under acceleration and under braking, but it had revised side panels and a completely shrouded rear end. Andretti was only half a second slower than Villeneuve's quickest time on the Friday session, but problems with the T80's engine mounts sidelined him for much of the session. Practice times were all down on the previous year's because of a freak incompatibility between both Goodyear's and Michelin's qualifying tyres and the track surface. Just as Friday's qualifying drew to a close, Andretti and Jochen Mass's Arrows A1 had a coming-together, damaging the Lotus 80's front left-hand corner, necessitating an on-the-spot repair with tin-snips, welding torch and pop-rivet gun. It was enough to make Andretti think twice about racing the T80 and, after trying his spare T79/5 on the Saturday morning, back-to-back with the T80, he opted to race the older car, starting from the third row. Reutemann, meanwhile, was back on row five, perhaps conscious of the lack of a newer model.

After a promising enough start, Andretti's race came to an end on lap 28 with a lack of brake-pedal pressure. Reutemann battled on to finish fourth behind Scheckter, Laffite and Pironi, while Villeneuve was unfortunate to run out of fuel half a lap from the chequered

Mario Andretti: The Racer's Racer

Mario Andretti arrived in the USA as the teenage son of Italian immigrants, and went on to become one of America's greatest racing drivers, in a career spanning over thirty-five years of top-level motor sport.

As a young man he raced on the hugely competitive US sprint and midget circuit with his twin brother Aldo, winning the championship in 1964. That year he made his debut in USAC single-seaters, winning the first of his four USAC/Indy Car titles in 1965, including third place on his Indy 500 debut. He was Sprint Car Champion again in 1966 and raced in this category for another three years to 1969, when he won the Indianapolis 500.

Colin Chapman was an astute talent spotter, and as early as 1969 he invited Andretti to drive for Team Lotus. The American duly put the winged Lotus 49 on pole for the US Grand Prix at Watkins Glen, and went on to drive in three Grands Prix for Team Lotus in 1969.

Andretti's conflicting commitments in USAC racing restricted his appearances in Formula 1 with both Lotus and March. He also competed in the international world championship for Makes, winning at Sebring and Watkins Glen for Ferrari in 1970, going on to emulate his boyhood hero Alberto Ascari by driving the Ferrari F1 car in 1971. It was a dream start as he won the South African GP followed by the non-title Questor GP in California. In the World Sportscar series the following year he scored four victories in the Ferrari 312P shared with Jacky Ickx.

Having spent the 1973 and 1974 seasons racing for the Vel's Parnelli squad in F5000 and USAC events, late in 1974 he debuted the team's F1 car, the VPJ14, coming seventh at Mosport. Like Peterson and Ickx at Team Lotus, Andretti spent a gritty year in 1975 with the Parnelli car, picking up a fourth place at Anderstorp and a fifth at Paul Ricard – along with a catalogue of retirements. When the team folded, in 1976, Andretti returned to Team Lotus where he and Chapman embarked on the ground-effect revival that would lead to the 1978 World Championship. He recalls the air of optimism that prevailed at that time. In 1977, Chapman had claimed that 'the Lotus 79 would make the 78 look like a London bus'. Andretti could hardly wait for the 79 to come out.

It has been said that Andretti's relationship with Chapman was similar to that which existed between

Mario Andretti had a long association with Team Lotus, going back to his first forays into F1 in the Type 49 in 1968. (Peter Riches)

the Lotus boss and Jim Clark. Andretti has the following opinion:

If it was anywhere close, I would think it was a great compliment. But I think Colin had these relationships when he was right in his stride, and when Lotus had a driver that obviously responded. Jim Clark was certainly one. My arrival at Lotus was perfectly timed, when there was a Colin Chapman resurgence. His ideas were just perfect for the time and revolutionary. Of course I embraced all that, because I love the technical side of it, and it was uncharted waters. And good results create the proper mood.

Mario Andretti: The Racer's Racer *continued*

There is no doubt that much of the credit for the success of the ground-effect Lotuses must go to Mario Andretti. He was able to galvanize the team around him, and he was extremely sensitive and mechanically adept. He could juggle all the finer points of the T78 and T79 and use them to the maximum. He was sensitive to the variables of tyre compound, tyre size and construction, anti-roll bar settings and spring rates, aerofoil loadings, suspension settings and camber angles, and able to achieve a compromise for all of these factors that would add up to consistently quick lap times.

After quitting Team Lotus, Andretti drove for Alfa Romeo in 1981; it was a case of 'out of the frying pan, into the fire'. He had just three more races in F1, for Williams and Ferrari, coming third at Monza in the 126C2 turbo in 1982. For the majority of that season he was back in Indy Cars, winning the title in 1984 and spending the next decade driving for the Newman-Haas team.

Despite retiring in 1994, Andretti was still up for a race, with an eye to equalling Graham Hill's achievement and adding Le Mans to his list of wins. As recently as 2000 he drove a Panoz at La Sarthe. The Andretti dynasty has continued to operate at the top end of the sport with Mario's son Michael, his grandson and nephew all taking part.

Mario Andretti, pictured in 79/5 at Kyalami in 1979, juggled the finer points of the ground-effect cars to his advantage and galvanized the team around him. (Ford Photographic Archive)

---

flag when lying third. The Zolder meeting was also the occasion for the presentation of the International Racing Press Association's (IRPA's) Orange Prize, awarded to the driver judged to be the most amiable among the F1 fraternity. For the second year running it was given to Mario Andretti.

The 50th Monaco Grand Prix took place on 27 May, and Team Lotus arrived with the single T80 and three T79s. In first practice, Reutemann hit the harbour-front barriers in 79/2 and demolished its left-front corner. He walked back to the pits to have a go in 79/4, only for the left front hub to give trouble after just one lap. The T80 ran out of fuel just before the pits – luckily the mechanics did not have to carry the fuel very far to get Andretti going again.

It was decided to fettle 79/4 properly for Reutemann and abandon 79/2, although the Argentinian's back was painful following the shunt. Quickest on Friday was Villeneuve, with his Ferrari team-mate Scheckter fastest on Saturday, both roughly 2 seconds quicker than Andretti and Reutemann. Lauda's Brabham-Alfa was right on the pace, as were the Ligiers of Laffite and Depailler. Jones and Regazzoni were in the Williams FW07s that were similar in design to the Lotus 79 and they too were a match for the Lotus pair. The Tyrrell 009s of Jarier and Pironi were equally formidable. It was clear that most of the opposition had

Soldiering On – The 1979 Season

Carlos Reutemann crosses his hands on opposite lock as he rounds Loew's hairpin during practice for the Monaco Grand Prix. Having knocked a front corner off 79/2, he drove 79/4 during the race. (Ford Photographic Archive)

caught up with Team Lotus and its previously dominant ground-effect cars. They started tenth and eleventh and, in a race of typical Monegasque mechanical attrition, Andretti's T80 rear suspension broke on lap 22, coinciding with a broken exhaust on Reutemann's car, slowing him down slightly. He received a nudge in the rear from Piquet at one point, without sustaining any damage.

Of the twenty cars that started, only eight finished, and Reutemann did well to bring 79/4 home in third place, less than 10 seconds behind Scheckter's winning Ferrari 312T4 and Regazzoni in the Williams FW07. John Watson was fourth in the McLaren M28, a very disappointing car, which Ronnie Peterson would probably have been driving had he survived. McLaren produced three evolutions of the M28, and the M28C was similar in some respects to the Lotus T80.

Occupants of Loew's Hotel get a grandstand view of proceedings during practice at the Monaco Grand Prix, as Mass's Arrows A1/05 precedes Jarier's Tyrrell 009/3 and Reutemann in Lotus 79/4. The Argentinian drove a stolid race to finish third. (Ford Photographic Archive)

Andretti asserted that the Type 80 chassis needed to be stiffened at the centre. He was unable to get T80/1 on the pace at Monaco, running out of fuel during first practice and having to start from the seventh row of the staggered grid. He retired on lap 22 when the rear suspension failed. (Ford Photographic Archive)

Andretti has a particular view of the Type 80:

> When the Lotus 80 came on the scene, much more was known about downforce, so the car had quite a bit more downforce than the 79. I started out with the 80, but this was when Colin and I started going off at one another. He failed, in my opinion, or didn't want to recognize the importance of a stiff chassis. He was interested in the aerodynamics, the downforce, but he didn't realize that to support that downforce, you needed to go to much stiffer springs. We were experiencing a lot of porpoising, because we were nowhere near the range of springs that we needed to be to deal with that downforce. We were testing, and I kept asking for stiffer springs. He said, 'You won't be able to corner,' but I felt that it didn't matter, because every time we put stiffer springs on we'd go faster. Then, when I finally convinced him of that, we were experiencing a very inconsistent car. We'd put stiffer springs on, then the chassis would start torsioning even more. We were popping rivets all over the place on the bulkhead. I told Colin that we needed a collar round the cockpit, to stiffen the car in the centre. He used to hit the roof when he heard me, as a driver, offering technical advice. We had arguments like you can't believe on that. Meanwhile, the competition, Williams and Patrick Head, once they understood the effects of ground-force, were doing the right thing. They had stiffer pods. Colin's big concern was the additional weight. He just didn't want to make the car heavier. The Lotus 80 was the same lady as the 79, but with a totally new dress. In other words, the chassis was basically the same with a lot bigger dress on. So the presence of it was enormous, and it had the initial effect, but somehow the body needed more vitamins!

July Races

After the loss of both top Swedish drivers in the latter part of 1978, the Swedish Grand Prix organizers failed to come up with the £250,000 bond required by FOCA before the deadline, so the race in Sweden was cancelled. This meant that there was no GP during June 1979.

The next event on the calendar was the French Grand Prix, staged on the fast autodrome of Dijon-Prenois on 1 July. Mario had a second T80 chassis at his disposal – 80/2 – and Carlos had 79/4 and 79/5 to chose from. On the afternoon of Friday qualifying, the underside of the nosecone of 80/2 had to be patched up with fibreglass, having worn itself away along the straight – evidence that the downforce was effective. The second T80 had much of its underside reshaped and the suspension members were angled backwards in

Soldiering On – The 1979 Season

A major disadvantage of the Type 80 was that, if the skirts jammed when riding the kerbs, 50 per cent of the downforce was lost. The French Grand Prix at Dijon was its last race. Andretti despaired of ever getting its set-up right, and was forced to pit with failing brakes due to a fluid leak from a split union in the frontal system. (Classic Team Lotus)

The skirts appear to be working properly as Andretti hurls the Type 80/1 through the fast left-right-left complex at Dijon-Prenois circuit, but it still failed to generate enough downforce for Andretti's liking. (Classic Team Lotus)

order to shift the centre of gravity forwards. The frontal skirts were absent, and it was tried without the upper aerofoil in place. Andretti recalls another problem area with the Type 80:

> It was a big disaster when the skirts jammed; you'd lose probably 50 per cent of the downforce. That's why we were at a disadvantage on a circuit like Jarama or Paul Ricard, where you must use the kerbs to get around. We couldn't do that, because all you had to do was slam through the kerb a few times and your skirts were jammed and that was that. We had advantages in some areas because of the cornering power, but we couldn't use the kerbs, so we were giving something away. We were struggling to be competitive with some of the non-ground-effect cars because of that.

While Andretti was content to continue with the development of the T80, Reutemann preferred to stick with the more reliable T79. He had troubles of a different kind during first practice, as an electrical fault in the wiring of the steering-wheel switch on 79/4 kept shorting and blowing a fuse. He opted to use 79/5 for the afternoon session while it was sorted out. After three timed sessions, Andretti still only qualified eleventh-fastest, with Reutemann thirteenth. Halfway down the grid had been unfamiliar territory during the past two seasons for the world champion.

Now that most drivers were experiencing the phenomenal physical effects of ground-effect, some were complaining of neck strain due to the G-forces caused on the corners. Andretti lamented that he wished the T80 would go fast enough to give him a pain in the neck! He abandoned 80/2 in favour of 80/1 while more work was carried out on the underside of the newer chassis. For now, it was the turn of the new Renault RS11 twin-turbo cars of Jabouille and Arnoux to set the pace, and it was these two, along with Villeneuve's Ferrari and Jones's Williams, that sparred for the lead as the race got under way. Although

Soldiering On – The 1979 Season

As the 1979 season progressed, the reigning World Champion's expression grew increasingly perplexed. (Ford Photographic Archive)

Jabouille scored a memorable victory for Renault and for turbocharging technology the scrap for second between Villeneuve and Arnoux provided the real excitement. As for the Lotuses, Andretti called it a day with the poorly handling and brakeless T80 on lap 52, while Reutemann stuffed his T79 into the back of Rosberg's Wolf WR8 when his brakes failed on lap 78, three laps from the end while running tenth.

At Silverstone for the British Grand Prix on 14 July it seemed that the Lotuses were going backwards. Andretti elected to run with 79/4 as his first choice car, using 80/1 as back-up, while Reutemann got 79/5 and 79/3 as his spare. While Alan Jones was making hay with the Williams FW07 – the T79 copy – the atmosphere in the Team Lotus enclave was one of bewilderment and misery. As *Motor Sport*'s Denis Jenkinson put it, 'The scene at Team Lotus was so sad that it is best to draw a veil over it, and it was pointless to ask what was the matter, because if Colin Chapman and Nigel Bennett knew, they would do something about it.' Andretti did try the T80, but was not enthusiastic about it. By this time much of the titanium suspension componentry had been replaced with steel items, which at least did not break.

As the grid formed up, Jones was on pole with Jabouille alongside him, and Reutemann was on row four, 2 seconds a lap slower, with Watson's McLaren, then Andretti on the row behind, accompanied by Laffite's Ligier. Andretti made a fantastic start to get up to sixth on the first lap, with Reutemann running ninth, but after three laps the American's race was run. The T79 came to a halt with wheel-bearing failure when it looked as if a decent points finish might have been on the cards. Eventual victory went to Regazzoni in the second Williams FW07

Reutemann drove 79/5 at Silverstone for the British Grand Prix in 1979, finishing eighth, two laps behind, having been delayed by the break-up of a ceramic tip to one of the Lotus's skirts. (Classic Team Lotus)

Soldiering On – The 1979 Season

At Zandvoort for the Dutch Grand Prix, the Lotus T79s abandoned their twin-plate rear bodywork, reverting to a central support for the rear wing. It was similar to the system used by Williams with its FW07, which was in most other respects an evolved version of the Type 79. (Ford Photographic Archive)

after Jones's engine blew up, and Reutemann came eighth in 79/5. Behind him in ninth place was Hector Rebaque in 79/1.

The Williams duo took over Lotus's role from the previous year, scoring a one-two victory at Hockenheim on 29 July and giving Jones his first taste of the top step of the podium. Now though, Team Lotus was floundering, with no sight of the T80 and each of its drivers using T79 chassis with slightly tweaked rear suspension. Andretti even had the angle of his steering wheel in 79/5 adjusted. Fortunes fluctuate, and initially at least, the Ligier squad that had opened the year so well were also puzzled at their own lack of form, although Laffite managed to get on the pace. Quickest was Jabouille in the Renault turbo once again. Reutemann drove 79/4 in practice but crashed very heavily at the far end of the circuit, so there was no option but to go with 79/3 for the race. Andretti started from the sixth row and Reutemann from the seventh rank. At the end of the first lap, Andretti had forged his way to ninth place, with Reutemann fifteenth. The Argentinean's gloom was short-lived however, as when he and Mass contested the second chicane on lap 2, the Lotus 79 struck the guard rails and knocked off the right-front corner. Andretti's race hardly lasted much longer, as a universal joint broke up in a drive shaft, the heat transferred from the inboard brakes causing the grease to run out.

Reworked Rear Ends

For the Austrian Grand Prix, held on 12 August, Team Lotus arrived with 79/2 and

79/4, both having reworked rear ends. These included outboard brakes and T80 rear wheels, new suspension members and, significantly, the Lotus-designed gearbox used in the T80. This implied a lengthening of the wheelbase by 2_in (6.25cm), hence the revised suspension geometry. The spare car was 79/5, still fitted with a normal Hewland transmission and regular rear suspension. In qualifying, however, neither Lotus driver could get within 3 seconds of the quickest runners, who were Jones on the Friday and Arnoux on the Saturday. Reutemann was beginning to make it clear that he wished to move teams, and matters were not helped when Andretti was quoted out of context by a Swiss journal, which implied that he placed the blame for the team's maladies on his Argentinian colleague.

While Team Rebaque was given a set of Reutemann's skirts to replace its broken ones, Andretti drove 79/5, decided that was better after all, and chose to do the race in it. He was on the eighth row and Reutemann in 79/4 was on row nine. Rebaque, after all, failed to qualify. Andretti need not have bothered either. As the lights changed and the grid roared away, his clutch refused to bite, and that was that. The cars behind him, including Reutemann's, were thrown into confusion as the number-one Lotus crawled away to the end of the pit lane to retire. After twenty laps, Reutemann brought his 79/4 in for fresh tyres, fitted in a leisurely pitstop, and then returned to the pits a couple of laps later to ask for the original ones to be put back. Chapman decided to call it a day, while Jones went on to score another win for Williams.

Prior to the Dutch Grand Prix, on 26 August, Team Lotus carried out more testing with the T80 but only took a trio of T79s to Zandvoort for the race. These were 79/2 for Andretti and 79/4 for Reutemann, with 79/5 as spare; in fact, Andretti used it only on the Saturday afternoon session. The Rebaque team had its usual 79/1, but was in the process of building a brand-new car. As an interim measure they had a Geoff Ferris-designed, Penske-built chassis on hand that closely resembled a T79 (albeit with reworked air-flow characteristics) and used much of its running gear. The two Team Lotus works cars – 79/2 and 79/4 – that had been modified for Austria were returned to their original specification, with Hewland transmissions and normal rear suspension fitted, but still with outboard rear brakes. Instead of the covered-in back end and twin tail-plates, they now sported uncovered rears and had their aerofoils mounted on a central pier, just like the Williams FW07.

It was all to no avail, since Reutemann was 2½ seconds off the pace, and Andretti a full 3 seconds away from Arnoux's pole-setting time. In fact, Andretti arrived on the grid without any side skirts on his car, causing rivals to imagine that Chapman had suddenly discovered a way forward. In fact, it was simply that they were still being adjusted in the pits and they were fitted to the car on the dummy grid. At the first corner there was a pile-up involving Regazzoni and Arnoux, and Jarier caught the front of Reutemann's Lotus as he took avoiding action. The steering was too badly damaged and the Argentinian crept round to retire. On lap 9, Andretti's Lotus was in the pits with a split oil tank, ruptured by a broken rear suspension arm, and it was left to Rebaque to carry the Lotus torch into seventh place, his 79/1 being the last car to go the full distance of seventy-five laps. It had been another triumph for Jones in the Williams, although this was the event probably best known as the one where Gilles Villeneuve really made his name, battling with the Australian for the lead and then vainly wrestling his Ferrari to the pits on three tyres.

At Monza, Andretti used 79/5 and Reutemann had 79/4; 79/2 was present as the spare but remained unused all weekend. The Rebaque squad debuted its HR100-001, and had 79/1 available in case it did not work. In the event, the new car was not quick enough

During 1979, Hector Rebaque's private team ran 79/1 with sponsorship from the Mexican Carta Blanca brewery. They started eight Grands Prix, non-qualifying in two, posting six retirements and achieving a best placing of seventh at Zandvoort. (Ford Photographic Archive)

to qualify. While the T80 had an unenviable reputation for porpoising, now it was the turn of the Ligier and Wolf cars to experience the phenomenon on the high-speed circuit. The pace was set by the Renault RS11s of Jabouille and Arnoux, which occupied the front row, although the performance characteristics of the turbo-powered cars was such that they could get bogged down at the start and become overhauled by the rest of the pack. The reigning World Champion – Mario Andretti, remember – claimed a spot on row five along with Lauda's Brabham-Alfa BT48. Separating the Lotuses on the grid were Pironi's Tyrrell 009 and Ickx's Ligier JS11, the Belgian ace standing in for Depailler for several rounds as the Frenchman was badly hurt in a hang-gliding accident. As Scheckter and Arnoux disputed the lead at the outset, Mario moved up to eighth place among the leading bunch. By lap 40 he was sixth, as drivers such as Laffite and Piquet fell by the wayside and, finally, fifth, with Jabouille out as well. Reutemann came seventh, the last car not to be lapped. At Monza it was the turn of the Ferraris to finish the race with dramatically close first and second places.

On 16 September a forty-lap non-championship race was held at Imola, as a prelude to running the San Marino Grand Prix there in 1980 and, apart from two Ferraris, the F1 teams participating despatched a single car, in most cases for their second driver. Reutemann drove the singleton Lotus 79/4. Villeneuve and Scheckter shared the front row with Reutemann and Lauda's Brabham-Alfa on the second row, with Patrese's Arrows A1 and Brambilla's Alfa Romeo 177 behind them. Reutemann suffered from rear-end vibrations from the outset and later from a broken exhaust, while the Ferraris were in tyre problems after ten laps. Lauda took the initiative, and traded the lead with Villeneuve until the latter drove into the back of the Brabham, and then performed a meteoric drive back up through the small field once a new nosecone had been fitted. Reutemann finished second to Lauda, with Scheckter third.

Soldiering On – The 1979 Season

Across the Pond

Once again the Canadian Grand Prix was held on the island circuit on the St Lawrence river in Montreal. Team Lotus dispatched 79/5 for Mario and 79/4 for Reutemann with 79/3 the designated spare. In practice the Argentinian found he preferred the spare chassis to his regular car and declared that he wanted to drive it in the race. Since it was meant to be available to Mario as his spare car as well, this caused a degree of friction within an already frustrated team. Jones was quickest on both days of practice, with Villeneuve and Regazzoni closest to him. There were a number of talking points. Lauda suddenly departed from the Brabham team, declaring that, like Hunt, he had had enough. The two works Alfa Romeos of Brambilla and Giacomelli – run by Carlo Chiti's Autodelta squad – were told they had to pre-qualify along with extra cars entered by Tyrrell and Fittipaldi (Copersucar) for 'novice' drivers, hardly front-runners; sensibly, the Italians declined. The organizers declared that they could not practise at all, but after protests from Ferrari and Renault they were allowed a single car.

Andretti started the race from the fifth row alongside the World Champion designate Jody Scheckter, while Reutemann was on the row behind with Stuck's ATS D3 next to him. In the race Reutemann passed his team-mate but retired on lap 23 with a split oil-tank mounting, while Andretti's car simply ran out of fuel on lap 67 out of seventy-two. Since both Lotuses had run out of petrol during practice, it seemed a curious oversight that it should also happen in the race. Winner was Jones who beat Villeneuve by a scant tenth of a second, the French Canadian having led for the first fifty laps.

The final outing for the works T79s was at Watkins Glen on 7 October for the US Grand Prix East, a relatively simple journey by semi-truck 350 miles (560km) to the south. The harder suspension settings in use as a result of ground-effect made life even more uncomfortable for drivers over the frost-damaged and undulating surface. To make matters worse, it rained heavily on the Friday practice session, and with only twenty-four cars allowed to start out of thirty entered, there were some grim faces in the pits. Reutemann did one lap and came back in, while Andretti did not venture out at all. Brambilla damaged his Alfa, but Villeneuve put on a display of absolute skill and bravery. On the Saturday the rain had stopped, but Andretti managed very few flying laps before his 79/5's engine blew, valve gear finding its way into the inlet tracts. Since Reutemann had commandeered the spare 79/3, the mechanics had to alter 79/4 to suit the American's smaller physique, adjusting the pedals and seat. He was still not happy, unlike Reutemann, who found the chassis of 79/3 stiffer and more to his liking. He ended up sixth-fastest, 2 seconds slower than poleman Jones.

In what was to be the final outing for Team Rebaque, Hector Rebaque failed to qualify. For the next two years, he received support from Mexican oil giant Pemex and drove Bernie Ecclestone's Parmalat Brabham BT49s, as well as making a foray into CART in 1982, before retiring completely.

For the 1979 US race at Watkins Glen, Andretti was back in his regular 79/5, but his lowly grid position on the ninth row reflected the torrid time he had had getting the 'spare' car to work for him. Before the race could start, the rain came down again and, while some went straight for wet tyres, the gamblers stuck with slicks. Chapman took this line with Andretti's car – not unreasonably, since he was so far down the grid – although Michelin wets were far superior to Goodyear's, and a Ferrari victory looked a foregone conclusion. This is exactly what happened. Villeneuve took off and was a speck in the distance, initially with Jones a distant second. Reutemann was lying third in the early laps, but lost control when the dry-battery pack that energized the fire extinguisher fell from its mounting and dropped between his knees, causing him to lose concentration for long enough to go off. Since it was clearly not going to stop raining, Mario came in for a set of wets on lap 10. On lap 17 a tooth broke off the Hewland transmission's fifth gear and jammed the selector mechanism. As luck would have it, the rain stopped after around twenty laps and a strong wind dried the track, making slicks once again the optimum choice.

End of the Line

The 1979 season for Team Lotus could only be described as, at best, disappointing; some would say it was frankly disastrous at times. This was partly due to the fact that other teams had leapfrogged the T79, but it was also due to the fact that the T80 wing car was not the beacon of light that Chapman had hoped it would be. Tyres were undoubtedly a factor, but in fact the T79 should probably have been improved rather than put to one side while the T80 was developed. The same could be said of the maligned Type 76, sidelined in favour of the old T72 back in 1974. With hindsight, Carlos Reutemann was perhaps not the best team-mate to have accompanied Mario Andretti, having nothing much in common with him, and the Argentinian was only too glad to move on and join Alan Jones at the Williams team for 1980.

Reutemann's replacement was the wealthy young Italian Elio de Angelis, who came out best in tests at Paul Ricard in November 1979, which also involved Nigel Mansell, Stephen South and Jan Lammers driving the T79. De Angelis went on to spend six seasons with Team Lotus, before being ousted by the dominant Ayrton Senna, and drove more Grands Prix for them than even Jim Clark. Meanwhile, Andretti stayed on as number-one driver for 1980, while Nigel Mansell was hired as test driver.

Mario said the Type 80 was 'the same lady as the 79, but with a totally new dress'. Here at Brands Hatch, her skirts trail on the ground. (Peter Riches)

10 Epilogue: The Final Years of Ground-Effect, 1980–81

The Successors

The story of ground-effect racing cars still had another three years to go before skirts were banned completely. It is instructive to show how Colin Chapman and Team Lotus attempted to fight their way out of the trough into which they had slipped in 1979; it is a classic story of what might have been. Typically, the route they took produced one of the most innovative chassis constructions ever seen.

In 1978, the Lotus 79 showed the way to go with ground-effect, and the following year most other teams had caught on. Team Lotus's own follow-up, the Type 80, fared badly, and its successor, the Type 81, was not much better. Originally intended only as a stop-gap while Chapman prepared his revolutionary twin-chassis car, the Type 81 consisted of a hybrid Type 79/80 chassis clad in straight-sided T79-type bodywork, and fitted with a DFV engine and Lotus gearbox from the T80. By now, con-

New Team Lotus recruit Elio de Angelis poses a little self-consciously before taking the wheel at Paul Ricard; aerodynamicist Peter Wright walks around to the left. Cars under development were run with a degree of secrecy. Note the flat sides and the position of the exhaust manifolds. (Peter Riches)

Epilogue: The Final Years of Ground-Effect, 1980–81

De Angelis at Brands Hatch, retiring at 16 laps with rear suspension failure. A vicious circle developed where, if the chassis was made stiffer, the suspension then was not stiff enough, and the mounting points had to be strengthened. Structural loads were going up faster than aluminium tubs could be adapted, and the Type 81 that Team Lotus raced throughout 1980 was a case in point. (Ian Catt)

cerns were being expressed about the huge G-forces to which drivers were subjected by ground-effect cornering speeds. The T81's suspension was redesigned, with upper rocking arms, lower wishbones and inboard coil springs and dampers front and rear.

The car was finished in Essex Petroleum's blue, red and grey scheme with chrome strips, and debuted at the first round of the 1980

Type 81 (1980–81)	
Designer	Martin Ogilvie
Chassis	aluminium honeycomb monocoque
Engine	Cosworth DFV
Gearbox	Lotus-Hewland FGA
Front suspension	upper rocking arms, lower wishbones, inboard coil spring/damper units, anti-roll bar
Rear suspension	upper rocking arms, lower wishbones, inboard coil spring/damper units, anti-roll bar
Wheelbase	9ft 0in (2743mm)
Front track	5ft 10in (1778mm)
Rear track	5ft 4in (1625mm)
Weight	11.32 cwt

world championship season at Buenos Aires in the hands of Mario Andretti and Elio de Angelis. Both cars retired, although de Angelis was second at Interlagos and, later in the season, fourth at Imola and Watkins Glen. Andretti scored just a single point all year for sixth place at Watkins Glen, and went on to join Marlboro Team Alfa Romeo for 1981. By the time of the Austrian Grand Prix in 1980, Team Lotus had constructed the T81B, which had a longer wheelbase, single rear-wing support and a front wing mounted on top of the nosecone. This car was used for the first few races in 1981, with Nigel Mansell finishing third at Zolder and de Angelis fifth. Thereafter the T87 was used while the saga of the radical new Types 86 and 88 unfolded.

The conventional Type 87 was a carbon-composite monocoque that had much in common with the T81, but it failed to prove competitive. Both cars retired at Monaco, then de Angelis and Mansell came fifth and sixth at Jarama, and sixth and seventh at Dijon. The Spanish race coincided with the timely return of John Player with a two-year sponsorship deal, and the departure of Essex Petroleum, whose flamboyant boss had been arraigned for alleged business irregularities (a charge that

Epilogue: The Final Years of Ground-Effect, 1980–81

was subsequently overturned). There was, nevertheless, a serious shortfall in the Essex sponsorship fund. The Italian's best result in the Type 87 was fourth at Monza, while the Englishman's was fourth at Las Vegas in the last race of the season.

(Incidentally, the type numbers 83, 84, and 85 were allocated to the wedge-shaped Lotus Elite, Eclat and Esprit S3 road cars.)

What Should Have Been

There is an element of 'closing the stable door after the horse has bolted' about the T81, since it was an admission of what Lotus should have built in 1979. Neither brilliant nor catastrophic, it was more like the Williams FW07, using the 1979 aerodynamics of the T80, but based on the problematic T79 monocoque. The structure of the car suffered as ground-effect came into play. As Peter Wright recalls,

> The suspension went stiffer and stiffer, the rocker arms then weren't stiff enough, the monocoque itself wasn't stiff enough, the suspension mounting points weren't strong enough. Basically the monocoques were all over the place. We found cracks, and that was simply because the loads were going up much faster than the structural integrity of aluminium tubs could cope with.

At the end of the 1970s, carbon-fibre was just becoming available as a real engineering material and the composite chassis came out of the Type 80, spawning the T86 and the T88 twin-chassis cars. Just as with ground-effect, the design team was learning on the hoof. As Wright describes it,

> We were playing around with it, and Martin [Ogilvie] suggested that we should build a monocoque out of the stuff. The first real carbon honeycomb structure we built was the under-tray for the T86, which was the precursor of the T88. That was where we learned that it was good stuff to use.

Writing in the journal *Race Car Engineering* in 2001, Wright mentions the genesis of what would become yet another significant milestone in F1 technology. In the laboratories at Cranfield College of Aeronautics, Wright was shown an artificial-feel control column, which

Mario Andretti is ready to go in his T81 at Zolder for the 1980 Belgian Grand Prix. He would retire with broken gear linkage on lap 42. (Ian Catt)

Epilogue: The Final Years of Ground-Effect, 1980–81

was being developed for a fly-by-wire research aircraft. It was demonstrated how the control computer could provide any spring rate, mass and damping for the system, and that the technology could produce a suspension system with unique properties. However, at that time Team Lotus already had the twin-chassis T88 up their sleeves, and Wright decided that 'active suspension' would be a project for another day.

Tony Rudd recollects an important underlying aspect of the era:

> By this time Chapman had fallen in with David Thieme from Essex Petroleum, and was going around with him, staying at the best hotels in the world and eating in posh restaurants. That wasn't how Chapman really was. A cup of coffee and a sandwich would keep him going for ages. But when he got his share of the DeLorean money, he hoped that Team Lotus would come up with a better car than the 79. The 80 didn't do it and neither did the 81. And finally, when he got back into the act, prodded by David Thieme, he innovated for the sake of innovation and made the twin-chassis 86 with skirts that became the 88. Peter Wright wasn't sure whether it was going to work, but he was dead sure if it did work they'd make it illegal. Once the 86 ran, the rules were changed.

The Twin-Chassis Car

The Concept

Many of the lessons learned from the Types 78 and 79 affected the F1 cars that came immediately afterwards. The idea for the twin-chassis car came to Peter Wright when he contemplated how to apply ground-effect to a high-performance road car such as the Esprit Turbo. Unconstrained by any performance regulations, he thought that there was no reason why a ground-effect under-body could not be connected directly to the outboard ends of the lower suspension members, and not to the sprung part of the car. In this way, the contradictory requirements of significant deflection of soft road springs and the undertray ride height and angle of attack remaining constant relative to the road surface, could be satisfied. Having read the regulations thoroughly, Wright highlighted the relevant sections and went to see Colin Chapman:

> One of the wonderful things about working for Chapman was that as soon as you put your idea to him, he picked it up and extrapolated to where it might lead, while at the same time scrutinizing it carefully for weaknesses. Within hours Martin [Ogilvie] and I had moved upstairs to a locked office in Kett Hall, and a veil of secrecy was drawn over what we were doing.

Above: *The hope was that the twin-chassis Type 88 could circumvent the rules banning moving aerodynamic parts, because the word 'chassis' can be construed as both singular and plural. (Classic Team Lotus)*

Epilogue: The Final Years of Ground-Effect, 1980–81

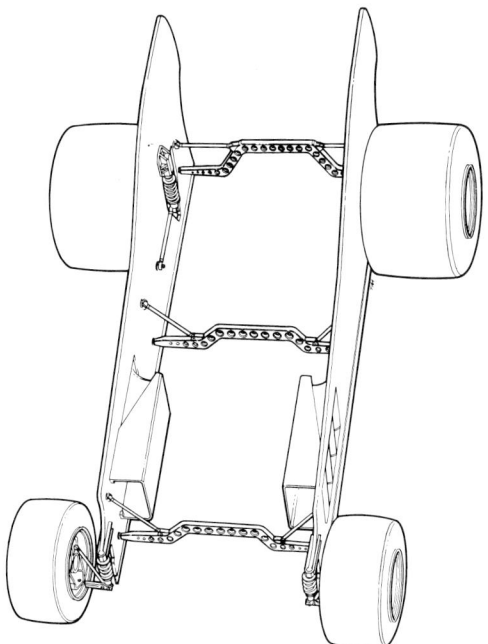

Above: *The primary chassis was of the ladder-type, with transverse beams connecting the side panels, and not connected to the inner chassis. It used stiff, independent outboard damper/coil spring suspension, and carried the radiators and the sides of the car that were instrumental in providing the aerodynamic ground-effect. (Classic Team Lotus)*

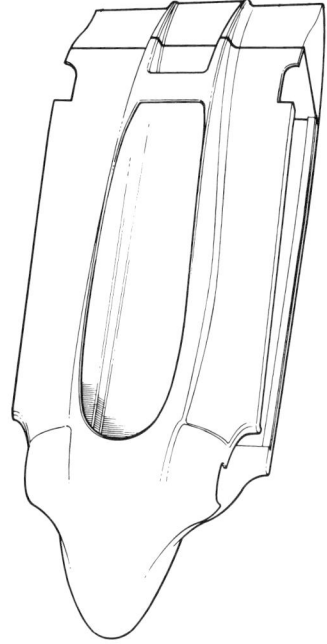

Above: *The T88's bodywork was secured rigidly to the primary chassis. As the car went along, the driver rode serenely in the secondary chassis while the lower chassis and bodywork were sucked towards the ground, exerting downforce on the car as a whole. (Classic Team Lotus)*

Team Lotus used the third Type 80 chassis as a mule to develop and prove the concept for what would become the Type 86. While Ogilvie prepared the drawings Wright implemented a wind-tunnel programme, feeding back critical features for the car's aerodynamics. These were based on those of the Type 80, with the full-length body and under-tray, plus the awkwardly curved sliding skirts. There was to be no rear wing, just a spoiler on the trailing edge of the body. It would thus be very similar aerodynamically to the Type 80 when it first appeared, except that the body would have to be bigger to

Left: *The secondary chassis was a monocoque of carbon and Kevlar – the 'Chapman tartan' – with softer, independent inboard suspension that provided the car's handling characteristics and isolated the driver from road shocks. (Classic Team Lotus)*

Epilogue: The Final Years of Ground-Effect, 1980–81

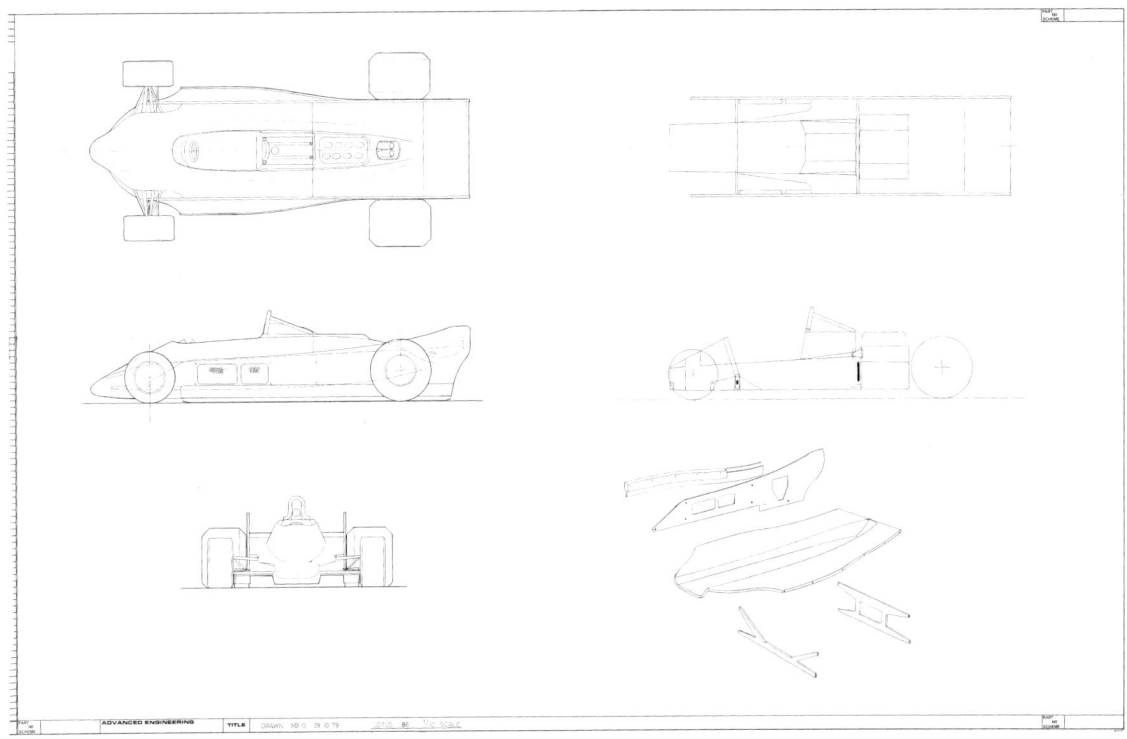

Martin Ogilvie's GA drawing for the Type 86 shows the undertray and bridging structure for the outer chassis. (Classic Team Lotus)

allow the sprung masses, consisting of the chassis, powertrain and radiators, to move relative to and inside the body. It would not be possible to build an empty shell for the body because there needed to be a structure spanning across it, and this had to be accommodated in holes through the chassis. Radiator ducting was also a problem, since the intake and the radiator needed to be able to move relative to each other. The suspension of the chassis part would be conventional, but the body could not be mounted directly on to the hubs, as Wright had proposed for a road car. The F1 car required a suspension, since the regulations stated that any part having an aerodynamic influence must be mounted to the entirely sprung part of the car. To make the concept more comprehensible, Chapman and Wright described the car as the 'twin-chassis' Type 86 rather than the 'twin-body' car.

The suspension characteristics they sought were very stiff, which amounted simply to hard bump rubbers. At this point, there was nothing in the rules to say they could not have a very stiff suspension.

The Type 86 consisted of a Type 80 tub, with the engine spaced off the back of the fuel tank to allow a crossbeam to pass between them. Two additional crossbeams passed through the monocoque, one under the driver's knees, and another over the gearbox. The body was manufactured in a carbon-fibre reinforced plastic (CFRP) and Nomex honeycomb sandwich, the first time Team Lotus had used such a formula. A better powertrain fit was achieved when Chapman persuaded Cosworth to rearrange the pumps on the DFV engine, tucking them closer in to the block, so that the under-tray could fit closer around the engine.

187

Epilogue: The Final Years of Ground-Effect, 1980–81

Chapman's bid to provide drivers with a comfortable ride at the same time as exploiting the ground-effect phenomenon was the Type 88, but Elio de Angelis had few opportunities to savour the softer ride provided by the twin-chassis car. (Ian Catt)

Testing and Further Development

Team Lotus booked an exclusive test session at Jarama, far away from prying eyes. There were initial problems with the revised oil pumps, and the car kept filling its under-tray with oil to the extent; it even gained the nickname 'Torrey Canyon' (after the oil tanker that hit rocks and spilled its cargo off the Cornish coast in 1967). Despite these setbacks, it showed great promise immediately. The curved skirts were problematic, as could be expected, but the downforce was there and the car did not porpoise. The decision was made to proceed to a new race car, based on these principles, and to include sliding skirts in the specification.

Then, out of the blue, FISA (as the sporting branch of the FIA was then called) banned skirts. To put this into practice, they ruled that all cars must have a ground clearance of at least 6cm. Crucially, they did not specify when this would be measured. To do it in the pits was obviously the only practical opportunity. As Peter Wright recalls,

> It took us about 30 seconds to realize that in the twin-chassis concept we had the perfect solution, provided we could come up with a suspension system for the body that raised it at slow pit-lane speeds, which would then allow it to sink down on to the bump rubbers at racing speeds.

The characteristics they sought were a very low rate, but with sufficient pre-load to raise the body by 6cm. They wanted it to go down fast, and come up slowly, to ensure that it stayed down if the car's speed dropped momentarily. To achieve this, it needed very soft bump damping, and very stiff rebound. These characteristics were available in the type of pressurized gas strut commonly used to support bonnets and boot-lids on road cars, and they found a supplier who was prepared to manufacture them to the exact characteristics they required.

As the Team Lotus drawing office and Ketteringham Hall workshops geared up to produce the Type 88s for the 1981 season, a blanket of security was placed over the whole project. The Jarama test started off the rumour mill, but Team Lotus's project was not revealed. The opposition grew paranoid, as was often the case when it seemed that Chapman was off on one of his tangents. Ferrari were so convinced that Team Lotus was building a Formula 1 kart that they managed to persuade FISA to add a last-minute regulation requiring F1 cars to have a suspension system. That regulation survives today, but Peter Wright claims that 'no designer ever wanted to build such a car'.

By now it was obvious that a monocoque chassis built in aluminium sheet was deficient in torsional stiffness and rigidity when subject-

Epilogue: The Final Years of Ground-Effect, 1980–81

ed to the loads imposed by ground-effect and suspension stiffness. Peter Wright describes the moment of transition at Team Lotus:

> One day, Martin [Ogilvie] took a piece of the T86's under-tray material and bent it until it folded along the failure line. The outer CFRP skin folded and the inner skin buckled inwards. He showed it to me and said, 'We could make a monocoque like this by cutting the inner skin, folding the sandwich material, and jointing the inner skin again with a lap joint.' I agreed, and Chapman leapt at the idea. That was in November 1979, and the first race was just five months away. Martin set about designing a monocoque using this construction technique. The skin of the monocoque would be folded up out of a single sheet of composite honeycomb, and then we had to figure out how to bolt in the machined aluminium bulkheads. Because of my previous experience with composites I had to find out how to make the composite sheet and develop a material specification for it and, fortuitously, I had Lotus's best composite people available to help.

Unlike McLaren's approach to its first CFRP (carbon-fibre reinforced plastic) monocoque, which employed the aerospace expertise of the Hercules Corporation and pre-preg (impregnated) CFRP, Team Lotus decided to develop their CFRP tub in house. There was no time to do otherwise. They decided to mould the flat sheet on a large piece of plate glass to achieve the desired precision and surface finish. The skins were hand-laid, using epoxy resin, and the Nomex honeycomb was vacuum-bagged to bond it to the skins. The first attempt demonstrated that they were not using the correct release agent, and Wright had to ask Chapman to authorize another sheet of expensive plate glass as the original one had shattered while the operators were trying to remove the moulded panel. The boss was not impressed. A suitable release agent was found the day before the first monocoque was due to be made.

Towering Impact

The designers at Team Lotus had little idea how CFRP would behave in an impact, so they decided they needed to develop a skin specification that would be at least as good in a crash as aluminium. There were no FIA frontal-impact tests to pass at that time. Wright asked Chapman if he could build a 50ft (15m) tower, with a pole down the middle, so that he could drop a 220lb (100kg) concrete block on to samples representing different monocoque constructions. He recalls Chapman's reaction:

> He rolled his eyes and then smiled – this was the sort of R&D he loved. We made box sections of aluminium, aluminium/honeycomb, carbon-fibre/honeycomb, Kevlar/honeycomb and hybrid

T88B at Silverstone, showing off its 'Chapman tartan' Kevlar composite tub. The Type 88 consisted of an inner chassis made of a carbon and Kevlar sandwich with Nomex paper-foil filling, riding on conventional suspension, while the outer chassis had a harder set-up and carried the aerodynamic side pods, wings and radiators. (Ian Catt)

Epilogue: The Final Years of Ground-Effect, 1980–81

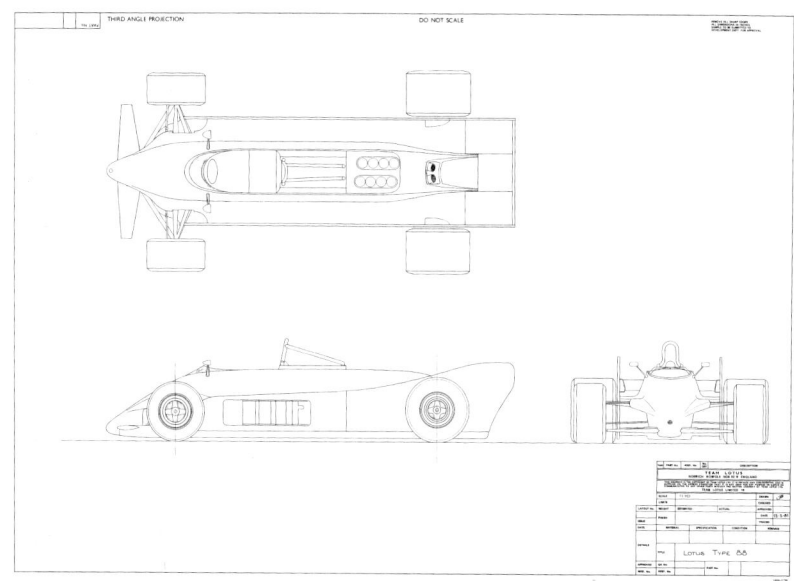

Plan view of the Type 88 emphasises the linear, almost rectangular, quality of the body and driver-forward cockpit. (Classic Team Lotus)

carbon and Kevlar/honeycomb and discovered that carbon-fibre was just as good at absorbing impact energy as aluminium, provided it was constrained to fail in the right way. The honeycomb content ensured that it crushed progressively.

They chose the hybrid carbon and Kevlar/honeycomb combination, as the Kevlar strands in Courtauld's specially woven fabric tended to hold the pieces together after an impact. The material was nicknamed 'Chapman Tartan', because of the yellow Kevlar strands that formed a pattern of 10mm squares.

The Type 88 inner chassis had conventional suspension, which ensured that the driver had a comfortable ride. The inner monocoque also contained machined aluminium bulkheads that doubled as mounting points for the suspension and powertrain. The outer chassis was in effect a ladder-type, which rode on a relatively soft suspension system that was connected to the main suspension set-up of the inner chassis. It also included the side pods, wings and radiators. The moulded carbon-composite Kevlar bodywork had been developed by Du Pont chemicals, and clad the outer chassis and performed the aerodynamic function.

The whole outer structure lowered itself when the car was travelling at speed to create the ground effect phenomenon. The driver meanwhile enjoyed a ride blissfully free of the serious pounding and bruising experienced in regular hard-ride ground-effect cars. It could be compared with the suspended cabs fitted on big modern trucks, where the driver is insulated from the bumpy ride normally associated with stiff truck suspension.

Outlaw Man

The Type 88 was announced in London at the Royal Albert Hall in February 1981 and was set to debut at Long Beach in March. The first test of the car was at Paul Ricard circuit. Peter Wright recalls the event:

> I remember that Alfa Romeo were also there to test their 179/C, and a few photographers were present, so we closed the garage doors to prevent them from prying. To keep them entertained, the mechanics

Epilogue: The Final Years of Ground-Effect, 1980–81

Above: At the 1981 British Grand Prix, the organizers invited Team Lotus to run the twin-chassis T88s, and arranged an early-morning photo call. (Ian Catt)

Following unsuccessful attempts to run the T88 at Buenos Aires, Long Beach and Silverstone, due to protests from other teams, the T88 was banned from racing. The subsequent appeal was rejected. (Ian Catt)

lifted the door shortly before the car was due to run, and four of them emerged wearing the body top, their heads sticking out of the long cockpit opening. It rained a lot, and when the car first ran, it was on a damp track. Alfa immediately sent out their own car to gauge the Type 88's performance and the T88 was about a second a lap quicker! That's when the campaign to prevent the T88 racing really started.

Team Lotus's fears of a ban grew when de Angelis recorded some impressive times in qualifying at Long Beach, and voices of protests began to be heard. Indeed, some teams threatened to boycott the race if the T88 was allowed to run. Chapman went to the US Automobile Competition Committee, which overturned the protests, declaring the T88 to be perfectly legal. However, this judgement was overruled by FISA. The T88 was again excluded at Jacarepagua and Buenos Aires, despite passing through scrutineering. Ferrari and Williams led the protesters. Chapman issued a scathing press release, for which FISA fined him $100,000 on the spot, although this was revoked ten days later. The Lotus boss then went to the FIA court of appeal in Paris, but still failed to get the T88 legitimized.

At Silverstone, the RAC encouraged Team Lotus to enter the T88s again and, now designated T88B, with additional panelling and gearbox oil cooler located to the outer chassis, the cars were passed by scrutineers. Resplendent in Courage Brewery colours for the occasion, the twin-chassis concept was again thrown out by the FIA after Ferrari threatened to withdraw its cars if the Lotuses raced. The T88s were hastily transformed into T87 guise. According to Bob Dance, this involved an all-night session, removing the T88 bodywork and relocating the radiators in the side pods. After de Angelis was

191

Epilogue: The Final Years of Ground-Effect, 1980–81

Type 88 (1980)	
Designer	Martin Ogilvie
Chassis	twin chassis, with inner of carbon-Kevlar monocoque, outer carbon-Kevlar body
Engine	Cosworth DFV
Gearbox	Lotus-Hewland FGA
Front suspension, inner chassis	upper rocking arms, lower wishbones and inboard coil spring/damper units, anti-roll bar
Rear suspension	upper rocking arms, lower wishbones, inboard coil spring/damper units, anti-roll bar
Outer chassis	independent outboard coil-sprung suspension
Wheelbase	8ft 11in (2438mm)
Front track	5ft 10in (1778mm)
Rear track	5ft 3in (1600mm)
Weight	11.52 cwt

black-flagged for overtaking under a yellow flag he wanted to hit the FIA steward he was so angry about the whole debacle.

The T87 lacked the development lavished on the T88, and was good enough in a straight line but poor on corners. It provided a basis for Peter Wright and Martin Ogilvie to develop the T91 for the 1982 season. In what could be construed as fickleness and a lack of conviction on the part of the rule-makers, the 6cm rule was rescinded for 1982, and flexible skirts again became acceptable. By this time, Renault and Ferrari were using 1.5-litre turbocharged engines, and the Cosworth-powered teams were hard pressed to keep up. Initially, Team Lotus had to resort once again to the T87, now known as the T87B, with wider track, 3in (7.5cm) longer wheelbase and broader side pods.

At Kyalami, after a threatened drivers' strike was averted, Elio de Angelis finished the race eighth and Nigel Mansell retired. The T87B then gave way to the new Type 91, resplendent once again in the livery of the sponsoring tobacco company JPS. Colin's son Clive Chapman pointed out that, 'After the Type 88, Team Lotus basically fell in line with what everyone else was doing. In fact, the Type 91 raced by Elio de Angelis and Nigel Mansell in 1982 was basically the Type 79 brought up to date.'

Within the Regulations

With hindsight, it is outrageous that the Lotus Type 88 twin-chassis cars were outlawed. Peter Wright provides a postscript in his piece in *Race Car Engineering*:

> Every independent technical judge and legal person judged that the Type 88 was allowed under the regulations. In the first FISA appeal the findings were proved to be incorrect, due to a wrong interpretation of the French-language version of the regulations. The English version is the definitive version. Chapman, being a logical engineer, believed that logic and right would prevail and he was fighting for the right to try new ideas, even if nine out of ten did not work. Quite simply, that was his reason for going racing. He was prepared to jeopardize Team Lotus's whole season, and possibly its entire future, for that right. He was particularly incensed that, while the T88 was judged illegal, Brabham were permitted to race a car that raised itself hydro-pneumatically to

The Type 87 was raced by Team Lotus throughout 1981, and was basically a single-chassis version of the T88. De Angelis drove the T87 at Silverstone in the 1981 British GP, but was black-flagged for overtaking under yellow flags. (Ian Catt)

pass the 6cm test in the pit lane, and then lowered itself on the track, and ran flexible skirts. In his view, 'The Brabham hydropneumatic self-lowering system was just a way round the regulations. It had nothing to do with the car's running.'

In fact, most of the cars had driver-controlled hydraulic or pneumatic raising and lowering systems and Vethane skirts by the start of the European season in 1981. The Vethane skirt was effectively a flexible rubbing strip and consisted of a strip of soft Vethane attached to the bottom of the side pod with a hard Vethane strip forming the rubbing edge. Its configuration was similar to the Type 78's suck-up skirt, but, according to Wright, it did not do the job properly:

> The argument was whether it should be allowed to flex. It was a fudge really. In any case, full ground-effect was back on the menu for another two seasons, making the Type 88 concept seem completely reasonable and within the rules.

After he lost the battle to have the twin-chassis car validated, in the face of a co-ordinated effort by his competitors and the sport's ruling body, Colin Chapman never really enjoyed Formula 1 racing again. He went off to develop his new interest, ultralight aircraft, immersing himself in it right up to the day he died, in December 1983.

In 1980 and 1981, FISA (the sporting arm of the FIA) and FOCA (Formula One Constructors' Association) were at war. The no-skirt regulation was part of that war, FISA introducing the rule without consultation with FOCA. They were possibly influenced by Ferrari, which was on the side of FISA and being beaten by the FOCA teams using ground-effect. The twin-chassis concept drove a wedge through that regulation, although it had not been originally conceived to do so. Peter Wright believes that both sides in the FISA-FOCA war agreed that it should not be allowed, in the interests of trying to gain some stability in Formula 1. In another year, the T88 might have survived.

Now, more than twenty years later, Steve Hitchins is demonstrating in the Thoroughbred Grand Prix series that it just might have revolutionized Formula 1 design. Peter Wright is philosophical about the legacy of ground-effect:

> The long-term consequence of ground-effect on motor racing has been disastrous. It's ruined motor racing. But you can't deny the existence of ground-effect, because you've got a body near the ground and you have to do something. It's either going to work against you if you do nothing, or it's going to work for you. Obviously you're going to elect for it to do something for you. But it hasn't improved motor racing, and I'm surprised they've allowed so much of it to remain. It's gradually being eroded, which is a good thing. I don't think pulling 4 or 5G is relevant to motor sport's entertainment value.

The Type 88 was Chapman's own take on the moveable aerodynamic parts rule. 'It wasn't a cheat,' affirms Martin Ogilvie:

> It really was founded on the rules, because the rules state that the aerodynamic devices had to be 'attached to the car's chassis'. Now, the plural of 'chassis' is 'chassis', and that's what we worked on. It just happened to be the second chassis, but two chassis is still 'chassis'.

In view of the regulation forbidding moveable aerodynamic devices, it's surprising that skirts were permitted at all, since they swept the track surface in their early incarnation and moved up and down later on, and their purpose was to harness aerodynamic effect. By 1982, most teams had figured out how to set up the cars with exceedingly stiff suspension, thus minimizing the gap between side pod and track, and restoring some of the lost downforce. The cars were so unpleasant to drive that flat bottoms were decreed for 1983. This in turn led to a much more pitch-sensitive aerodynamic arrangement, which continues to hold sway some twenty years on. This situation may not last for ever. In

Epilogue: The Final Years of Ground-Effect, 1980–81

order to create closer racing and thus more overtaking opportunities, F1 may have to follow the example set in the USA by the CART and IRL single-seater categories, where controlled ground-effect through restricted venturii has been retained, without any form of skirt. This configuration was imposed to avoid pitch sensitivity on high-speed ovals such as Indianapolis.

Even though the FIA-mandated flat-bottomed F1 cars only five years after the Lotus 78 started the ground-effect revolution, Chapman's innovative brilliance focused the attention of the racing world on the importance of under-car air flow, a legacy that endures to the present day. And there can be no going back. From the days when simply cladding a chassis in a streamlined body was sufficient, ground-effect placed aerodynamics on an equal footing with engine performance, suspension and chassis set-up, tyre grip and weight reduction, in the hierarchy of factors that define a racing car's specification.

End of the Hard Ride

With Colin Chapman heavily involved in his Group Lotus business, it was the job of chief engineer Peter Wright to oversee the development of the Type 91. Externally, it differed markedly from its predecessor in having an aerodynamically superior shape, drawn by Martin Ogilvie. It was some 10 per cent lighter than the Type 87B on which it was based, with a carbon Kevlar monocoque and fixed skirts, now with rubbing strips along the bottom edges. Front suspension uprights were of cast magnesium, and a strengthened rear suspension system and gearbox casing allowed for variations in wheelbase and track dimensions. The ride quality was rock hard, and drivers were subjected to even higher G-loads in corners. Along with most other teams, especially the normally aspirated brigade, Lotus opted for water-cooled brakes. This was a system open to abuse as the tanks could be drained or topped up to affect the car's weight – by this means the Cosworth-powered runners could recoup some of their horsepower deficit to the turbos. Both Piquet and Rosberg, in Brabham and Williams respectively, were disqualified by the FIA after such infringements in Brazil in 1982.

That year, Elio de Angelis was still number-one driver, although Nigel Mansell was rapidly improving and able to match the Italian. The pair were fourth and fifth at Monaco, de Angelis was fourth at Montreal and Brands Hatch, while Roberto Moreno and Geoff Lees stood in for Mansell for two races after he injured his left wrist in Canada. De Angelis tried out the pull-rod front suspension system at Brands Hatch, running third until he ran out of fuel on the last lap.

The T91 suffered from a lack of grip, understeering on slower circuits and porpoising on bumpy ones. The open curves of the Österreichring suited it better, and it was here that de Angelis scored his maiden GP victory, fighting off Rosberg's Williams at the last corner. For Team Lotus it was the first taste of victory in four seasons, although that was to be the full extent of its good fortune for the rest of the year.

As the 1982 season ended, the FIA declared that ground-effect was indeed banned, and thereafter cars had to have flat bottoms. Lotus responded with the T92, powered by the Cosworth DFY. The T92 was based on the T91's carbon-Kevlar tub, and one car was equipped with computerized active-ride suspension. Test driver Dave Scott was evaluating this set-up at Snetterton on 16 December when news reached Team Lotus that Colin Chapman had died of a heart attack, having just returned to Hethel the previous evening from a FISA meeting in Paris. The loss of his fertile and innovative mind marked the end of an era. Team Lotus would soldier on for more than a decade, much of it under the control of competitions manager Peter Warr and the Chapman family. There were highlights in the years to come, notably with Ayrton Senna driving the turbocharged Renault- and Honda-powered cars, but it was the ground-effect years that were to mark the final flowering of Team Lotus's fortunes.

Appendix I
Chronology of Team Lotus F1 Cars

Team Lotus could trace its origins back to 1948 when Colin Chapman built his first Austin 7-derived trials special. During the mid-1950s Team Lotus built and ran a succession of streamlined sports-racing cars from the Mk 8 of 1954 to the Type 15 of 1958. Their many race successes included a class win and Index of Performance victory with a Mk Eleven at Le Mans in 1957. As well as F1, Team Lotus ran in most other categories of the sport, including F2, F3, sports racing and GT, and touring cars.

1957–58:
Mk 12: first single-seater Lotus, F2 car. Spaceframe chassis. Aluminium body. Engine: 1500cc Coventry Climax. Grand Prix debut at Monaco 1958. Driven by Allison and G. Hill.

1958–60:
Type 16: first Lotus F1 car. Spaceframe chassis, aluminium and fibreglass body. Engines: 2500cc Coventry-Climax. Driven by Allison, Ireland, G. Hill and Stacey.

1960–61:
Type 18: first rear-engined single-seater Lotus. Engines: 2500cc Coventry-Climax. Driven by Ireland, Stacey, Surtees, Flockhart, Clark, Larreta; Moss won Monaco GP in Rob Walker car, Lotus's first GP success.

1961:
Type 21: Formula 1 car, spaceframe chassis, developed from 18. Engine: 1498cc Coventry-Climax. Driven by Ireland, Clark, Taylor.

1962–64:
Type 24: single-seater Formula 1, spaceframe chassis. Engine: 1498cc Coventry-Climax V8. Driven by Clark, Taylor.

Type 25: world's first monocoque Grand Prix car debuts at Zandvoort. Single-seater Formula 1, aluminium monocoque. Engine: 1.5-litre Climax V8. Driven by Clark, Taylor, Spence, Rodriguez. Jim Clark and Team Lotus won the world championship.

1964–67:
Type 33: single-seater Formula 1 monocoque developed from Type 25 with revised suspension and steering, wider wheels and tyres. Engine: 1.5-litre Coventry-Climax V8. Driven by Clark, Spence, Arundell, G. Hill, etc. Clark won world title in 1965.

1965:
Type 39: F1/Tasman car. Engine: intended for flat-16 Coventry-Climax; 2.5-litre Climax FPF 4-cylinder engine fitted for 1966 Tasman series. One unit built, classified as Type 33/R12. Driven by Clark.

1966:
Type 43: truncated monocoque. Engine: 3.0-litre BRM H16, acting as stressed chassis member. Driven by Clark, Arundell.

Chronology of Team Lotus F1 Cars

1967–70:
Type 49: powered by 3.0-litre Cosworth-Ford DFV V8, acting as stressed chassis member. Transition in aerodynamics from no wings to massive aerofoils and back to chassis-mounted wings; Team Lotus adopts Gold Leaf livery of new sponsors John Player & Son. Driven by Clark, Hill, Oliver, Rindt, Miles, Fittipaldi, Andretti, Attwood, etc.

1970–75:
Type 72: four-wheel drive. Driven by G. Hill, Rindt, Miles.

Type 72: Maurice Phillippe-designed wedge, driven by Rindt, Miles, Fittipaldi, Peterson, Ickx, Wisell, Charlton, Walker, Henton, Crawford, Watson, etc. Gold Leaf and JPS livery. World drivers' championship-winning car in 1970, 1972 and constructors' world championship in 1973.

1971:
Type 56B: Pratt & Whitney gas-turbine wedge, resurrected Indianapolis car. Driven by Fittipaldi, Walker.

1974:
Type 76: Bi-plane rear wing, four-pedal, automatic clutch John Player Special-branded F1 car, designed by Ralph Bellamy. Intended replacement for Type 72. Driven by Peterson, Ickx, Schenken.

Ronnie Peterson drives the Type 78, first of the ground-effect generation, at Monaco in 1978. (Ford Photographic Archive)

Chronology of Team Lotus F1 Cars

1976:
Type 77: aluminium monocoque designed by Geoff Aldridge, driven by Peterson, Evans, Andretti, Nilsson.

1977–78:
Type 78: first F1 ground-effect car, designed by Peter Wright, Ralph Bellamy. Driven by Andretti, Nilsson, Peterson.

1978–79:
Type 79: Martin Ogilvie-designed full ground-effect F1 car, driven by Andretti, Peterson, Jarier, Reutemann. Mario Andretti won world title in 1978.

1979:
Type 80: full sliding skirts, with Martini sponsorship. Driver: Andretti.

1980–81:
Type 81: F1 car in Essex Petroleum livery. Driven by Andretti, de Angelis, Mansell.

1981:
Type 86: still-born twin-chassis car. Skirts banned by FISA, 6cm ground clearance rule imposed.

Type 88: twin-chassis car, banned by FISA after protests. Essex livery. Driven by Mansell, de Angelis.

Type 87: single-chassis version of T88. Essex, Tissot, Courage and JPS sponsorship. Driven by de Angelis, Mansell.

1982–83:
Type 91: 'flat-bottom' car produced due to final ban on skirts and shaped under-trays. Designed by Peter Wright, Martin Ogilvie, driven by de Angelis, Mansell, Lees. Last F1 car of Chapman era.

1983:
Type 92: computerized hydraulic 'active-ride' suspension. Pull-rods first appear in suspension system. Driven by de Angelis, Mansell.

Type 93T: powered by 1.5-litre twin-turbo Renault V6 engine replacing Cosworth-Ford DFV V8. Driven by de Angelis.

Type 94T: designed by Gerard Ducarouge, based on Type 91 chassis, driven by de Angelis and Mansell.

1984:
Type 95T: completely new carbon-Kevlar monocoque, Renault turbo power, driven by de Angelis, Mansell.

1985:
Type 97T: evolved from 95T, retained Renault power, driven by Senna, de Angelis.

1986:
Type 98T: carbon-Kevlar monocoque. Driven by Senna, Dumfries.

1987:
Type 99T: powered by Honda V6 twin-turbo engines, Camel sponsorship, yellow paint scheme. Computerized active suspension reintroduced. Driven by Senna, Nakajima.

1988:
Type 100T: Honda power, Camel, Elf, Epson, Courtauld sponsorship, driven by reigning champion Piquet, Nakajima.

1989:
Type 101: powered by normally aspirated 3.5-litre Judd V8 engines. Frank Dernie replaces Gerard Ducarouge. Team manager Peter Warr leaves, new management team includes Tony Rudd. Driven by Piquet, Nakajima.

Chronology of Team Lotus F1 Cars

1990:
Type 102: power from 3.5-litre Lamborghini 3512 V12 engine. Driven by Warwick, Donnelly, Herbert. At season's end, several key staff leave.

1991:
Type 102B: powered by Judd V8 engines, driven by Hakkinen, Bailey, Herbert. Team Lotus under Peter Collins and Peter Wright's control.

1992:
Type 102D: powered by Ford Cosworth HB V8 engines. Driven by Hakkinen, Herbert.

Type 107: designed by Peter Wright, Chris Murphy, used semi-active suspension, Ford Cosworth HB engines.

1993:
Type 107B: active ride, powered by Ford Cosworth HB engines, driven by Herbert, Zanardi, Lamy.

1994:
Type 107C: Mugen-Honda V10 engines. Active suspension banned by FIA, wooden 'plank' under cars mandatory. Driven by Herbert, Lamy, Zanardi.

Type 109: powered by Mugen-Honda ZA5C engine. Driven by Herbert, Zanardi, Adams, Bernard, Salo. Team Lotus faces bankruptcy. Name acquired by David Hunt.

Andretti holds off Villeneuve at Brands Hatch in the 1979 Race of Champions. (Peter Riches)

Appendix II
Race Record of Lotus Types 78 and 79

Race/Date/Circuit
Chassis/Race no./Driver/Result

Key: DNQ = did not qualify; DNS = did not start; ret = retired

1977

Argentine GP, 9 January, Buenos Aires
No 5, Type 78/2, M. Andretti, fifth
No 6, Type 78/1, G. Nilsson, DNS

Brazilian GP, 23 January, Interlagos
No 5, Type 78/2, M. Andretti, ret – electrics
No 6, Type 78/1, G. Nilsson, fifth

South African GP, 5 March, Kyalami
No 5, Type 78/2, M. Andretti, ret – accident
No 6, Type 78/1, G. Nilsson, twelfth

Race of Champions, 20 March, Brands Hatch
No 5, Type 78/2, M. Andretti, ret – electrics

US GP West, 3 April, Long Beach
No 5, Type 78/3, M. Andretti, first
No 6, Type 78/2, G. Nilsson, eighth

Spanish GP, 8 May, Jarama
No 5, Type 78/3, M. Andretti, first
No 6, Type 78/2, G. Nilsson, fifth

Monaco GP, 22 May, Monte Carlo
No 5, Type 78/3, M. Andretti, fifth
No 6, Type 78/2, G. Nilsson, ret – gearbox

Belgian GP, 5 June, Zolder
No 5, Type 78/3, M. Andretti, ret – accident
No 6, Type 78/2, G. Nilsson, first

Swedish GP, 19 June, Anderstorp
No 5, Type 78/3, M. Andretti, sixth
No 6, Type 78/2, G. Nilsson, ret – wheel-bearing

French GP, 3 July, Dijon-Prenois
No 5, Type 78/3, M. Andretti, first
No 6, Type 78/2, G. Nilsson, fourth

British GP, 16 July, Silverstone
No 5, Type 78/3, M. Andretti, ret – engine failure
No 6, Type 78/2, G. Nilsson, third

German GP, 31 July, Hockenheim
No 5, Type 78/3, M. Andretti, ret – engine failure
No 6, Type 78/2, G. Nilsson, ret – engine failure

Austrian GP, 14 August, Österreichring
No 5, Type 78/3, M. Andretti, ret – engine failure
No 6, Type 78/2, G. Nilsson, ret – engine failure

Dutch GP, 28 August, Zandvoort
No 5, Type 78/3, M. Andretti, ret – engine failure
No 6, Type 78/2, G. Nilsson, ret – accident

Race Record of Lotus Types 78 and 79

Italian GP, 11 September, Monza
No 5, Type 78/3, M. Andretti, first
No 6, Type 78/2, G. Nilsson, ret – accident

US GP East, 2 October, Watkins Glen
No 5, Type 78/3, M. Andretti, second
No 6, Type 78/4, G. Nilsson, ret – accident

Canadian GP, 9 October, Mosport Park
No 5, Type 78/3, M. Andretti, ninth – engine failure
No 6, Type 78/4, G. Nilsson, ret – accident

Japanese GP, 23 October, Fuji
No 5, Type 78/3, M. Andretti, ret – accident
No 6, Type 78/4, G. Nilsson, ret – gearbox

1978

Argentine GP, 15 January, Buenos Aires
No 5, Type 78/3, M. Andretti, first
No 6, Type 78/2, R. Peterson, fifth
No 18, Type 78/1, H. Rebaque, DNQ

Brazilian GP, 29 January, Jacarepagua, Rio
No 5, Type 78/3, M. Andretti, fourth
No 6, Type 78/2, R. Peterson, ret – collision damage
No 18, Type 78/1, H. Rebaque, ret – driver fatigue

South African GP, 4 March, Kyalami
No 5, Type 78/3, M. Andretti, seventh
No 6, Type 78/2, R. Peterson, first
No 25, Type 78/1, H. Rebaque, tenth

Daily Express **International Trophy**, 19 March, Silverstone
No 5, Type 79/1, M. Andretti, ret – accident
No 6, Type 78/2, R. Peterson, ret – accident

US GP West, 2 April, Long Beach
No 5, Type 78/3, M. Andretti, second
No 6, Type 78/2, R. Peterson, fourth
No 25, Type 78/1, H. Rebaque, DNQ

Monaco GP, 7 May, Monte Carlo
No 5, Type 78/3, M. Andretti, eleventh
No 6, Type 78/2, R. Peterson, ret – gearbox
No 25, Type 78/4, H. Rebaque, DNQ

Belgian GP, 21 May, Zolder
No 5, Type 79/2, M. Andretti, first
No 6, Type 78/2, R. Peterson, second
No 25, Type 78/4, H. Rebaque, DNQ

Spanish GP, 4 June, Jarama
No 5, Type 79/3, M. Andretti, first
No 6, Type 79/2, R. Peterson, second
No 25, Type 78/1, H. Rebaque, ret – broken exhaust

Swedish GP, 17 June, Anderstorp
No 5, Type 79/3, M. Andretti, ret – engine failure
No 6, Type 79/2, R. Peterson, third
No 25, Type 78/4, H. Rebaque, twelfth

French GP, 2 July, Paul Ricard
No 5, Type 79/3, M. Andretti, first
No 6, Type 79/2, R. Peterson, second
No 25, Type 78/4, H. Rebaque, DNQ

British GP, 16 July, Brands Hatch
No 5, Type 79/3, M. Andretti, ret – engine failure
No 6, Type 79/2, R. Peterson, ret – fuel leak
No 25, Type 78/4, H. Rebaque, ret – gearbox

German GP, 30 July, Hockenheim
No 5, Type 79/3, M. Andretti, first
No 6, Type 79/2, R. Peterson, ret – engine failure
No 25, Type 78/4, H. Rebaque, sixth

Austrian GP, 13 August, Österreichring
No 5, Type 79/3, M. Andretti, ret – accident
No 6, Type 79/2, R. Peterson, first
No 25, Type 78/4, H. Rebaque, ret – clutch

Dutch GP, 27 August, Zandvoort
No 5, Type 79/4, M. Andretti, first
No 6, Type 79/2, R. Peterson, second
No 25, Type 78/4, H. Rebaque, eleventh

Italian GP, 10 September, Monza
No 5, Type 79/3, M. Andretti, sixth
No 6, Type 78/3, R. Peterson, ret – accident
No 25, Type 78/4, H. Rebaque, DNQ

US GP East, 1 October, Watkins Glen
No 5, Type 79/4, M. Andretti, ret – engine failure
No 55, Type 79/3, J.P. Jarier, fifteenth
No 25, Type 78/2, H. Rebaque, ret – clutch

Canadian GP, 8 October, Montreal
No 5, Type 79/4, M. Andretti, tenth
No 55, Type 79/3, J.P. Jarier, ret – oil leak
No 25, Type 78/2, H. Rebaque, ret – clutch

1979

Argentine GP, 21 January, Buenos Aires
No 1, Type 79/4, M. Andretti, fifth
No 2, Type 79/2, C. Reutemann, second
No 31, Type 79/1, H. Rebaque, ret – suspension failure

Brazilian GP, 4 February, Interlagos
No 1, Type 79/4, M. Andretti, ret – fuel leak, fire
No 2, Type 79/2, C. Reutemann, third
No 31, Type 79/1, H. Rebaque, DNQ

South African GP, 3 March, Kyalami
No 1, Type 79/5, M. Andretti, fourth
No 2, Type 79/2, C. Reutemann, fifth
No 31, Type 79/1, H. Rebaque, fourteenth

US GP West, 8 April, Long Beach
No 1, Type 79/5, M. Andretti, fourth
No 2, Type 79/2, C. Reutemann, ret – broken driveshaft
No 31, Type 79/1, H. Rebaque, ret – accident

Race of Champions, 15 April, Brands Hatch
No 1, Type 79/3, M. Andretti, third

Spanish GP, 29 April, Jarama
No 1, Type 80/1, M. Andretti, third
No 2, Type 79/2, C. Reutemann, second
No 31, Type 79/1, H. Rebaque, ret – engine failure

Belgian GP, 13 May, Zolder
No 1, Type 79/5, M. Andretti, ret – brake problem
No 2, Type 79/2, C. Reutemann, fourth
No 31, Type 79/1, H. Rebaque, ret – broken driveshaft

Monaco GP, 27 May, Monte Carlo
No 1, Type 80/1, M. Andretti, ret – rear suspension failure
No 2, Type 79/2, C. Reutemann, third

Gunnar Nilsson Trophy, 3 June, Donington Park
No 1, Type 79/5, M. Andretti, third

French GP, 1 July, Dijon-Prenois
No 1, Type 80/2, M. Andretti, ret – brake & handling problems
No 2, Type 79/4, C. Reutemann, thirteenth
No 31, Type 79/1, H. Rebaque, twelfth

British GP, 14 July, Silverstone
No 1, Type 79/4, M. Andretti, ret – wheel-bearing failure
No 2, Type 79/5, C. Reutemann, eighth
No 31, Type 79/1, H. Rebaque, ninth

German GP, 29 July, Hockenheim
No 1, Type 79/5, M. Andretti, ret – universal joint failure
No 2, Type 79/3, C. Reutemann, ret – accident
No 31, Type 79/1, H. Rebaque, ret – handling problems

Race Record of Lotus Types 78 and 79

Austrian GP, 12 August, Österreichring
No 1, Type 79/5, M. Andretti, ret – clutch failure
No 2, Type 79/4, C. Reutemann, ret – dissatisfied with tyres
No 31, Type 79/1, H. Rebaque, DNQ

Dutch GP, 26 August, Zandvoort
No 1, Type 79/2, M. Andretti, ret – rear-suspension failure
No 2, Type 79/4, C. Reutemann, ret – accident
No 31, Type 79/1, H. Rebaque, seventh

Italian GP, 9 September, Monza
No 1, Type 79/5, M. Andretti, fifth
No 2, Type 79/4, C. Reutemann, seventh

Canadian GP, 30 September, Montreal
No 1, Type 79/5, M. Andretti, ret – ran out of fuel
No 2, Type 79/3, C. Reutemann, ret – split oil-tank mounting

US GP East, 7 October, Watkins Glen
No 1, Type 79/5, M. Andretti, ret – gearbox failure
No 2, Type 79/3, C. Reutemann, ret – spun off

Hector Rebaque was the only privateer to run ex-works 78s and 79s concurrently with Team Lotus. (Ford Photographic Archive)

Appendix III
Cast of Characters

Colin Chapman: founder of Lotus, chassis designer and architect of the Racing Team's fortunes in Formula 1
Tony Rudd: former BRM team manager, technical director at Lotus and facilitator of the ground-effect programme
Peter Wright: aerodynamicist, Team Lotus engineer and designer
Ralph Bellamy: Team Lotus designer, Types 76, 78
Martin Ogilvie: Team Lotus designer, T79, T81, T87, T91
Geoff Aldridge: Team Lotus designer, T77, T80
Eddie Dennis: former Team Lotus chief mechanic, in charge of construction of T78, T79
Peter Riches: in charge of construction of T79, T80, T81
Andrew Ferguson: Team manager
Bob Dance: Team Lotus chief mechanic
Nigel Bennett: Team Lotus engineer
Mario Andretti: Team Lotus driver, 1969, 1976–80
Gunnar Nilsson: Team Lotus driver, 1976–77
Ronnie Peterson: Team Lotus driver, 1973–76, 1978
Carlos Reutemann: Team Lotus driver, 1979
Glenn Waters: mechanic to Mario Andretti, 1977–79
Phil Denney: mechanic to Mario Andretti
Rex Hart: mechanic to Ronnie Peterson
Bobby Clarke: mechanic to Ronnie Peterson

Team Lotus mechanic Glenn Waters makes a point about the car's set-up during a discussion with Andretti, Peterson and Chapman during practice for the 1978 Austrian Grand Prix. The amiable rapport within the winning team is clearly evident. (Glenn Waters)

Appendix IV
Where Are They Now?

Type 78 chassis
78/1   S. Pietro Ratti, c/o F1 Storiche, Italy. Racing in Thoroughbred Grand Prix series.
78/2   Imperial Tobacco, on loan to National Motor Museum, Beaulieu.
78/3   Classic Team Lotus Ltd. Destroyed after Ronnie Peterson's accident at Monza, 1978. Team Lotus rebuilt the car with a replacement tub.
78/4   Junro Nishida, Japan; driven regularly in demonstrations.

Type 79 chassis
79/1   Joel Finn, USA; running condition.
79/2   Classic Team Lotus Ltd.
79/3   Classic Team Lotus Ltd; restored, used at events like Goodwood Festival of Speed.
79/4   Duncan Dayton, USA; raced regularly in historic motorsport events.
79/5   Piers Dawson-Damer, Australia; running condition.

Type 80 chassis
80/1   Sid Hoole, England; restoration planned 2002.
80/2   Classic Team Lotus Ltd.

Type 86 chassis
86/1   Classic Team Lotus Ltd.

Type 88 chassis
88/1   Classic Team Lotus Ltd.
88/2   Steve Hitchins; competes in Thoroughbred Historic F1 series.

Note: 88/1 completed 1,425 turbulent miles (2280km). For the 1981 British GP Team Lotus presented composite chassis numbers 2 and 4 in Type 88 specification. When the twin-chassis concept was banned they were converted to Type 87 specification for the race.

Further Reading

Jabby Crombac, *Colin Chapman – The Man and his Cars* [PSL, 1986]

Hugh Haskell, *Colin Chapman Lotus Engineering* [Osprey automotive, 1998]

Frederick Petersens, *The Viking Drivers* [William Kimber, 1979]

Nigel Roebuck, *Mario Andretti* [Hamlyn, 1979]

Tony Rudd, *It was Fun* [Haynes, 1993]

John Tipler, *Ronnie Peterson* [Coterie Press, 2003]

Peter Wright, *Racing Car Technology* [SAE International, 2002]

Index

Ahrens, Kurt 142
Alfa Romeo 15, 71, 172, 180, 183, 190, 191
Amon, Chris 142
Anderstorp circuit 15, 71, 119, 127, 128, 131, 132, 161, 171, 174
Andretti, Mario 6, 7, 9, 10, 12-14, 18, 25, 26, 29-32, 35-39, 42, 47, 52, 54, 58, 59, 62, 63, 65, 67, 71-74, 79, 81-84, 86, 89-91, 94-136, 138-143, 145-181, 183, 184, 198, 203
Andretti, Michael 172
Arnoux, René 175, 176, 178, 179
Arrows cars, A1 94, 97, 113, 119, 125, 133, 151, 157, 170, 173
Ascari, Alberto 171
ATS cars
    D1 155
    D3 180
Autocar 116
Auto Union 15

Barcelona, Montjuich Park circuit 13, 18
Barnard, John 52
Barrichello, Rubens 140
Bell, Derek 142
Beltoise, Jean-Pierre 153
Bonnier, Jo 163
Brabham Racing Team 31, 40, 128, 157, 159, 161, 180, 193
Brabham cars
    BT18 142
    BT30 161
    BT34 161
    BT45 102, 109
    BT46 15, 70, 103, 104, 106, 108, 112, 119, 124, 125, 130, 132-134, 136, 138, 141, 148, 150, 161
    BT48 164-166, 167, 169, 172, 179
    BT49/49C/D 180, 181, 193, 194
    BT52B 70
Brakes
    Ferodo pads 107, 151
    Girling master cylinder 169
    Lockheed calipers 81, 151, 156

Brambilla, Vittorio 108, 136, 153, 155, 180
Brands Hatch circuit; 13, 14, 103, 110, 134, 137, 140, 141, 153, 161, 166, 167, 183, 194, 198
BRM 9, 16-18, 25, 94
Buenos Aires circuit 10, 67, 97, 98, 101, 115, 162, 163, 183, 191

Campbell, Sir Donald 15
CART (Championship Auto Racing Teams) series (Champ cars) 7, 10, 82, 171, 180, 194
Caterham Seven 46
Catt, Ian 134
Chiti, Carlo 180
Chaparral cars 14, 38, 134
Chevrolet cars
    Camaro Z28 113
Chevron cars 22, 142, 163
Clark, Jim 16, 70, 142, 160, 171, 181
Connaught 15
Copersucar F6A (Fittipaldi) 169, 180
Courtaulds 190
Crabbe, Colin (Antique Automobiles) 20, 142
Crane-Fruehauf 128
Cranfield College of Aeronautics 90, 184
Crowland, Paul 49, 51, 74, 75
CSI (Commission Sportive International) 134, 150

Daily Express International Trophy 61, 63, 73, 120
Daily Mail Race of Champions 88, 103, 110, 166, 167
Daly, Derek 128, 150, 153, 169, 180
Dayton, Duncan (Highcroft Racing) 84
De Angelis, Elio 181-184, 188, 191, 192, 194
De Havilland Mosquito 22
DeLorean 87, 185
Depailler, Patrick 108, 113, 114, 116, 119, 124-127, 129, 134, 140, 148, 150, 153, 155, 156, 159, 164, 168-170, 172, 179
Differentials 104

Dijon-Prenois circuit 60, 106, 108, 142, 174-176, 183
Ducarouge, Gérard 164
Duckworth, Keith 28, 70
Du Pont chemicals 190

Ecclestone, Bernie 97, 150, 161, 180
Elford, Vic 14, 20
Engines
    Cosworth 1600 FVA 70
    Cosworth-Ford DFV 10, 52, 61-63, 68, 70, 71, 77-79, 81, 85, 92, 111, 113, 115, 121, 122, 126, 129, 131, 134, 136, 169, 182, 183, 187, 192
    Cosworth-Ford DFV development engine 71, 104, 109, 111, 118, 122, 134, 140
    Cosworth-Ford DFY 194
    Eurorracing-built DFV (Peter Hass) 71, 134
    Nicholson-McLaren built DFV 48, 104, 105, 110, 122, 126, 134, 146
    Pratt and Whitney PT6 gas-turbine 77, 79
    Swindon Racing Engines-built DFV (John Dunn) 71, 134
Ensign cars (Mo Nunn)
    N177 96
    N179 169
    N180-B 48, 94
Evans, Bob 63, 88

Fangio, Juan-Manuel 116
Ferrari Scuderia 20, 38, 58, 70, 71, 114, 128, 159, 180, 188, 191-193
Ferrari cars 83, 96, 103, 104, 109-111, 116-118, 124, 127, 129, 141, 142, 150, 151, 156, 164, 165-167, 169, 171, 172, 173, 175, 179, 198
Ferris, Geoff 178
FIA (Federation International Automobile) 13, 188, 189, 191, 193, 194
FISA (Federation International Sport Automobile) 188, 191-193
Fittipaldi, Emerson 7, 54, 111,

205

Index

118, 120, 148, 150, 156, 157
FOCA (Formula One Constructors Association) 125, 134, 150, 157, 174, 193
Ford Motor Company 70
Ford cars 15, 161
Franklin, William 60
Fuji International Speedway 63, 113, 114

Galica, Divina 128
Gearboxes
    Hewland FG400 61, 63, 65, 66, 68, 76-79, 81, 83, 108, 116, 119, 121, 122, 140, 169, 178, 181
    Lotus-Getrag 68, 76-80, 116, 118, 122, 140
    Lotus-Hewland FGA 85, 178, 182, 183, 192
    Lotus 'queerbox' 77
    ZF 77, 79
Giacomelli, Bruno 180
GKN 77
Goggomobile 76
Goodwood circuit 16, 23
GPDA (Grand Prix Drivers' Association) 156
Granatelli, Andy 19
GRD cars 20, 97
Gurney, Dan 122

Hall, Jim 14
Hardy-Spicer 79
Hayes, Walter 70
Head, Patrick 174
Henry, Alan 116, 166
Herd, Robin 16, 18, 20
Hesketh Racing 88, 128, 163
Hewland, Mike 76
Hill, Phil 14
Hill, Graham 16, 18, 54, 62, 142, 172
    Embassy Hill Team 62
Hockenheim circuit 31, 42, 72, 109, 141, 143, 161, 177
Hulme, Denny 14, 20
Hunt, James 63, 96, 103, 107-114, 116, 117, 126, 129, 131, 132, 138, 140, 150, 151, 155-157, 180

Ickx, Jacky 60-62, 110, 142, 153, 171, 179
Imola circuit 179, 181, 183
Interlagos circuit 36, 62, 98, 101, 161, 162, 164, 181, 183
IRL (Indy Racing League) 7, 194

IROC (International Race of Champions) 113
IRPA (International Racing Press Association) 172
Irving, Frank 21
Irwin, Chris 15

Jabouille, Jean-Pierre 136, 147, 149, 151, 158, 164, 165, 175-177, 179
Jacarepagua circuit 116, 118, 161, 191, 194
Jarama circuit 32, 42, 81, 97, 128-130, 168, 169, 175, 183, 188
Jarier, Jean-Pierre 18, 111, 153, 154, 157-159, 164-167, 169, 172, 173, 178
Jaussaud, Jean-Pierre 136
Jenkinson, Denis 104, 110, 160, 176
Johnson-Evinrude outboard motors 20
Jones, Alan 110, 114, 124, 140, 143, 150, 151, 158, 169, 172, 175-178, 180, 181

Keegan, Rupert 111
Kent, Geoffrey 26
Kojima KE009 114
Kottulinsky, Freddy 97
Kyalami circuit 13, 18, 30, 33, 38, 61, 99, 101, 103, 104, 117-119, 134, 153, 161, 164, 165, 192

Laffite, Jacques 102, 104, 107, 108, 110-112, 114, 129, 131, 132, 136, 145, 150, 163, 170, 172, 176, 179
Lammers, Jan 181
Las Vegas circuit 184
Lauda, Niki 63, 101, 104, 107-110, 114, 116, 117, 119, 124, 126, 129, 131, 132, 136, 138, 140, 141, 143, 146, 149, 150, 156, 157-159, 161, 167, 172, 179, 180
Lees, Geoff 194
Ligier cars,
    JS7 96, 104, 107, 110, 111, 114, 136
    JS11 72, 164, 165, 168-170, 172, 176, 177, 179, 181
    JS21 153
Lobro CV joints 79
Loctite sealant 83
Lola cars 20
Long Beach circuit 86, 95, 102, 104, 112, 121, 122, 161, 167, 169, 191
Lotus Cars Ltd 88
    Eclat 184
    Elite 184
    Esprit 184, 185
Lotus racing cars,
    Type 15 77
    Type 16 77
    Type 25 12
    Type 30 27
    Type 47 27, 54
    Type 48 54
    Type 49 12, 18, 70, 163
    Type 56 12, 77
    Type 70 7
    Type 72 7, 20, 21, 23, 40, 41, 43, 44, 56, 57, 60, 61, 84, 110, 142, 181
    Type 73 41
    Type 74 Texaco Star 50
    Type 76 20, 23, 41, 43, 44, 48, 50, 60, 61, 181
    Type 77 25, 26, 30, 31, 40, 41, 43, 44, 48, 50, 52, 57, 62-66, 68, 94
    Type 78 6, 7, 9, 10, 17, 21, 22, 24-26, 28, 31, 32, 34, 38, 40, 41, 43-46, 48, 50, 52-57, 60, 64-69, 71-76, 80-84, 90, 94-128, 130, 134, 136, 137, 140, 143, 148, 150, 151, 153, 155, 161, 163, 185, 193, 194, 202
    Type 79 6, 7, 9, 10, 15, 26, 27, 31-38, 40, 42-49, 51-53, 55-57, 68, 71-76, 79-85, 87-92, 94, 110, 119, 120, 122, 125-138, 140, 141, 143, 146, 148, 150-182, 184, 185, 192, 198, 202
    Type 80 7, 9-11, 36-38, 42, 43, 53, 54, 58, 59, 84-91, 161, 166-179, 181, 182, 184-186
    Type 81/B 34, 91, 181-187
    Type 86 183-187
    Type 87/87B 34, 183, 184, 191, 192, 194
    Type 88 10, 183-186, 189-193
    Type 91 192, 194
    Type 92 194
    Type 93T 7,
    Type 100 40
Lotus personnel,
    Aldridge, Geoff 9, 10, 40, 41, 43, 45, 46, 48-53, 62, 63
    Bamber, Jim 56
    Bellamy, Ralph 9, 20, 21, 23-25, 28, 29, 40, 41, 43, 48, 50, 60, 65, 66, 68
    Bennett, Nigel 86, 94, 98, 120,

Index

128, 140, 176
Burchall, Arthur 94
Bushell, Fred 28
Campbell, Ian 27
Chapman, Clive 54, 192
Chapman, Colin 9, 10, 12, 13, 18, 20, 22-26, 28, 30, 31, 40, 41, 43, 44, 46, 48-54, 56, 58, 62, 63, 67, 70, 71, 73, 74, 76, 77, 79, 84, 86-88, 91, 92, 94, 96, 98, 101, 104, 106-109, 111, 112, 116, 119-121, 125, 127, 128, 129, 132, 134, 138, 139, 143, 145, 148, 150, 156-158, 160, 163, 166, 171, 174, 176, 178, 180-182, 185, 187-194, 203
Chapman, Stan 67
Clarke, Bobby 94, 139, 140
Cook, Mike 40, 48, 50, 56, 79
Cubitt, Frank 41
Dance, Bob 9, 10, 14, 30, 37, 38, 87, 89, 94, 97, 100, 103, 107, 120, 121, 128, 134, 164, 166, 169, 191
Dawson, Ian 94, 99, 100, 116
Denney, Phil 94, 120
Dennis, Eddie 9, 10, 33, 38, 49, 54-57, 65, 74-76, 84, 86, 90, 92
Ferguson, Andrew 9, 94, 96, 98
Franks, Roy 49, 56, 89
Garner, Dougie 23
Gray, Eric 55, 56
Hart, Rex 94, 139, 140
Hicks, Clive 58, 59, 96, 98
Kinkaid, Darryl 99
Lane, Keith 40
Leighton, Keith 23
May, Stevie 23
Monaghan, Billy 56, 89
Moses, John 95, 96
Murphy, Mike & Anne 96
Ogilvie, Martin 9, 10, 15, 23, 27, 28, 40, 41, 43-53, 62, 63, 68, 76, 77, 79, 85, 183-187, 189, 192-194
Paravani, Nick 56
Phillippe, Maurice 12, 41, 52
Prior, Charlie 21, 24, 51
Riches, Peter 10, 86, 87, 88
Rudd, Tony 9, 17, 18, 20-26, 29, 30, 40, 65, 67, 77, 79, 86, 88, 185
Sills, Gilbert 94, 125
Southgate, Tony 94, 98, 100, 113, 125
Spooner, Brian 43, 48, 77
Stanbury, Noel 96
Szymanski, Kenny 58, 139

Terry, Len 12, 63
Truman, Mike 94
Underhill, Reg 49, 55, 73, 94
Van Dongen, Tony 94
Wade, Martin 41, 52
Warr, Peter 23, 194
Waters, Glenn 10, 23, 35, 39, 43, 56-59, 63, 66-69, 72, 80, 83, 88, 91, 94, 96, 98-101, 106-108, 114, 118, 119, 125, 143, 148, 151, 157-159, 203
Weston, Trevor 94
Wight, Peter 9, 10, 12, 15-18, 20-24, 28-31, 33, 34, 38-40, 51, 53, 57, 59, 90, 119, 182, 184, 185, 187-194
Lotus, Team 7, 10-12, 17, 20, 22-25, 27, 49, 54, 61, 63, 79, 81, 83, 88, 93, 94, 97, 111, 114, 122, 124, 125, 127, 128, 130, 134, 142, 151, 153, 159, 163, 167, 176, 181-183, 185, 188-192, 194
Lotus, Classic Team 54
    Hethel test track 57, 73, 138, 140
    Ketteringham Hall 22, 24, 25, 30, 40, 43, 48, 54-56, 73, 86-89, 185, 188
Lunger, Brett 111, 120, 153
Lyons, Pete 84

Mansell, Nigel 181, 183, 192, 194
March Engineering/Racing Team 18, 20, 63, 104, 119, 134, 142
March cars,
    701 18, 26, 153
    711 142
    712 142, 153
    731 153
    732 18, 22, 153
    743 97
Mass, Jochen 96, 101, 104, 107, 108, 113, 114, 170, 173, 177
Matra International Racing Team 70, 153
May, Michael 15
McLaren, Bruce/Racing Team 16, 18, 40, 52, 63, 70, 96, 104, 114, 128, 134, 150, 151, 189
McLaren cars,
    M6B 16
    M7A 20
    M7C 18, 19, 20
    M8D 14
    M23 96, 97, 103, 104, 105, 108, 109, 111, 112, 113, 117
    M26 124, 129, 131, 134, 136, 153,

M28 168, 173, 176
Mercedes-Benz 15
Merzario, Arturo 111
Messerschmitt kabinenroller 79
Mexico City circuit 70
Minardi 70
Momo steering wheel 75, 90
Monaco circuit 25, 44, 46, 47, 54, 76, 77, 103, 104, 122, 123, 125, 126, 142, 161, 172-174, 183, 194
Montreal circuit 153, 154, 155, 157-159, 180, 194
Monza circuit 6, 7, 69, 83, 88, 89, 109, 111, 142, 148-151, 153, 155-157, 172, 178, 179, 184
Moonraker cabin cruisers (JCL Marine) 20, 28
Moreno, Roberto 194
Mosport circuit 63, 71, 113
Moss, Stirling 16
Motor Sport 104, 110, 160, 176
Motoring News 116
Murray, Gordon 15, 133

Neve, Patrick 111
New London Theatre 60
Newman-Haas Team 172
Nicholson, John (Lyncar) 134
Niguardia hospital 155
Nilsson, Gunnar 7, 15, 30, 44, 63, 67, 79, 90, 94, 97-99, 101-114, 127, 128, 129, 159, 174
Nürburgring circuit 15, 20, 62, 97, 109, 153

Oils
    Texaco 49
    Valvoline 49
Oliver, Jackie 13, 18, 113
Osborne, Alec 18
Österreichring circuit 63, 89, 97, 109, 138, 144, 145, 147, 157, 161, 177, 178, 181, 183, 194, 203

Panoz cars 172
Parnelli Racing Team, Vels 63, 171
Patrese, Riccardo 114, 119, 131, 133, 136, 140, 150, 151, 157
Paul Ricard circuit 43, 62, 66, 134, 136, 138, 140, 142, 153, 161, 166, 169, 171, 175, 181, 182
Penske cars,
    PC4 111, 153, 178
Petersen, Fredrik 119, 156
Peterson, Ronnie 7, 9, 38, 40, 42, 54, 57, 60-63, 69, 81, 88-90, 94, 109, 111-113, 115-122, 124-134, 136-151, 153, 155-

207

Index

157, 159, 161, 163, 167, 171, 173, 174, 203
Phillippe, Maurice 165
Phipps, David 31
Piquet, Nelson 70, 157, 166, 167, 173, 179, 194
Pironi, Didier 136, 148, 150, 153, 164, 165, 170, 172, 179
Pook, Chris 122
Porsche, Professor Ferdinand 15
Porsche cars,
    Typ 80 16
    Typ 550 Spider 15
Postlethwaite, Harvey 38, 74, 125
Pryce, Tom 101, 102

RAC (Royal Automobile Club) 191
Race Car Engineering 184, 192
Ralt 63
Ransomes-Hoffman-Pollard (RHP) 66, 79
Rebaque, Hector 115, 116, 125, 132, 134, 145, 150, 155, 163, 164, 169, 177-180, 202
Rebaque HR 100-001 178
Rees, Alan 113, 142
Regazzoni, Clay 73, 101, 120, 124, 153, 155, 172, 173, 176, 178, 180
Renault cars,
    4 van 57, 76
    RS01 70, 136, 147, 151, 164, 165, 169
    RS11 175, 177, 179, 180
    RE30B 192
    A442 136
Reutemann, Carlos 9, 11, 89, 108, 110, 111, 114, 116, 117, 124, 125, 127-129, 131, 140, 141, 145, 147-151, 153, 156, 158-170, 172-181
Revson, Peter 153
Ribeiro, Alex-Dias 97, 180
Rindt, Jochen 7, 18, 54, 142
Road & Track 84
Rodriguez, Pedro 17
Rolls-Royce 88
Rondel Racing 161
Rosberg, Keke 120, 150, 155, 176, 194
Rover-BRM 16
Royal Albert Hall 190
Royal Garden Hotel 66, 67

Scheckter, Ian 111
Scheckter, Jody 71, 98, 104, 105, 107-109, 111, 113, 114, 117, 119, 122, 124, 127, 134, 140, 143, 145, 147, 150, 153,

156-159, 164, 165, 169, 170, 172, 173, 179, 180
Schenken, Tim 142
Schumacher, Michael 110, 140
Sebring circuit 171
Senna, Ayrton 110, 181, 194
Shadow Racing Team, UOP 94, 153
Shadow cars,
    DN8 73, 110, 114
    DN9 120, 124, 125
Siffert, Jo 142
Silverstone circuit 11, 57, 61, 70, 73, 74, 97, 108, 176, 189, 191, 192
Snetterton circuit 29, 88
South, Stephen 181
Spark plugs,
    NGK 101
Sparshott, Bob (BS Fabrications) 88
Specialised Mouldings
    (Peter Jackson) 17, 18, 20
Spence, Mike 14
Sponsors
    Carta Blanca 169, 179
    Courage 191
    Essex petroleum 9, 10, 165, 183, 184, 185
    Martini & Rossi 9, 10, 88, 160, 161
    NGK 128
    Olympus 128, 160
    Pemex 180
    Player & Son, John 9, 26, 62, 93, 128, 134, 136, 138, 160, 183, 192
    Tissot 160, 161
    Valvoline 128, 160, 161
Stanbury-Foley 138
Stewart, Sir Jackie 14, 38, 136, 142
Stollery, John 15, 16, 17
Stuck, Hans 102, 109, 112, 150, 153, 156, 180
Surtees, John/Team 17, 18, 94, 134
Surtees cars,
    TS20 108, 136, 153
Svenby, Staffan 62, 112

Tambay, Patrick 134, 136, 168, 169
Tecno 142
Temporada race series 161
Theodore Racing 94
Thruxton circuit 161
Travco, Dodge 93, 96, 129
Trimmer, Tony 120
Tyres
    Bridgestone 143
    Goodyear 20, 48, 57-59, 96, 105, 106, 109, 112, 116, 122, 124,

129, 132, 139, 140, 143, 150, 164, 169, 170, 180, 181
    Michelin 58, 106, 116-118, 143, 156, 165, 170, 180
Tyrrell Racing Team 20, 22, 57, 128, 134, 150, 159
Tyrrell cars,
    P34 62, 97, 105, 109, 112, 113, 142
    008 116, 119, 134, 136
    009 153, 164, 165, 167, 172, 173, 179, 180
    012 70

Vanwall 15
Villeneuve, Gilles 83, 115, 117, 122, 124, 127, 129, 131, 148-151, 156, 158, 159, 164-167, 169, 170, 172, 175, 176, 178-180, 198
Volvo F89 128

Walker, Murray 132
Watkins Glen circuit 14, 70, 111, 112, 152, 153, 157, 158, 161, 171, 180, 181, 183
Watson, John 103, 105-108, 116, 124, 126, 131, 133, 136, 138, 140, 141, 148, 150, 156-159, 173, 176
Wheels
    Speedline 98
Williams, David 90
Williams Racing Team 20, 134, 172, 174, 181, 191
Williams cars,
    FW06 143, 151, 158
    FW07 46, 53, 72, 84, 92, 161, 172, 173, 175-178, 184, 194
Windsor, Peter 116
Winkelmann Racing, Roy 54, 142
Wisell, Reine 142
Wolf Racing Team, Walter 151, 159
Wolf cars,
    WR1 96, 104, 105, 109, 111, 113, 117, 124
    WR4 156
    WR5 74, 125, 134, 153
    WR7 169
    WR8 176, 179

Zandvoort circuit 9, 18, 63, 64, 70, 89, 110, 111, 146, 149, 150, 177, 178, 179
Zanon, Count Ghughie 112
Zolder circuit 37, 38, 77, 82, 97, 104, 105, 125, 127, 128, 142, 161, 170, 172, 183, 184
Zorzi, Renzo 101